INSTITUTIONALIZING
THE JUST WAR

INSTITUTIONALIZING
THE JUST WAR

ALLEN BUCHANAN

OXFORD
UNIVERSITY PRESS

OXFORD
UNIVERSITY PRESS

Oxford University Press is a department of the University of Oxford. It furthers
the University's objective of excellence in research, scholarship, and education
by publishing worldwide. Oxford is a registered trade mark of Oxford University
Press in the UK and certain other countries.

Published in the United States of America by Oxford University Press
198 Madison Avenue, New York, NY 10016, United States of America.

CIP data is on file at the Library of Congress
ISBN 978-0-19-087843-6

1 3 5 7 9 8 6 4 2

Printed by Sheridan Books, Inc., United States of America

CONTENTS

PREFACE

There is a sense in which this book wrote itself, piecemeal, over a period of almost eighteen years. Each chapter is based on a previously published article that was crafted to stand on its own. Yet the articles and even more so the chapters of this book represent a systematic treatment of most of the central topics in the morality of recourse to war—and an equally systematic view about how to do Political Philosophy. The order of the chapters of the book is determined by systematic considerations and does not reflect the order in which the original articles were written. After the Introduction, which clarifies the unifying project and the links among the chapters, the sequence of chapters moves from the more abstract to the concrete: Chapters One through Six lay out the conceptual framework and methodology that ground the specific proposals for institutional innovation that are developed in greatest detail in the final two chapters.

My usual procedure in writing books is to first write a few freestanding articles that are intended to serve as the basis for core chapters of a planned book. That's what happened in this case, except that there was no plan for a book. It was only after the fact, when I looked back over the articles, that I realized that together they constituted a coherent whole. Each chapter contains most of the material of the corresponding article, but I have made modifications in each case, both to make the connections among the chapters more evident and because my thinking has changed (and, I hope, improved). Each chapter can be read on its own, but each helps to enrich the others.

As the title suggests, this volume is an endeavor to think institutionally about the morality of recourse to war. But it is more than that: it is an attempt to reconceive Political Philosophy in a way that takes institutions and the impact of institutions on morality seriously.

I think it is fair to say that throughout my career—which now spans more than four decades—I have been more attentive to institutional realities and possibilities than most contemporary analytic philosophers. That was due in part to the fact that in two fields in which I have worked, Political Philosophy and Bioethics, I have had the good fortune to work with policy-makers both at the national and international levels. This engagement with the real world has involved a diverse and rich set of experiences, including advising Meles Zenawi's Transitional Government on the writing of the secession clause of the Ethiopian Constitution, writing a paper commissioned by the Canadian Government on a Supreme Court Decision on the possible secession of Quebec, advising the High Commissioner on National Minorities of the Council of Europe on the development of intrastate autonomy regimes for national minorities, serving on the staffs of or as a consultant to four US Presidential Bioethics commissions, and being a member of the Advisory Council for the National Human Genome Research Institute. These experiences forced me to engage more with the facts, to learn from people in other disciplines, and to appreciate the importance of institutions.

In the past fifteen years, my interest in thinking institutionally has developed considerably, due in no small part to my having developing a rewarding collaborative relationship with the renowned International Relations scholar Robert O. Keohane. That relationship ripened into co-authorship of five articles so far, two of which appear, with modifications, as Chapters Seven and Eight of this volume. I am deeply grateful to Keohane for giving me the opportunity to work with him and to learn better how to think institutionally. I could not have had a better co-author or a better teacher.

ACKNOWLEDGMENTS

The thinking that went into this volume benefited from the work and generosity of many people and the support of the philosophy departments of the University of Arizona and Duke University. Among the individuals who were most helpful in providing comments on drafts of the articles that form the basis for this book are Samantha Besson, Julian Culp, Jeff Holzgrefe, Robert O. Keohane, James Nickel, Seth Lazar, and Leif Wenar. I am especially indebted to Jeff Holzgrefe, both for his interest and encouragement for my work over the years and for having introduced me to Robert O. Keohane when he invited me to contribute to a volume on humanitarian intervention that he and Keohane were putting together. My biggest single intellectual debt is owed to Bob Keohane. In the process of co-authoring five articles with him, including two that are included, with modifications, in this volume, he generously tutored me in international relations theory and helped me learn to think more clearly about the importance of institutions.

I also wish to express my appreciation to the editorial leadership of four journals: *Ethics & International Affairs; The Journal of Political Philosophy; Philosophy & Public Affairs*; and *Politics, Philosophy & Economics*, for providing venues for the sort of work represented in this volume. Unfortunately, too often the journals in which moral and political philosophers publish tacitly endorse a philosophical methodology that is fact free, as well as oblivious to both relevant work in other disciplines and to the ways in which institutions can change the moral landscape. Finally, but importantly, I am grateful to Peter Ohlin of Oxford University Press for his encouragement and efficiency in bringing this volume to press.

Chapter One is based on an article of the same title that appeared in *Philosophy & Public Affairs*. Chapter Two is based on my contribution to *The Oxford Handbook of the Ethics of War*, edited by Helen Frowe and Seth Lazar (Oxford University Press, 2017). Chapter Three largely replicates my contribution to an *Oxford Studies in Political Philosophy* volume edited by Peter Vallentyne (Oxford University Press, 2017). Chapter Four, with modifications, is from an article entitled "Reciprocal Legitimation: Reframing the Problem of International Legitimacy," which appeared in *Politics, Philosophy & Economics* 10, no. 1 (2011): 5–19. Chapter Five significantly modifies an article with the same title that appeared in *The Journal of Political Philosophy* 7, no. 1 (1999): 71–87. Chapter Six is largely based on my contribution to *Humanitarian Intervention: Ethical, Legal, and Political Dilemmas*, edited by J. L. Holzgrefe and Robert O. Keohane (Cambridge University Press, 2003). Chapters Seven and Eight, with modifications, are taken from "The Preventive Use of Force: A Cosmopolitan Institutionalist Proposal," *Ethics & International Affairs* 18, no. 1 (March 2004): 1–22; and "Precommitment Regimes for Intervention: Supplementing the Security Council," *Ethics & International Affairs* 25, no. 1 (2001): 41–63, both co-authored with Robert O. Keohane.

INSTITUTIONALIZING
THE JUST WAR

INTRODUCTION

How the World Looked, 1999–2016

During the period in which much of the thinking that went into this book occurred, the world looked strikingly different from what we see today. The growth of multilateralism, defined as the coordination of national policies in groups of three or more states, was evident. Transnational networks of regulatory officials, judges, and legislators were proliferating and trade agreements of unprecedented scale were achieved. The most inclusive treaty-based multilateral institution for furthering international peace and security, the UN Security Council, expanded its mission to include the authorization of humanitarian military interventions even in cases in which international peace and security were not at risk. Environmental treaties outlined multilateral responses to pressing problems of ozone depletion and global climate change. Globalization in its manifold dimensions was increasing. The obstacle to more comprehensive mulitilateral institution-building and to the extension of human rights regimes that the Cold War had posed had been removed by the dissolution of the Soviet Union. Although some multilateral institutions remained informal, there was also a trend toward legalization (though perhaps without much reflection as to whether greater formal legality is always better). Just as evident, of course, was the continuing turmoil in weakly governed areas of the world and the power of conflicts there to affect even the stablest countries, both through the export of terrorism and through the often unintended results of military interventions that purported to enhance security and stability but which instead fueled rivalries among states and among groups within them. The world at that time was also characterized by political divergence (rather than convergence on liberal constitutional democracy as Fukuyama and others had predicted at the end of the Cold War). Yet while some objected to the growth of multilateral institutions, until 2016 their voices were far from dominant and the burgeoning of multilateral institutions proceeded apace.

In that world, the clearest and most coherent theoretical foundation of multilateralism was a marriage of liberal cosmopolitan moral principles gleaned from contemporary Political Philosophy and institutionalism as characterized in Liberal International Relations Theory. The latter purports to show that international relations can be informed by liberal cosmopolitan moral principles, including human rights norms, through the leadership of democratic states in the construction of multilateral institutions. Contemporary Political Philosophy articulates more explicitly and defends more rigorously the principles that liberal international relations theorists think should inform the procedures of multilateral institutions and the goals to be promoted by them.

For the most part, this volume is a response to the world as I then perceived it. The chapters are based on articles written during that period, though in each case the current versions reflect new refinements and in some cases substantial development of my ideas. As this Introduction will make clear, the ideas in the various chapters, even though they developed over a considerable period of time and first appeared in stand-alone articles, are systematically connected. Taken as a whole, they provide a first start at engaging in just war theorizing, and more generally Political Philosophy, in a new way.

As I was writing the original articles, it seemed to me that the conditions during the first decade and a half of the twenty-first century called for three main responses: (1) the development of an understanding of political legitimacy suitable for multilateral institutions and for states as participants in multilateral institutions; (2) a re-theorizing of just war theory that takes seriously the possibility that well-designed institutions could improve the decisions leaders make regarding recourse to war and alter the moral status of certain types of wars; and (3) more generally, a demonstration of the potential benefits of innovative institutional proposals grounded in an appreciation of the realities of power, sound principles of institutional design, and liberal cosmopolitan moral principles.

The World as it Appears Now

In 2016, a sea change occurred—or rather reached a critical threshold and became salient: the withdrawal of the United Kingdom from the European Union; the upsurge of author-itarian, antidemocratic, anti-immigrant political parties in Europe; and the election of Donald Trump, with his promises to "make America great again" by raising trade barriers, rad-ically restricting immigration, withdrawing from the North American Free Trade Zone agreement and from the Paris Accord on climate change, and withdrawing from NATO if other members fail to pay their "fair share." Perhaps most sig-nificantly, the now President Trump repeatedly asserts that the existing multilateral order the United States had taken such pains to create in the decades since the end of World War II does not serve her interests but instead facilitates her exploita-tion by other countries.

There is a heavy irony in Trump's complaint: those who have even a modicum of knowledge of the post-World War II interna-tional order typically say that it is too skewed toward furthering US interests. That is hardly surprising, given that the United States wielded disproportionate power in creating that order. It is in fact implausible—and contrary to what is known about the behavior of states—to assert that the United States has used its hegemonic power to create an order that facilitates its own exploitation by other nations. Nonetheless, Trump's message that multilateral in-stitutions are playing the United States for a sucker apparently resonates with many Americans—enough, perhaps, to empower him to do significant damage to the existing international order.

In blunter terms, the world today is more xeonophobic, more nationalistic, and more cynical about the prospects for mutually beneficial cooperation among states. It is therefore more hostile to existing and proposed multilateral institutions than perhaps at any time since the 1930s.

Does this transformation make the thinking embodied in this volume irrelevant or hopelessly utopian? On the contrary, the current retreat from multilateralism and the assault on liberal cosmopolitanism make my approach more, not less relevant. An effective effort to retain the best features of the existing world order and to preserve the possibility for eventually rebuilding institutions now under assault is likely to succeed only if a better understanding of the strengths of multilateralism built on liberal cosmopolitan values and sound principles of justice is achieved. Just as important, defenders of multilateralism must be careful to admit the limitations as well as the virtues of multilateral institutions and, above all, to make the case for their legitimacy in a convincing way. For after all, the present turning away from multilateralism is among other things a crisis of legitimation: many people who previously endorsed the project of establishing a world order based on multilateral institutions and informed by liberal cosmopolitan principles or who at least acquiesced in it are now disenchanted, angry, and resentful. Many also no longer respect the agents of domestic and international institutions and question their authority.

The time is ripe, then, for serious inquiry into what legitimacy means in the case of multilateral institutions, for developing a clear understanding of the conditions that must be satisfied if they are to be legitimate and widely perceived to be so, and for understanding the relationship between the legitimacy of international institutions and the legitimacy of states. It is also a critical time for making the case that well-designed, morally principled multilateral institutions can be an important component of effective responses to some of the most pressing problems of our world. This volume should prove useful, then, not only for resisting an ill-considered, wholesale rejection of the existing multilateral world order, but for rebuilding and extending that order in a better way when the predictable reaction to its dismantling begins. Each chapter weds liberal cosmopolitan Political Philosophy with a liberal institutionalist approach to International Relations, while taking to heart the valid insights of Realism, but without its acquiescence in the status quo.

Multilateralism Tempered with Realist Insights

This volume is not an uncritical, or qualified endorsement of multilateralism. All of its chapters reflect an unblinking recognition that liberal cosmopolitan institutionalists must heed three related central points made by Realists regarding world politics. (1) Institutional design must take seriously the actual, as opposed to the ideal distribution of power, with the implication that well-designed institutions must provide effective incentives for all participants, and especially the most powerful ones, not only to formally "sign-on," but also to follow through, rather than reneging on their commitments or gaming the institutional rules. (2) Legalism, understood as including both an uncritical faith in the efficacy of law (not qualified by an appreciation of the effects of power and interests on both the creation of law and its actual operation) and the assumption that progress always involves strict adherence to existing law, is counterproductive and even dangerous. (3) Moralism, understood as overconfidence in the ability to ascertain what is universally right combined with an exclusive focus on ideal moral thinking to the neglect of practical strategies for incremental moral improvement, is not just unhelpful for solving real world problems; it can actually be an impediment to doing so. What is more, moralism's inevitable failures are also likely to reinforce the extreme Realist's disdain for the idea that morality can play a significant role in world politics.

In positive terms, two themes run through all of the chapters in this volume. The first is that moral progress in international relations requires institutional innovation. The second is that to achieve the right sort of institutional innovation it is necessary to integrate a grasp of the fundamentals of effective institutional design and a fact-based understanding of the limitations and resources of existing institutions, on the one hand, with moral analysis informed by liberal cosmopolitan principles, on the other. In other words, it is crucial both to appreciate the flaws and limitations of existing institutions and to be willing to make realistic but morally progressive proposals for better ones.

If one simply looked at how most contemporary political philosophers invest their energies, one would have to conclude that they think that the greatest deficiency of our world, or at least the deficiency that should most fully occupy their attention as philosophers, is the failure to have in hand an adequate theory, a systematic and well-argued Political Philosophy that speaks to a range of issues including the morality of war and more generally justice in international relations. My diagnosis, and hence the focus of my efforts is quite different. I think the most glaring deficiency at present is the lack of institutions capable of implementing widely agreed upon, rather philosophically uncontroversial principles of justice. I also think that philosophers can play a distinctive and vital role in evaluating existing institutions and formulating proposals for better ones. But to do this, philosophers will have to revise their own methodologies. They will need to learn to think institutionally.

Taken together, these chapters make the case that if political philosophers wish their work to have a decent chance of contributing to moral progress, they must first admit that the traditional analytic philosopher's toolkit is inadequate. This means departing from their comfort zones and learning new skills. I do not underestimate the difficulty of persuading philosophers to do this. I have been unpleasantly surprised by how quick many are to ignore—or to react with hostility to—my request that they make their work more useful by thinking institutionally.

It would be a mistake to gloss my suggestion as merely a plea to try to think about how to use institutions to implement moral conclusions that can be arrived at by thinking noninstitutionally. My point, rather, is that institutional realities and possibilities make a difference as to what we should think about the morality of war and of international relations more generally.

My proposals for institutional innovation are, of course, informed by a normative perspective. All proposals for improvement must be, for without a normative perspective one cannot distinguish improvement from change. The moral principles I invoke as premises in my arguments are, however, relatively unproblematic, at least across a broad range of liberal cosmopolitan views. This refusal to take a stand on a number of important disputes within the liberal cosmopolitan camp reflects neither lack of intellectual courage nor theoretical uncertainty; it is instead a virtue when it comes to providing a moral foundation for the design of new institutions.

Nonetheless, my focus on institutions enables me to advance some novel normative conclusions. For example, I argue, contrary to the mainstream of contemporary thinkers who have dealt with the issue, that preventive war can be justified—but only if the decision to engage in it comes about through an institutionalized procedure aptly designed to reduce the special risks of relying on "the Preventive War Justification." Similarly, I argue, again contrary to the mainstream of opinion, that it would be justifiable for a state or group of states to intervene militarily to prevent the destruction of a democratic government, even without UN Security Council authorization and without the *current* consent of that government or the people—if the intervention was duly authorized by a valid "precommitment" contract for intervention. To take another example: I argue that under certain conditions, it can be permissible and even morally obligatory to improve international law by violating it and that a violation of existing law may exhibit the virtue of law-abidingness if it is undertaken as part of a well-thought-out scheme of institutional development that embodies a commitment to the rule of law. My methodological strategy is to work from relatively uncontroversial *basic* (but usually unhelpfully abstract) principles of liberal cosmopolitan morality toward much more controversial and more specific moral conclusions, via proposals for institutional innovation.

To be useful, proposals for institutional innovation need not be immediately feasible to implement, but they must not be too distant from the current feasibility horizon. To be "close enough" to feasibility, proposals for institutional innovations must not only be realistic in the sense of being compatible with the actual distribution of power and the interests that motivate the exercise of power, but also able to marshal broad moral support. More specifically, it must be possible to make the case that if the proposed institutions were created they would be legitimate according to criteria for legitimacy that are grounded ultimately in a Political Philosophy that can command broad allegiance and that is well-developed, coherent, and adequately defended. At present, liberal cosmopolitanism satisfies those desiderata better than any alternative. In my judgment, liberal cosmopolitanism is also the most morally plausible view presently on offer.

I believe that taken together these chapters make a compelling case for a new, genuinely interdisciplinary approach to thinking about multilateral institutions generally and in particular regarding their potential for regulating war. The main ideas of each chapter and how they serve to illustrate this fundamental theme can be summarized as follows.

Before proceeding to the summary, a word about the title is in order. Significant work has been accomplished in the last century and a half, beginning with the establishment of the International Committee of the Red Cross, in institutionalizing some important aspects of the *jus in bello*, the part of just war theory that concerns how wars are to be conducted. For that reason I chose a sculpture honoring Henry Dunant, founder of the ICRC, for the front cover image of this book. Dunant's deep empathy for the suffering of unattended wounded soldiers he encountered in the aftermath of the battle of Solferino prompted his conscience. The ultimate result was not only the creation of an international organization to provide succor to the victims of armed conflict, but a new body of international law—the humanitarian law of war—with a complex array of institutions to clarify and help implement it.

The institutionalization of the *jus ad bellum*, the part of just war theory that consists of principles prescribing the conditions under which recourse to war is just or right, has been less effective and much less developed. The UN Charter, the most important single document of international law regarding recourse to war, prohibits the use of military force across borders except in self-defense (or defense of other countries) unless it is authorized by the United Nations Security Council. Since the 1990s this law has been interpreted in a broader fashion, so as to allow Security Council authorization of wars of humanitarian intervention, in cases where massive violations of the human right to physical security have occurred or are eminent. But international law, and the institutions that support it, still provide inadequate control over the initiation of war. Notoriously, the Security Council has failed to authorize humanitarian intervention in recent cases of genocide.

There is a more general failure, however, that is the focus of my thinking in this volume: international law and institutions do little to help ensure that state leaders will make morally sound and factually informed decisions regarding recourse to war. Nor do domestic institutions provide serious protections against the predictable errors and abuses of recourse to war decision-making. Yet even if domestic institutions were much better in this regard than they are, there is good reason to think that they would be inadequate unless they were properly supported by the right sort of international institutions. This is true even in the case of democratic domestic governments operating under laudable constitutional constraints and within the boundaries of the rule of law. Democracy by definition includes institutional devices for helping to ensure that government officials, including the commander in chief who ultimately makes the decision to go to war, are accountable *to the people of that polity*; but that is no assurance that the rights and interests of foreigners will be accorded due regard. On the contrary, being accountable only to their own fellow citizens puts leaders at risk for slighting the rights and interests of the citizens of other countries.

This volume is in part an effort to elevate the discussion of how further principled institutionalization of the *jus ad bellum* might be achieved. In other words, it offers proposals that could help achieve better compliance with widely agreed-upon principles concerning recourse to war, by achieving their more effective implementation through reliance on suitable institutions. In that sense, this is addressed to government officials and NGO workers who recognize that the most pressing human problem regarding war is not the lack of a fully developed *theory* of the morality of war, but rather a failure to put into effect what we already know about the morality of war. But it is also an intervention designed to encourage *jus ad bellum* theorists to take seriously the practical task of constraining recourse to war. A central message of this volume is that if just war theorizing is to make human life better, it must engage with the limitations and potential value of institutions. To do this, just war theorists will have to descend from the lofty heights of ideal theory to think about how the presence or absence of institutions makes a difference to the morality of going to war. This central point can be put in an even more provocative way: philosophers should quit acting as if they thought that just war theory is a theory for the state of nature—a condition in which there are no institutions worth mentioning and in which questions of institutional innovation simply do not arise.

Summary of Chapters

Chapter One, "Institutionalizing the Just War," advances a basic thesis that informs all the subsequent chapters: traditional just war theory was developed on the implicit assumption of *negligible institutional capacity* for improving decisions to engage in war and explores how the moral possibilities enlarge once this assumption is abandoned. This amounts to assuming that just war theory is a theory for people in the state of nature as it was traditionally conceived in the Social Contract tradition—a condition in which in effect all issues of morality are issues of individual morality. (Hence the tendency of many contemporary just war theorists to begin by eliciting intuitions about the rightness of acts of violence among individuals, abstracted from any institutional context.)

Once we take seriously the idea that institutions can reshape the moral possibilities, a second major thesis of the chapter comes clearly into view: the proper object of assessment for just war theory is not norms considered in isolation, but rather norm/institution packages, due to the fact that whether a norm is valid can depend upon whether it will function within a particular institution. For example, the widely held view that wars with the object of forcibly democratizing another country are never justified is plausible only if one assumes (1) that the validity of norms does not depend upon institutional context; or (2) that existing institutional resources for constraining decisions to initiate such wars are inadequate *and* the creation of better institutional resources is either not feasible or would be an improvement, all things considered. But neither of these two assumptions, I argue, is valid. Failing to consider how institutional innovation can change the moral landscape of war serves to support a morally suboptimal status quo, while at the same time fostering an arbitrarily restrictive understanding of the scope of just war theorizing.

This chapter does not advocate forcible democratization; instead it argues that while this type of warfare could be justifiable under certain demanding institutional constraints, in the absence of significant institutional innovations, there is a very strong presumption against it. One goal of this first chapter, then, is to gain greater clarity about exactly why forcible democratization (under current conditions) is unjustified. The conclusion reached is that it makes no sense to argue either that forcible democratization is justified or that it is not without specifying the institutional setting within which norms regarding the use of force to achieve democracy would be applied.

The fundamental methodological implication of this chapter is clear: practically relevant work in this and other departments of just war theory cannot be restricted to formulating abstract norms to capture intuitions elicited by consideration of hypothetical cases presented in an institutional vacuum. A knowledge of existing institutional capacities combined with a realistic appraisal of the opportunities for institutional innovation grounded in an understanding of principles of institutional design are also needed. Otherwise, we will be left with moral norms that are so abstract that they provide little guidance for responding to the real problems of war.

Chapter Two, "A Richer *Jus ad Bellum*," draws out further implications of Chapter One's thesis that traditional just war theory was developed on the assumption of negligible institutional capacity—whether domestic or supranational—for regulating recourse to war. In other words, traditional just war theory typically addresses its principles to the conscience of state leaders, while remaining silent on the question of whether different principles might be appropriate if leaders made decisions within institutional structures aptly designed to improve their decision-making. I argue that contemporary mainstream just war theorizing suffers this limitation as well: it proceeds as if the institutional context of decisions to initiate war need not be considered in developing a systematic account of the morality of war. The result is an arbitrarily narrow understanding of the domain of just war theorizing, a truncated set of issues to which the just war theorist ought to address. Among the important moral issues that a comprehensive theory of just war ought to address but which are not even broached by traditional or contemporary mainstream just war theory are these: (1) whether and if so under what conditions leaders should not apply the objective criteria for right war-making actions directly, but should instead rely on heuristics designed to reduce the risk of abuse and error in their decision-making that arises from their imperfect information and conflicting motives and incentives; (2) what is the proper division of labor between heuristics and institutional constraints on decision-making as distinct but potentially complementary ways of reducing the risk of abuse and error; (3) what are the proper criteria for evaluating the actual decision-making of leaders, including an account of the virtues that are appropriate for individuals empowered to initiate and conduct war; and (4) whether a morally sound social practice of offering public justifications for going to war ought to regard certain types of justifications as illegitimate due to the high risk that their use will result in erroneous or duplicitous decisions to initiate war.

The first two chapters set the stage for the third, "Institutional Legitimacy": if some of the most important issues just war theory should address can only be sensibly engaged by recognizing the limitations of existing institutions and being willing to contemplate institutional innovations, then a understanding of what makes an institution legitimate is needed. Further, the needed understanding of institutional legitimacy must encompass both the state and its internal institutions, as well as international institutions.

This chapter refines and augments an analysis of institutional legitimacy designed to illuminate both the legitimacy of states and of international institutions first advanced in a widely cited essay I co-authored with Robert O. Keohane: "The Legitimacy of Global Governance Institutions." It begins by distinguishing between normative and sociological legitimacy. It then proceeds on the assumption that institutions designed to further liberal cosmopolitan values can only do so if they are widely perceived to be legitimate, because the raw exercise of power without at least the trappings of legitimacy is rarely effective in the longer run, and that, therefore, when the legitimacy of actual or proposed institutions is called into question, an effective response on their behalf will rely in part on plausible arguments to show that they satisfy reasonable criteria for legitimacy. A virtue of the "Metacoordination" View of institutional legitimacy developed in this chapter is that it is general enough to illuminate the legitimacy of both states and of multilateral institutions that are quite unlike states, but sufficiently contentful to provide guidance for developing sound criteria for legitimacy that are tailored to specific types of institutions. This chapter offers a complex standard for legitimacy: a set of criteria that are relevant for assessing the legitimacy of a wide range of international and domestic institutions, including those that are designed to improve decisions regarding the initiating of war. These criteria will be shown to be useful in subsequent chapters, when specific institutional innovations are proposed.

The understanding of institutional legitimacy developed in this chapter is called the Metacoordination View to emphasize that the distinctive practical role of the concept of normative legitimacy is to facilitate coordination, based on certain types of moral reasons, regarding the assessment of whether an institution is worthy of particular forms of respect. A key feature of this analysis is the recognition that institutional legitimacy must be understood ecologically: that whether a particular institution is legitimate can often depend upon its relationship to other institutions.

Chapter Four, "Reciprocal Institutional Legitimation," further explores the idea, first advanced in the preceding chapter, that institutional legitimacy is ecological, by explaining through the use of pertinent examples how the legitimacy of an institution may depend upon the role it plays in an institutional division of labor and more specifically on whether other institutions operate in such a way as to enhance its legitimacy and vice versa. A key example is the fact that a state's participation in international human rights institutions can enhance its legitimacy, inter alia, by providing an independent determination of whether that state is respecting the human rights of its own citizens. Conversely, to the extent that international human rights institutions are created by states that are democratic and respect human rights, this enhances their legitimacy. Similarly, whether a multilateral regime for humanitarian intervention is legitimate may depend upon how it functions in a division of labor to which other legitimate institutions contribute. The idea of reciprocal institutional legitimation is exploited in the last two chapters of this volume, which offer respectively, proposals for the institutional regulation of humanitarian military interventions and military interventions to protect democracies.

Chapter Five, "The Internal Legitimacy of Humanitarian Intervention," is a significantly modified version of an earlier published article of that title, supplemented to emphasize the need for institutional change not only at the international but also at the domestic level, if humanitarian intervention is to be justified. It addresses a problem that is generally neglected in the literature on humanitarian intervention: how are state leaders to justify *to their own fellow citizens* the decision to use the country's armed forces and its material resources for the sake of helping foreigners, when doing so does not further the interests of those citizens and is not required for the protection of their rights?

This fifth chapter first argues that making the case for the internal legitimacy of humanitarian intervention depends upon the rejection of a simple but prima facie attractive conception of what the state is for: if the state is only an institutional resource for furthering the interests of its citizens and protecting their rights, then humanitarian intervention is not legitimate (except in cases where it serves the interests of the citizens or protects their rights). I then go on to argue that this highly constraining understanding of what the state is for, which I call The Discretionary Association View, is mistaken. The chief conclusion of Chapter

Five is that for humanitarian intervention to be legitimate, the decision to intervene must be made through an institutional process that is more robustly democratic than those through which the decision is currently made or it must be authorized by an explicit and suitably crafted constitutional provision.

Chapter Six, "Reforming the International Law of Humanitarian Intervention," connects themes from the preceding chapters regarding the multilateral institutional regulation of recourse to war with an inquiry into the nature of the relationship between institutions, international law, and morality. More specifically, it challenges the widely held assumption that moral improvements in international law and institutions can—or should—always be achieved without violating existing international law.

Using as a case study the 1999 NATO intervention in Serbia to halt the start of large-scale violence against ethnic Albanians in the province of Kosovo, this chapter challenges the assumption that moral progress in international law can or must always be achieved without illegality. A key distinction, emphasized earlier in Chapter Three, is drawn between legality (conformity to law as it is) and lawfulness (a commitment to the rule of law, where this includes a willingness to attempt to improve existing law, even if this requires breaking it, through the creation of new, legitimate institutions that exhibit the virtues of the rule of law). The central idea is that in a system of law like the international legal system, one that is seriously morally deficient and which also affords very limited possibilities for progress through strictly legal actions, violating the law can be consistent with lawfulness, but only if the violators are committed to institutional innovations that satisfy appropriate criteria for legitimacy and express respect for the rule of law. This means that NATO's intervention would have been less morally problematic if that institution—instead of claiming a privilege to act without Security Council authorization that it denied to others—had publicly committed to transforming itself into the sort of accountable multilateral institution that could be trusted to engage in humanitarian interventions when the Security Council fails to authorize them.

Once again, the point is that the morality of armed conflict, in this case military humanitarian intervention, is not institution-independent: acts that would otherwise be morally impermissible violations of international law can be not only morally permissible, but also lawful in the sense of expressing a proper appreciation of the importance of law, in spite of their illegality, if they are part of an effort to improve the law through institutional innovation. In terms of what Realists get right, the point is that an exceptionless, fetishistic commitment to legality can be an impediment to developing morally better law in a system as imperfect as the international legal order. Yet developing better international law regarding humanitarian military intervention requires that the violation of existing law be undertaken in the context of a project of institutional innovation. Ad hoc violations of international law, bereft of a commitment to lawfulness, are unlikely to be morally justifiable. Given President Trump's disdain for law generally and especially for international law, this sixth chapter is if anything more relevant than when it first appeared.

Chapter Seven, "Justifying Preventive War, Institutionally," the original version of which was co-authored with Robert O. Keohane, develops further the idea that institutions matter for the morality of war by making an institutionalist case for the permissibility of preventive war, understood as war undertaken not to avert an imminent harm (preemptive war), but rather to eliminate a threat of harm that is temporally distant and therefore inevitably uncertain as to its realization. The question of whether preventive, as distinct from preemptive war, is justifiable was vividly posed by the Iraq War that began in March of 2003, because the Bush administration argued that the war was necessary to avert the threat that at some unspecified time in the future weapons of mass destruction said to be in Saddam Hussein's possession would be used against the United States or its allies. This chapter first disposes of the view that preventive war is never permissible because war is only justified against parties who have already actually done wrong by showing that under certain conditions conspiring to inflict temporally distant future harms counts as wrong-doing. The key point here is that creating a dire threat of wrongful harm *is* doing something wrong, even if the threat is not likely to be immediately realized. Chapter Seven then goes on to explain the inadequacies of widely employed consequentialist arguments against preventive war, arguments designed to show that preventive war is too morally risky, due to the extraordinary potential for error and abuse that recourse to the idea of preventing temporally distant and uncertain harms poses. The crucial point is that these risks are not fixed: they can be reduced to acceptable levels if the decision to engage in preventive war is made within well-designed institutional constraints, procedures aptly designed to improve the epistemic context of decisions and counteract leaders' incentives to exaggerate the seriousness of threats of temporally distant harms. This chapter concludes that although preventive war would be justifiable if the decision to engage in it were made through the right sort of institutional procedures, the US decision in 2003 to invade Iraq in order to prevent possible future harms was not justified. That decision was made in the absence of the demanding institutional constraints that alone could make the decision to engage in preventive war justified. There is a clear link between this chapter and Chapter Two, which emphasized, inter alia, that *jus ad bellum* theory should address the moral evaluation of practices for justifying going to war: a social practice that regards the appeal to prevention as a legitimate kind of justification for going to war is morally defective unless it operates in the context of a suitably designed institution for ameliorating the inherent risks of appealing to this sort of justification for war-making.

Chapter Eight, "Precommitment Regimes for Intervention," like the preceding chapter, is a modified version of an article co-authored with Robert O. Keohane. It explains how an institutional innovation that is compatible with existing international law concerning the rights of sovereignty could facilitate timely intervention to protect democracies from authoritarian coups or from a resurgence of internal violence, through pre-authorization. The practical urgency for such a proposal stems from the fact that interventions to protect democracies from authoritarian coups or prevent the resumption of ethno-national violence are unlikely to receive Security Council authorization due to the exercise of the permanent member veto by two authoritarian regimes, China and Russia. This essay outlines a precommitment regime, to be created by treaty, by which a legitimate government can in effect avail itself of an insurance policy by authorizing a particular state or group of states to intervene if there is an attempt to overthrow it by force or if there is a resumption of large-scale ethno-national violence. The precommitment contract is a kind of rational self-binding mechanism that is properly viewed as a prudent exercise of sovereignty by a democratic government on behalf of its people, rather than an abdication of sovereignty. The chief virtue of the idea of a precommitment regime for intervention is that it provides a way of supplementing, not rejecting, the authority of the Security Council to authorize intervention, by providing for the possibility of intervention when the exercise of the permanent member veto precludes it and doing so without adopting a broad—and highly dangerous—norm allowing intervention whenever democracy or internal peace and security are threatened. And it provides this benefit without violating state sovereignty; instead, precommitment regimes provide a new way for vulnerable democracies to protect themselves through the exercise of sovereignty, by entering into a treaty that authorizes intervention in advance.

A Plea for a Change in Methodology

The interdisciplinary but explicitly normative institutionalist approach employed in this volume can be applied to a wide range of multilateral institutions designed to cope with a diversity of problems. The specific institutional proposals advanced focus on the problem of regulating recourse to war, but the theory of institutional legitimacy offered and the methodological strategy followed throughout are of much broader applicability.

Accordingly, my hope is that this volume will do something to bring about a significant change in the intellectual culture of contemporary political philosophers, prompting them to think institutionally and to recognize that their favorite technique of eliciting intuitions about hypothetical cases involving individuals (and not individuals as institutional agents!), without a specification of institutional realities and possibilities, can only take one so far.

To be frank, my suspicion is that "so far" is not very far at all. When contemporary just war theorists produce extremely complex criteria for determining when an act of going to war is right—including remarkably complicated requirements regarding as many as three distinct types of "proportionality"—they ignore the fact that the epistemic demands for applying their criteria may be too great for flesh and blood leaders. They also ignore the fact that leaders are unlikely to act in ways that are consistent with valid moral norms unless they have sufficient incentives to do so and that different institutions create different incentives. So long as political philosophers confine themselves to articulating and defending moral norms that are so abstract as to be valid irrespective of institutional context, they need not concern themselves with institutional analysis, nor with a consideration of whether sound decision-making regarding war should be constrained and structured by institutions that are designed to prevent leaders from attempting to apply directly appropriate criteria for the rightness of war-making acts. But the price of this "advantage" is that there will remain an enormous gap between the highly abstract moral norms they endorse and the development of morally sound practical responses to the problems. In other words, even if decision-makers ingested and internalized the basic norms of the best just war theory, they would still face a host of unanswered questions; they would still not know what to do. Unless something is done to bridge this gap, just war theorizing will remain an intellectual exercise for a small number of specialists rather than an example of how expertise in moral reasoning can make a positive difference in the world.

My worry can be put in another way. I fear that mainstream just war theory has become largely a matter of different theorists intervening in a dialogue among themselves that is so narrowly framed as to ensure its almost total irrelevance to the problems that actual individuals face when confronted with the possibility or reality of war. In other words, they are responding more to problems identified in their literature—and in particular to the question of criteria for right acts of war-making—rather than to the full range of moral problems of war. Suppose, as I have argued, that the morality of war contains much more than the identification of criteria for right acts of war-making. Suppose, as I argue in Chapters One and Two, that it also includes the articulation of sound heuristics and institutional procedures for decision-making, the identification of sound social practices regarding what are regarded as legitimate public justifications for going to war, and an account of the virtues of war leaders, where this includes practical knowledge of when to rely on heuristics and how far they should be bound by institutional procedures for decision-making and by existing international law. If that is so, then any approach to just war theory that confines itself to articulating criteria for right war-making acts that are valid irrespective of institutional context and without regard to the epistemic and motivational limitations of human beings will be of limited value.

CHAPTER 1

Institutionalizing
the Just War

Momentous events, especially wars and revolutions, have a way of awakening theorists from their slumbers (dogmatic or otherwise). The US invasion and occupation of Iraq stimulated a vigorous scholarly debate over the justification of preventive war and forcible democratization. Justifications for preventive war and forcible democratization both challenge the Traditional Just War Norm (henceforth TJWN), according to which war is permissible only in response to an actual or imminent attack.[1] Preventive war justifications hold that it can be permissible to

---

[1] I proceed on the assumption that the dominant stream of contemporary just war theory endorses this norm. In its earlier versions, just war theory included the idea that war could be waged to punish wrongs. However, in recent times the idea of war as punishment has fallen into disfavor, for good reasons. Nonetheless, one might argue that what I have called the Just War Norm includes an exception: war may be waged (as a last resort) to rectify wrongful conquest. Whether this is an exception depends upon how one construes "armed attack" in the TJWN. If this includes an unjust occupation as an ongoing attack on the people of the unjustly conquered state, then war to rectify wrongful conquest is not an exception to the TJWN but rather is encompassed by it. If one believes that this is an implausible construal of "armed attack," then the TJWN can be reformulated to include this exception. The two justifications I am concerned with in this article, the Preventive Self-Defense Justification and the Forcible Democratization Justification, are challenges to the TJWN regardless of whether it is understood to cover war to rectify unjust conquest or not.

make war to avert a temporally distant harm; forcible democratization justifications hold that it can be permissible to make war to achieve a temporally distant good, namely, democracy.

However, the debate has proceeded within the confines of a rarely stated framing assumption: that the key question is whether to abandon the TJWN in favor of a more permissive norm regarding the use of force.[2] I shall argue that the assumption that the choice between competing norms is mistaken. The proper choice is between adherence to the JWN and the creation of new institutions that would allow for a more permissive norm. Not just alternative norms but also alternative combinations of norms and institutions need to be evaluated.

The chief practical aim of just war theory is to constrain warmaking for the sake of morality. The *jus ad bellum* part of just war theory tries to do so by articulating norms that, if adhered to by state leaders, would constrain their decisions about whether to go to war. However, constraint on the resort to war can be achieved not only by state leaders adhering to narrowly drawn norms, but also by a division of labor between more permissive norms and institutions aptly designed to reduce the risks that reliance on more permissive norms would otherwise entail. Therefore, focusing only on competing norms rather than on combinations of norms and institutions only makes sense if one assumes either (1) that the validity of norms does not depend upon institutional context, or (2) that existing institutional resources for constraining war are negligible *and* the creation of new institutional resources is either not feasible or not worth the cost.

In Section I, I argue that the first assumption is false. I show that which norms are valid can vary, depending upon the institutional context. Section II explains the best rationale for the TJWN: it rules out war to avert temporally distant harms or to

---

[2] An exception is Allen Buchanan and Robert O. Keohane, "The Preventive Use of Force: A Cosmopolitan Institutionalist Perspective," *Ethics & International Affairs* 18, no. 1 (2004): 1–22.

achieve temporally distant goods in recognition of the fact that reliance on such inherently speculative justifications entails extraordinary risks of error and abuse. I then explain how adherence to the highly constraining TJWN as a way of avoiding these extraordinary risks comes at a high cost, given certain assumptions about the new conditions of terrorism. Next, I argue that the attempt to avoid these costs by simply abandoning the TJWN in favor of a more permissive norm that allows preventive force is a mistake, because it ignores the extraordinary risks that the TJWN's prohibition on preventive war is calculated to avoid. I show that the proper choice is not between adhering to the TJWN and abandoning it in favor of a more permissive norm, but rather between adhering to the TJWN and adopting a more permissive norm embedded in an institutional framework that reduces the risks of a more permissive norm. I then argue that which option is better depends both upon the costs of continuing to adhere to the TJWN and the feasibility and costs of creating institutions that would make reliance on a more permissive norm acceptable. Next, I show that whether it is worthwhile to try to create institutions in which a more permissive norm would be valid cannot be decided by philosophical argument alone, but requires empirically based institutional analysis.

In order to make clear that these results are not confined to the controversy over preventive war, but have broader implications for how we conceive of theorizing the morality of war, I then examine the proposal that the TJWN should be relaxed so as to allow for war to achieve democracy. I show that here, as in the case of preventive war, the controversy cannot be resolved simply by comparing alternative norms. Whether the TJWN's blanket prohibition of wars of democratization should be adhered to depends upon whether the extraordinary risks involved in the use of the Forcible Democratization Justification can be adequately ameliorated by embedding a more permissive norm in new institutional arrangements, and whether the costs of continued adherence to the TJWN are sufficiently high to warrant the costs of developing such institutions. I therefore conclude that it is a mistake simply to assume that the creation of a more permissive norm along with an appropriate new institutional context is either infeasible or would be too costly. Taken together, these explorations of preventive war and forcible democratization support the conclusion that some of the most serious controversies about the morality of war cannot be resolved without an inquiry into the feasibility and desirability of institutional change.

Section III draws the implications of this conclusion for the broader question of the viability of just war theory. I argue that just war theory thus far has assumed that institutional resources for constraining war are negligible; consequently, it *cannot* answer the question of whether the TJWN should be abandoned in favor of a more permissive norm embedded in a system of institutional safeguards. I then conclude that there are two ways to interpret this result. On one interpretation, just war theory has a much more limited domain than one might think: it is only a theory of the morality of war for the circumstances in which institutional resources for constraining the decisions of state leaders are negligible, theory for the state of nature. On this view, if institutional resources significantly improve, then we have moved beyond the domain of just war theory. This interpretation is plausible, indeed tautological, if one assumes that the domain of just war theory is *war* in the following technical sense: armed conflict among states that are in a state of nature vis-à-vis one another, where one important feature of the state of nature is lack of institutional capacity. On the second interpretation, just war theory has a more ambitious aim: to provide an account of the morality of large-scale military conflict among states, covering both situations in which there is significant institutional capacity and situations in which there is not. If my arguments are sound, then just war theory is either not a comprehensive moral account of large-scale armed conflict, or it is comprehensive but mistaken. Either it is limited to a domain in which institutional resources are negligible and can tell us nothing about what norms would be valid under different circumstances or whether we should try to build institutional capacity; or it purports to cover a domain that includes institutional as well as noninstitutional circumstances, but fails to take seriously the fact that the validity of norms can depend upon institutional context.

Finally, I argue that once the relationship between the validity of norms and institutions is understood, it becomes clear that contemporary just war *theorizing* is methodologically flawed, because it is insufficiently empirical. In arguing in favor of the TJWN, theorists often implicitly employ empirical premises about the bad consequences of abandoning the TJWN in favor of a more permissive one. However, their empiricism is arbitrarily incomplete. They fail to appreciate the fact that the risks of abandoning the TJWN are not fixed, but can vary depending upon institutional context. So, if just war theory is to be a comprehensive theory of large-scale military conflict, Just War theorizing must become more empirical. Arguments for and against proposed use-of-force norms must include factual premises about how various institutions work and about the feasibility and costs of creating them. This methodological implication is of considerable consequence; it means that a comprehensive just war theory cannot rely exclusively on philosophical argument as it is usually understood. The integration of moral philosophy and institutional analysis is required.

I. *How the Validity of Norms Can Depend on Institutions or Their Absence*

Whether a norm is valid can depend upon institutional context. For example, where we can rely on the police and courts to protect us from attacks by other individuals, a more narrowly drawn norm of justified self-defense is valid, other things being equal; where we must depend solely on our own efforts, there may be more latitude as to the measures we may take to protect ourselves. Similarly, it may be appropriate for police to have wider search or surveillance powers when there is reliable judicial review of their activities and where every citizen has access to competent legal counsel than where these institutional safeguards are lacking.

It is that connection between institutions and norms I wish to emphasize: better institutions can make more permissive norms valid. Constraints on agents can be achieved not only by their adherence to narrowly drawn norms but also by a combination of more permissive norms and institutions. This simple point has large implications for how to think about the morality of war. The next section draws out those implications in dialectical fashion, by critically evaluating the current controversy about the justification of preventive war and forcible democratization.

II. *Preventive War and Forcible Democratization*

Some critics have assumed that the Bush administration's appeal to the idea of preventive force in order to justify the invasion of Iraq in March of 2003 relies on a form of argument that enjoyed considerable popularity (at least among state leaders) during the eighteenth and nineteenth centuries in Europe, when the idea of the balance of power was ascendant. According to David Luban, this form of argument relies on the following premises:

1. Some state of affairs X (e.g., the balance of power in Europe) preserves some important value V ("European liberties") and is therefore worth defending even at some cost; and
2. To fight early, before X begins to unravel, greatly reduces the cost of the defense of V, while waiting does not avoid war (unless one gives up V) but only results in fighting on a larger scale at worse odds.[3]

---

[3] David Luban, "Preventive War," *Philosophy & Public Affairs* 32, no. 3 (2004): 207–48, at 220.

On Luban's reading, the Bush administration's version of this argument substitutes "US dominance" (remaining the one hyperpower) for "the balance of power."

Let us call a Preventive War Justification that relies on these two premises: the Traditional Preventive War Justification. Luban argues persuasively against this justification that its acceptance would be likely to lead to many wars and lead us to regard war as ordinary, that is, to fail to appreciate the almost incomprehensible, distinctive evil of war. To use the Traditional Preventive War Justification, he concludes, is simply too risky. However, as is usually the case with those who employ consequentialist reasoning to determine which just war norms are valid, he provides no explicit account of the relationship between the nature of the argument and the characteristics of the agents that are likely to employ it to spell out exactly what those risks are.[4]

Nor does Luban consider the possibility that the risks in question are not fixed, but instead vary, depending upon the institutional framework within which the justification is actually deployed to justify the act of going to war. In that sense, Luban, like virtually all Just War theorists, is incompletely empirical in his theorizing. He acknowledges the relevance of empirical assumptions by relying on arguments about the consequences of adopting this or that norm, but he does not recognize that institutions can make a difference as to the consequences of acting on norms and hence to the validity of norms. Finally, though he suggests that the Traditional Preventive War Justification ought not to be used, he does not consider the role that institutional constraints might play in preventing its use, for example, by

---

[4] Richard Miller's valuable discussion of humanitarian military intervention is a notable exception. Richard W. Miller, "Respectable Oppressors, Hypocritical Liberators: Morality, Intervention, and Reality," in *Ethics and Foreign Intervention*, eds. Deen K. Chaterjee and Don E. Schied (Cambridge, UK: Cambridge University Press, 2003), 215.

institutionally backed rules of public deliberation that explicitly exclude it. Instead, he again remains within the noninstitutionalist strictures of just war theory, apparently relying upon the persuasive effects of an institutionally disembodied consequentialist argument on the conscience of state leaders or on right-minded citizens who may then exert pressure on their leaders to behave properly.

Two Distinct Justifications for Preventive War

Some Bush administration statements are consistent with the Traditional Preventive War Justification. However, some of the administration's rhetoric suggests a more restricted and plausible appeal to preventive force. The Bush "National Security Strategy" can be read as claiming that under the new conditions of terrorism, the right of self-defense encompasses the use of preventive force: ". . . the United States . . . will not hesitate to act alone, if necessary, to exercise our right of self-defense by acting preemptively against . . . terrorists, to prevent them from doing harm against our people and our country."[5] The reason given for acknowledging this expanded right of self-defense is straightforward: we now live in a world in which weapons of mass destruction are widely available and can be deployed covertly and suddenly, and in which there are agents who are willing to use them against innocent persons and who are not subject to the 'logic of deterrence' to which state leaders typically conform. Under these new conditions, the administration concludes, preventive force in self-defense is justifiable.

[5] "National Security Strategy of the United States of America September 2002," 6; available at http://www.globalsecurity.org/military/library/policy/dod/nds-usa_mar2005. This document misleadingly uses the term 'preemptive,' which in standard international legal usage refers to efforts to thwart an *imminent* attack, to cover preventive self-defense, that is, defensive action against a temporally distant anticipated harm.

On a charitable interpretation, this passage from the National Defense Strategy appeals to what I shall call the Preventive Self-Defense Justification, according to which preventive war can be justified as an exercise of the right of self-defense, but only when the target against whom they engage in preventive war is *wrongfully imposing a dire risk*. On this view, the right of self-defense allows preventive war, but it does not allow preventive force to be used whenever using it would prevent some harm or other and waiting to address the harm at a later date would be more costly and risky. Instead, the Preventive Self-Defense Justification limits the resort to preventive war in two crucial ways. First, unlike the Traditional Preventive War Justification, it does not allow appeal to anything so broad as the preservation of "important values," or even to the prevention of harms, but instead limits action to the prevention of the most serious of harms. In the case of states, this would mean something much more serious than economic loss or loss of military dominance.[6] Second, the risk of harm must be *wrongfully imposed*. The mere fact that B poses a threat to A, even a dire threat, does not justify A's acting to prevent the threat from being realized. For example, if A has already unjustly attacked B, A is not justified in attacking B again to prevent B from rallying its forces and attacking A, even if the threat B poses is dire. In this case, B poses a dire threat to A, but not a wrongfully imposed dire threat.

Once the distinctive character of the Preventive Self-Defense Justification is understood, it becomes clear that the Traditional Preventive War Justification is not properly described as invoking the right of self-defense at all. Not all action to protect "important values" counts as self-defense. Nor are all threats of future harm wrongfully imposed.

---

[6] Luban's view of justified preventive war, which I critique below, incorporates something like the notion of a dire harm, but does not include the crucial requirement that the risk of harm must be wrongfully imposed.

Consequentialist and Rights-Based Arguments
against Preventive Self-Defense

There are two main arguments against the thesis that the right of self-defense allows preventive war under certain circumstances. The first, consequentialist objection is analogous to Luban's complaint about the Traditional Preventive War Justification: the use of such a justification for war is too risky. The second, rights-based objection, is that preventive war necessarily violates the rights to life of those against whom it is waged because, by hypothesis, they have not (yet) done anything wrong and therefore retain the right to life that the "innocent" have. Later I will argue that the consequentialist objection to the Preventive Self-Defense Justification, as typically framed, is incomplete, because it fails to consider whether the risks of using this justification could be adequately ameliorated by appropriate institutions. First, however, I want to focus on the rights-based objection.

The most obvious rebuttal to the rights-based objection is that it is not true that the target of preventive force, by hypothesis, has done nothing wrong. On the preventive force justification under consideration, she has done something wrong: she has wrongly imposed a dire risk on another, even though the harm is not imminent.

Both the law of conspiracy and the law of attempts provide useful analogies for understanding how a wrongly imposed dire threat need not be imminent. In both cases, the elements of the crime capture the idea that the agents in question have done something wrong, but in neither case must there be an imminent harm. In the law of conspiracy, two or more persons, working in concert, must have formed a "specific intention" and a plan to commit a crime, and (in most jurisdictions) something must have been done toward carrying out the plan.[7] In the law of attempts,

---

[7] Arnold H. Lowey, "Conspiracy," in *Criminal Law in a Nutshell* (St. Paul, MN: West Group, 2000), 260; and Joshua Dressler, "Inchoate Offenses," in

the individuals must have taken some substantial step toward committing a crime, but this need not result in the crime being imminent.[8]

Of course, both the law of attempts and that of conspiracy can sometimes be poorly framed in statute and there can be abuses in the enforcement of each as well. Nevertheless, there is nothing in the basic conception of either type of law that entails that enforcement of them, even with lethal force in extreme circumstances, *necessarily* involves violations of the rights of those against whom they are applied. In neither case can it be said that force is being used against someone who has not yet done anything wrong. If this is so, then there is no fundamental moral bar to holding that force can sometimes be justified in order to avert a future wrongful harm that is not yet imminent.[9]

Cases and Materials in Criminal Law, 2nd ed. (St. Paul, MN: West Group, 1999), 765.

[8] Russell Powell, "The Law and Philosophy of Preventive War: An Institution-Based Approach to Collective Self-Defense in Response to Mega-Terrorism" (unpublished manuscript), builds on the Institutionalist approach to preventive force developed in Buchanan and Keohane and argues that the law of attempts is the more useful analogy because, unlike the law of conspiracy, it does not require two or more parties working in concert. Powell's paper provides valuable critical overview of the international legal issues regarding preventive force.

[9] It might be argued that there is still a problem: at least some of the enemy soldiers who may be targeted by the preventive action may not, in any significant sense, be part of the conspiracy. I argue that there are two distinct conditions under which such individuals may be legitimate targets: when they are culpable for putting themselves at the disposal of governments whose behavior indicates that are likely to engage in conspiracies to commit aggression; or when the unjust harm that will occur if preventive action is not taken is so great that it is justifiable to attack them in spite of their lack of culpability, given that reasonable efforts have been made to apprise them that the action about to be taken against them is not an unjust attack but rather a justified preventive action and that they have been given the opportunity to surrender or step aside. Allen Buchanan, "The Justification of Preventive War," in *Preemption: Military Action and Moral Justification*, eds. Henry Shue and David Rodin (Oxford: Oxford University Press, 2006), 126-42.

In the case of enforcing the laws of conspiracy and of attempts, force is employed only under the direction of judicial institutions; private enforcement of such laws would be so risky as to be morally impermissible. What this shows is that a justification for preventive self-defense that draws on the analogy of conspiracy and attempts would have to include recourse to institutions that would adequately ameliorate the risks of private enforcement in the absence of an international judiciary. Later in this chapter I shall sketch such an institution. In Chapter Seven I fill in the details of the proposal.

A full account of the Preventive Self-Defense Justification for preventive war would have to spell out precisely what counts as wrongfully imposing a dire risk and make a fully convincing case that this does not require imminent harm. My aim here is not to produce such an account. Instead I have only tried to say enough to indicate its plausibility and by doing so make it clear that one cannot disregard the possibility of preventive self-defense by merely asserting that it necessarily violates the rights of the target because the target, by hypothesis, has not yet done anything wrong.

Why Imminence Is Not Necessary

Luban offers his consequentialist criticism of the much less plausible Traditional Preventive War Justification and then goes on to propose a more constraining justification for preventive war. According to Luban, preventive war is justifiable only when it is necessary to avert a harm that is "probabilistically imminent," though this need not involve being temporally imminent. In other words, Luban retains the TJWN according to which a state may make war only to stop an occurring or imminent attack, but construes imminence expansively, to cover *both* temporally proximate and temporally distant harms, if they are "all but certain."[10] He then suggests that this criterion for justified preventive

10 Luban, "Preventive War," 230.

war is equivalent to restricting the Traditional Preventive War Justification to cases where the target of preventive war is a "rogue state," on the assumption that the characteristics that define rogue states make it "all but certain" that they will act aggressively at some point in the future.[11]

Luban wrongly assumes that what justifies preventive force is the existence of an "imminent" threat, by which he means an *"all but certain"* prospect that something like what I have called a dire harm will occur. This analysis omits something that is essential to the idea of the right of self-defense and that accounts for the plausibility of the claim that preventive war, if it can be justified at all, is justifiable only in cases of self-defense: namely, that the dire risk to be averted is *wrongfully imposed*.

A harm's being imminent in the sense of being "all but certain" does nothing to justify using preventive force of any kind, much less preventive war. Consider the following variation on the case discussed above. A unjustly attacks B and then attacks B again, to prevent B's launching an "all but certain" lethal attack (in justified self-defense) against A.[12] The fact that B's acting to harm A is "all but certain" does nothing to justify A's second attack on B, and this is true even if the harm B would inflict on A is as serious as possible. Conversely, preventive force may be justified to avert a harm that is considerably less than "all but certain" if the harm is sufficiently great and the imposition of the risk of that harm is deeply wrong. For example, if I viciously plan to kill you and you have good evidence that I am committed to carrying out the plan, you may be justified in using lethal force against me, if this is the only way to prevent your murder, even if my plan is considerably less than foolproof. To expect you to refrain from using force to protect yourself unless the risk of deadly harm I wrongly impose on you is "all but certain" would be to construe the right of self-defense in a way that places an unreasonable burden of restraint

---

[11] Luban, "Preventive War," 229–31.
[12] I thank Jeff McMahan for this example.

on the innocent to protect themselves, at least in circumstances in which you cannot rely on effective help from others. Of course, if you and I happen to live in a society with an effective police and court system, you do not have to rely exclusively on your own actions to protect yourself from my sinister plan, and under these conditions a more restricted understanding of your right of self-defense may be compelling.

It can be argued that even the rather constrained legal right of individual self-defense that presupposes such backup institutions does not require anything so strong as Luban's notion of "all but certain" harm. However, even if it did, matters are quite different on the international scene, where at present there is nothing approaching an effective police force.

The results of the argument of this section thus far can be summarized as follows. (1) Luban's consequentialist criticism of the Traditional Preventive War Justification is cogent (though for the reasons noted, incomplete). (2) The Preventive Self-Defense Justification, explicated in terms of the use of force is to avert a wrongfully imposed dire harm, is more plausible than Luban's attempt to accommodate preventive war within the constraints of the TJWN by stretching the notion of imminence. (3) The Preventive Self-Defense Justification cannot be ruled out on the grounds that it allows the use of force against those who have not done anything wrong, because it limits the use of preventive force to circumstances in which the target has in fact already done something wrong (by initiating the execution of an aggressive plan). (4) So, because the "rights-based" objection fails, if the Preventive Self-Defense Justification is unsound, the argument against it must be consequentialist in nature. The next step, then, is to explicate the Preventive Self-Defense Justification in its most plausible form and then develop more carefully and evaluate the objection that it is too risky to use. To do this it is first necessary to understand how the new conditions of terrorism are supposed to make the idea of preventive self-defense more plausible.

The Significance of the New Conditions of Terrorism

As I observed earlier, the Bush administration National Defense Strategy suggests that the new conditions of terrorism call for an expanded understanding of the scope of the right of self-defense, one that encompasses preventive war. How are the "new conditions" supposed to change the scope of the right of self-defense? The New Conditions Justification would go like this:

1. The scope of the right of (national) self-defense depends upon what risks of harm a country can reasonably be expected to bear by forgoing actions that it could undertake to protect itself against wrongfully imposed dire risks.
2. Under the "new conditions," it is unreasonable to expect a country, in its efforts to protect itself against wrongfully imposed dire risks, to restrict itself to using force against presently occurring or imminent attacks (i.e., to adhere to the TJWN and thereby foreswear preventive war).
3. (Therefore,) under the new conditions, the scope of the right of self-defense does *not exclude* preventive war.

Notice that the appeal to the new conditions of the "war on terrorism" *cannot* establish the conclusion that the United States (or any country) is morally justified in using preventive force in order to defend itself whenever it deems such force to be necessary to avert a wrongfully imposed dire risk, even harm that is "all but certain." At most, it only establishes a much weaker conclusion: that a *blanket prohibition* on the use of preventive force in self-defense is unacceptable. In other words, a proper appreciation of the "new conditions" at most implies that there may be circumstances in which the use of preventive force is morally justifiable as an exercise of the right of self-defense. It does not specify what the conditions are.

In fact the New Conditions Justification does not even establish that the Traditional Just War Norm's (TJWN's) blanket prohibition on preventive self-defense should be abandoned, unless the crucial premise (2) can be supported. What is clear is that the "new conditions" increase the costs of adherence to the TJWN. However, from that it does not follow that those increased costs are unreasonable. Whether they are unreasonable depends upon how high the costs of abandoning the TJWN are likely to be. Even if the costs of adhering to the TJWN are now high, due to the "new conditions," the costs of abandoning it may be higher still, unless something is done to ameliorate the extraordinary risks of acting on the Preventive Self-Defense Justification.

The problem with simply assuming premise (2) is that doing so ignores the reason why the TJWN's prohibition of preventive war seemed plausible in the first place. Recall that the best justification for the TJWN is that adherence to it avoids the extraordinary risks that are entailed by relying on inherently speculative justifications such as the Preventive Self-Defense Justification. Given how serious those risks are, we cannot assume that because the costs of adhering to the norm that avoids them have *increased* adherence to that norm is no longer justified.

We seem to be in a very difficult situation, then. On the one hand, due to the "new conditions," the costs of adhering to the TJWN have increased; on the other hand, the costs of abandoning the TJWN so as to allow preventive war are high. Whether we should adhere to the TJWN or abandon it in favor of one that permits preventive self-defense depends upon a comparison of these costs. However, it is not clear that anyone is in a position to make an accurate comparison.

I now want to argue that there is a way out of this impasse. It may be possible both to avoid the extraordinary risks of simply adopting a new norm according to which preventive self-defense is sometimes permissible and to avoid the costs of adhering to the TJWN in the "new conditions." One can have one's cake and eat it, too, if a more permissive norm than the TJWN can be properly embedded in an institutional arrangement that adequately reduces the risks that attend the inherently speculative character of the Preventive Self-Defense Justification.

My aim in this chapter is not to make a rock-solid case for this institutionalist solution to the problem of preventive war. I only want to show that the controversy over the justifiability of preventive war cannot be resolved without considering the possibility of an institutional solution and that doing this requires moving beyond the framing assumptions of Just War theorizing. Nevertheless, to make it clear what an institutionalist solution would look like and to show that it should not be dismissed out of hand as unrealistic, I will sketch a proposal for institutionalizing decisions concerning preventive self-defense that Robert O. Keohane and I explored recently and which will be presented in much greater detail in Chapter Eight.

We outline the main features of an appropriate institution that would make it permissible for leaders to appeal to the right of self-defense in order to justify preventive war.[13] Instead of recapitulating the details of that argument here, I will sketch only the main features of this institutionalist approach, adding some important premises that were overlooked or not sufficiently emphasized earlier, and then see whether it can be extended to encompass the second major challenge to the TJWN as well, the Forcible Democratization Justification. The key idea is that for preventive force to be justified as an exercise of the right of self-defense, the decision to use preventive force must be made within a multilateral framework designed to reduce the special risks of error and abuse that are involved in attempts to justify the use of force by appeal to speculative reasoning about possible future harms.[14]

The special risks involved in relying on the idea that self-defense can include preventive war are due to the way the inherently speculative character of this justification interacts with the cognitive and moral limitations of the agents who are likely

---

[13] Buchanan and Keohane, "The Preventive Use of Force: A Cosmopolitan Institutionalist Proposal."

[14] Buchanan and Keohane, "The Preventive Use of Force," 10–16.

to invoke it. Because the harm to be averted is speculative, there are ample opportunities for honest mistakes in prediction, bias in the interpretation of evidence and hence in estimating both the magnitude and the probability of the anticipated harm. And this means there are also ample opportunities for self-deception as well as deception of others.

In addition, those who occupy the role of state leader are subject to incentives that encourage them to overestimate risks to their own country and to underestimate the costs of the preventive action (especially the costs to foreigners), or even to misrepresent deliberately the facts in order to justify aggressive actions under the cover of self-defense. To the extent that the leader is held accountable only to her own citizens, she is likely to construe her fiduciary obligation to act in the "national interest" in a near absolute fashion, sharply discounting, if not simply disregarding, the interests of foreigners. Even if the leader acknowledges that she ought to take the interests of foreigners seriously, from her standpoint there is a marked asymmetry between two kinds of possible errors she might make. Failing to prevent a serious harm to her own people is politically much more damaging than engaging in unnecessary preventive action, at least if the costs of the latter fall chiefly on foreigners.

These special risks of justifying war by appeal to preventive self-defense are exacerbated if two conditions are satisfied. First, the agent has *congruent interests*, interests that speak in favor of engaging in the action in question independently of whether the Preventive Self-Defense Justification itself provides adequate support for the action. In the Iraq war case, congruent interests most likely included some or all of the following: deterring other present or future "strongman" rulers in the Middle East from undertaking actions that are deemed contrary to US interests; disabling potential threats to Israel; demonstrating to the world that the United States has and is willing to use overwhelming military power and dispelling the common assumption that the US government will not undertake military operations that involve significant casualties to US troops; and having permanent military bases in the Middle East to protect US access to oil, especially after anti-US terrorism made the continued presence of large numbers of US troops in Saudi Arabia untenable. Second, the agent is not willing to appeal publicly to the congruent interests in publicly justifying the action in question.

In cases in which an agent has significant congruent interests, but is not willing to publicly appeal to them to justify her actions, there is a risk that the agent will proclaim to others, and perhaps even come to believe, that the justifying conditions specified in the justification the agent publicly embraces are satisfied, when in fact they are not. Under these conditions, the risk is that the justification will become a mere rationalization for furthering congruent interests that the agent is not willing to appeal to publicly. Call this the *Mere Rationalization Risk*.

In the Iraq case, both of the conditions for the Mere Rationalization Risk seem to have been satisfied. The Bush administration persisted in its appeal to the right of preventive self-defense even after the renewed International Atomic Energy Agency inspections found no evidence of nuclear weapons and in spite of the fact that the UN team headed by Hans Blix reported that it had found no biological or chemical weapons and was receiving greater cooperation from Iraqi officials. The fact that the Bush administration persisted in the Preventive Self-Defense Justification in spite of this evidence that it had initially overestimated the risk of Iraqi WMDs suggests that it believed that invading Iraq would serve other important interests. If these other interests included any of those listed above, it is hardly surprising that the Bush administration would not have been willing to cite them in a public justification for going to war. It is one thing to tell the people of the United States that they must go to war to protect themselves from a devastating terrorist attack, quite another that they must do so to protect Israel from a potential threat or to convince the world that the United States is willing to use its overwhelming military force or to secure military bases in Iraq because a large US presence in Saudi Arabia is no longer an option.

Where the decision-maker has strong congruent interests that she is not willing to invoke in public justification, there is also a risk that the decision will be made on the basis of motivated false beliefs (in this case about the presence of WMDs in Iraq). Where the type of justification the decision-maker employs gives extraordinary opportunities for the sorts of errors of judgment that motivated false belief encourages, as is the case with the inherently speculative Preventive Self-Defense Justification, the risk is all the higher.

The Bush administration *could* have reduced these risks in either of two ways. First, it could have accepted the French government's proposal to postpone the invasion for several months while Blix's inspections continued. Doing this would have provided a safeguard against possible biases or errors in its initial intelligence concerning the presence of WMDs in Iraq, thereby reducing the risk that the decision to go to war would be the result of motivated false belief, facilitated by the presence of strong congruent interests the administration was not willing to appeal to in a public justification. Second, if, as some argued, weather conditions made postponement of the invasion impractical, the administration could have pre-committed to a post-invasion evaluation of its actions by an impartial body empowered to impose costs on the United States if it turned out that there was a serious discrepancy between the evidence the administration cited to justify preventive war and the facts that came to light after the invasion. By doing neither, the Bush administration failed to take seriously the extraordinary risks of reliance on the Preventive Self-Defense Justification. Later I will argue that once the complexities of the Forcible Democratization Justification are understood, it becomes clear that it too carries an extraordinary risk of being a mere rationalization.

In the earlier article, Keohane and I argued that the special risks of relying on the Preventive Self-Defense Justification can only be adequately reduced by requiring that the decision to engage in preventive action be made through a multilateral institutional procedure that ensures the accountability of both the party that proposes preventive force and those who are to approve or disapprove its request for authorization to use it. Ensuring accountability requires that the party proposing to use preventive force must agree, ex ante, to an ex post evaluation of its actions by a comparatively impartial body that will have full access to the occupied territory. If the evaluation is negative, significant costs must predictably fall on the party that proposed the use of preventive force. For example, that party must bear a greater proportion of the costs of the war and of postwar reconstruction and/or have less of a say in how the reconstruction is carried out.

The standard of evaluation employed ex post would not require that all the statements the proposer of preventive force makes ex ante be fully accurate, because the possibility of nonculpable errors cannot be eliminated. Instead, the body undertaking the evaluation would focus on whether the decision ex ante was reasonable all things considered, employing something like the legal notion of due diligence or the concept of reasonable belief that is employed in the law of individual self-defense.

Two points bear special emphasis. First, the case for creating such an institution is comparative. The relevant question is not whether it would produce perfect decisions but rather whether it would be an improvement over the status quo. Furthermore, its being an improvement does not depend upon the possibility of creating and empowering a strictly impartial body to make the post-conflict evaluation, but rather upon whether such a body would be sufficiently impartial to create incentives for better decision-making. Including representatives of reputable transnational nongovernmental organizations, in particular human rights organizations, would be one way to combat partiality. Second, the accountability regime Keohane and I sketch does not operate through enforcement of norms, where this means achieving compliance through coercion. Hence it does not require the currently utopian assumption that sovereign states will consent to anything resembling an international criminal court with police powers capable of defining and enforcing a norm specifying what counts as aggressive war. Instead, it is designed to build on the incentives that states actually have and to utilize the prospects of costs other than coercive enforcement, in order to improve decision-making.

At this point it might be objected that state leaders would not allow themselves to be constrained in these ways, that they would not cooperate in the creation of such institutions. Whether this is so is an empirical question, but it is worth noting that there are two incentives for creating such an institution, or at least not blocking efforts to create it, to which even the most ardent practitioners of *Realpolitik* may be subject. First, because the use of the Preventive Self-Defense Justification is so subject to error and abuse, any state leader who invokes it faces a serious credibility problem. Unless this credibility problem is solved, the state that invokes the Preventive Self-Defense Justification may find it difficult to secure military allies or cost-sharers. Subjecting itself to an accountability regime for making decisions about the use of preventive force or forcible democratization can help solve the credibility problem. Second, in democratic countries the demand for the creation of such institutions could become a focal point for the efforts of citizens who are concerned, both on moral and prudential grounds, about the risks of invoking the Preventive Self-Defense Justification. Determining the conditions under which these incentives will dominate is, of course, an empirical matter.

Keohane and I argued that this sort of accountability mechanism, along with procedural requirements designed to foster principled deliberation, could elicit more accurate information about risks and benefits and reduce the risk of strategic behavior, deception, self-deception, and manipulation. We emphasized that such an institution should be multilateral on the commonsensical grounds that no country, including and perhaps especially the world's one hyperpower with its complex geopolitical interests, can be trusted to determine unilaterally when preventive force would be justifiable as a matter of self-defense.[15]

Two Basic Strategies for Achieving Responsibility in Justification

There are, then, two quite different ways in which one can take into account the extraordinary risks of relying on the Preventive Self-Defense Justification for war. First, one can do what the TJWN advocates: urge adherence to a blanket prohibition on preventive force. The attraction of this response is that it simply takes one especially risky kind of justification off the table. As the New Conditions Justification shows, however, under present conditions the costs of continued adherence to a blanket prohibition are considerable.

Alternatively, one can invoke a more permissive norm, thus avoiding the increased costs of adhering to the TJWN, but try to reduce the extraordinary risks of preventive self-defense by embedding the more permissive norm in a decision-making process that includes appropriate safeguards. This second response recognizes that striking the right balance between restraint and the ability to prevent harm can require a kind of division of labor between the content of a norm regarding self-defense and the institutional arrangements within which the norm is to be invoked. What is disturbing about the Bush administration's reliance on the Preventive Self-Defense Justification is that it abandoned the protection against the special risks of preventive action that are provided by the TJWN without any acknowledgment that doing

---

[15] In saying that preventive self-defense is justifiable only if the decision to use it is made within such institutional constraints, we were *not* endorsing the view that preventive force is only justified if the decision to use it receives Security Council authorization. On the contrary, we argued that the Security Council does not satisfy the accountability requirements we outline, chiefly because there is no effective accountability for the exercise of the permanent member veto.

so entailed serious risks, and apparently without taking any measures to reduce them.

Keohane and I not only argued that institutional innovation is a *necessary* condition for justified preventive self-defense; we also opted for the institutionalist solution (though we stopped short of endorsing one particular institutional arrangement). We did so because we assumed that under the "new conditions," the costs of the alternative strategy of barring all appeals to preventive self-defense were too great.

Our argument was incomplete. As I have already indicated, it is not enough to note that the costs of continued adherence to the TJWN have increased, due to the new conditions, and that a new institutional arrangement could avoid those costs as well as reduce the risks of relying on the TJWN. That might be so, yet it might still be the case that we should continue to adhere to the TJWN, if the costs of abandoning it were higher still. That would be the case if the costs of building a new institution were sufficiently high or if there were a significant risk that the new institution would not perform as intended.[16]

For present purposes, I need not defend the assumption that the costs of continued adherence to the TJWN are intolerably high. My aim here is not to endorse the institutionalist option in this case, but rather only to demonstrate its plausibility in order to show how taking the relationship between norms and institutions seriously transforms thinking about the morality of war. The crucial point is that the controversy over preventive war cannot be resolved conclusively without a serious consideration of the institutional alternatives to the status quo. Because just war theory simply assumes that institutional resources are negligible, it is inherently conservative and arbitrarily so. Because Just War theorizing does not take up the burden of an empirical inquiry into the feasibility of institutional change and the comparative

---

[16] I am indebted to Rachel Zuckert for making this point clear to me.

costs and benefits of adhering to norms designed to function in the absence of institutions versus developing new institutions, it is methodologically flawed.

I now want to bolster these conclusions by applying the institutionalist approach to another challenge to the TJWN: the attempt to justify war to create democracy. Again, my purpose is not to resolve the controversy, but rather to show that it cannot be resolved within the cramped framing assumptions of just war theory but instead requires supplementing abstract philosophical argumentation with empirically based institutional design. As with preventive self-defense, it will not be necessary to show that institutional innovation would make forcible democratization justifiable. Instead, I need only make a strong prima facie case that institutionalization is necessary for justifiability.

The Second Challenge to the Traditional Just War Norm: The Forcible Democratization Justification

This justification expands greatly what are generally recognized as the conditions for justified armed humanitarian intervention. Instead of restricting those conditions to actual or imminent massive violation of basic human rights, it asserts that armed humanitarian intervention of the most destructive sort, a full-scale war to topple a regime and occupy an entire country, can be justified if undertaken for the sake of creating democracy. The structure of the problem is the same as that of preventive war. On the one hand, the inherently speculative character of the justification carries extraordinary risks. Adhering to the TJWN avoids these risks by taking the Forcible Democratization Justification off the table, just as it rules out preventive self-defense as a justification for war. However, avoiding these risks in this way comes at a cost: no one is allowed to intervene militarily to break the yoke of tyranny.

Here, too, the proper question to ask is not whether the TJWN should be replaced with a more permissive one that allows forcible democratization, but whether (1) there is a feasible institutional arrangement that could adequately ameliorate the extraordinary risks of using a Forcible Democratization Justification; and whether (2) the costs of continued adherence to the TJWN, which excludes forcible democratization, are sufficiently high, relative to the costs of creating the new institution, that we should bear the costs of institutional innovation.

No amount of philosophical argumentation, by itself, can answer this question. As in the controversy over preventive self-defense, an approach that combines moral philosophy and empirically informed institutional analysis is required. To show that this is so, however, it is first necessary to explain why continued adherence to a use-of-force norm that excludes forcible democratization entails serious costs and then to show that there is no basic moral obstacle to forcible democratization.

Taking Cosmopolitan Commitments Seriously

It may be tempting for those who consider themselves cosmopolitans to dismiss the Forcible Democratization Justification simply because it has been invoked by what they take to be an extremely anticosmopolitan administration to justify what they take to be an unnecessary war. This temptation ought to be resisted. Cosmopolitans should try to distinguish between the question of whether forcible democratization was justified in the case of Iraq from the more general question of whether the Forcible Democratization Justification can be properly institutionalized so as to ameliorate its extraordinary risks, and whether the costs of adhering to a blanket prohibition on forcible democratization are sufficiently high to warrant opting for the institutionalist solution.

To the extent that cosmopolitans hold the following beliefs, they should not simply dismiss the idea of forcible democratization. First, sovereignty, and hence immunity from external force, is conditional; states earn it by doing a credible job of protecting basic human rights. Second, democracy is the most reliable arrangement for securing basic human rights.[17] Third, "one-off" humanitarian intervention to stop violence that has already become large-scale is often insufficient, merely postponing the killing until the intervener has withdrawn; basic regime change may be necessary. Fourth, to the extent that cosmopolitans are heirs of the liberal theorists of revolution of the seventeen and eighteenth centuries, they believe that a people may go to war to establish its own democratic institutions. But if war is morally permissible for the sake of establishing democracy for ourselves, could not war to establish democracy in another country that is so thoroughly repressive as to make revolution virtually impossible also be a moral option? Finally, if, as I have already argued, the JWN that war is only justifiable in response to actual or imminent attack is not a fundamental moral principle but at most a contingent moral rule, one whose validity may vary with institutional context, then there is all the more reason to take seriously

---

[17] Some might object to this assumption, contending that non-democratic states can do a creditable job of protecting basic human rights, in spite of the fact that the most massive violations of citizens' basic human rights by their governments in modern times have been perpetrated by dictatorships, not democratic governments. The plausibility of this objection depends in part upon how high one sets the bar for being democratic. If one's definition of 'democracy' includes the requirement that major government officials are subject to accountability through periodic elections, then a strong case can be made that even basic human rights are insecure where democracy is not present. See, for example, Amartya Sen's empirically based argument that famines do not occur in democracies. Amartya K. Sen, *Poverty and Famines: An Essay on Entitlement and Deprivation* (New York: Oxford University Press, 1981); "Development: Which Way Now?" *The Economic Journal* 93, no. 132 (1983): 745–62; Amartya K. Sen and Jean Drèze, *Hunger and Public Action* (Oxford: Clarendon Press, 1989). See David Beetham, *Democracy and Rights* (Cambridge, UK: Polity Press, 1999), 89–114. (It may not be an accident that Rawls's example of a non-democratic state that protects basic human rights is an imaginary society, "Kazanistan." See John Rawls, *The Law of Peoples* (Cambridge, MA: Harvard University Press, 1999), 5, 64.) In my judgment, the view that basic human rights are insecure without democracy is sufficiently plausible to make worthwhile the project of trying to ascertain the conditions under which forcible democratization would be justified.

the idea that there may be circumstances in which going to war to create the form of government that best protects human rights would be justified.

For all these reasons the Forcible Democratization Justification cannot simply be dismissed, at least not by sincere cosmopolitans. Instead, the proper course of action is to articulate the justification carefully, take stock of its special risks, try to determine whether feasible institutional arrangements could adequately reduce them, and then determine whether the costs of adhering to a norm that takes forcible democratization justifications off the table are sufficiently high to warrant the costs of developing the new institutional arrangements.

In the discussion that follows I do not attempt to set out all the conditions that would have to be satisfied if forcible democratization were to be justifiable. Instead, I want to say just enough about them to make it clear that using this sort of justification carries extraordinary risks and that the only reasonable prospect for adequately ameliorating these risks would be to create new institutions to structure the decision-making process. In other words, I want to show that institutional innovation would be a *necessary* condition for relaxing the TJWN to allow for forcible democratization, not that the best course of action is to start building the new institutions. This will suffice to confirm my chief conclusion: that theorizing about the morality of war must go beyond philosophical argumentation as traditionally understood to include empirically based reasoning about institutional alternatives. If it turns out that the sorts of institutions that would be required are not feasible, given the array of power and interests in our world, then the conclusion to be drawn is that war for democratization is not morally justified.

Justifying Forcible Democratization

The Forcible Democratization Justification presents war as a necessary means to achieving a good for the people of the country that is to be invaded. However, merely focusing on the good to be achieved for them is clearly inadequate: to justify attacking the non-democratic leaders of the state and those who support them, more than the prospect of providing a benefit to the people is needed. As in all cases of justifying war, those who are the targets of military action must be, in Jeff McMahan's phrase, "liable" to have military force used against them.[18]

For the Forcible Democratization Justification to get off the ground as a distinct justification for making war, it must be the case that those who rule undemocratically *are forcibly preventing the people from creating democratic institutions*. For brevity, let us call those who meet this description Despots. The question, then, is whether being a Despot makes one a legitimate target for war-making, even in the absence of the sorts of massive violations of human rights under which ordinary humanitarian intervention can be justified.

At least in the mainstream of the liberal tradition, it is thought that the people themselves can be justified in going to war against Despots; that is, that revolution as forcible democratization *from within* can be justified. The assumption is that simply by ruling undemocratically and forcibly resisting the people's efforts to create democracy, one can become a legitimate target of war-making by the people themselves. (The most obvious explanation of why being a Despot makes one liable to revolutionary force is that Despots violate the people's right of self-government, either as a collective right or as the right of each individual to participate in self-government.) So unless one is willing to deny that there is a right to revolution against Despots, then one must acknowledge that being a Despot can make one a legitimate target of war-making. Conversely, unless revolution against Despots is justifiable, it is hard to see how one could begin to make the case for forcible democratization. I will simply assume, for the sake

[18] Jeff McMahan, "The Ethics of Killing in War," *Ethics* 114, no. 4 (2004): 693–733.

of the argument to follow, that revolution against Despots can be justified.

At this point there are two opposing views to be considered. According to the first, being a Despot only makes one a legitimate target of war-making *by those whose right of self-government one is violating*. According to the second, under certain circumstances being a Despot can also make one a legitimate target of war-making by others than those whose right of self-government one is violating, if those others act so as to vindicate the right of self-government of one's victims. Call the former the *Constrained View* and the latter the *Permissive View*.

Assuming that revolution against Despots can be justifiable, the Constrained View must be false, for it would rule out making war to support a democratic revolution under conditions in which all of the oppressed people have explicitly requested such support. The question, then, is whether there are circumstances other than those of explicit authorization in which Despots are legitimate targets of war-making by external forces.

Notice that the worry about whether attacks on a Despot by external forces are justified where there is no explicit authorization is not that such attacks would violate the rights of the Despot. Clearly, whether the Despot's rights are violated could not be affected by authorization one way or the other, for the simple reason that the moral barrier against attack that all persons originally enjoy cannot be removed merely by someone else's granting permission to a third party to attack them. Instead, the worry about unauthorized intervention to secure democracy for an oppressed people is that it involves unwarranted paternalism toward or failure to show proper respect for the intended beneficiaries.

What must a would-be forcible democratizer do, then, to avoid unwarranted paternalism or disrespect, in circumstances in which their explicit authorization of his action is not possible? I am not sure how to answer this question, but it seems to me that at minimum the would-be forcible democratizer would have to have good reason to believe that the intended beneficiaries could reasonably accept the risks that the forcible democratization process poses for them. Call this the *Respect* (or *Antipaternalism*) *Principle*.

The attraction of the Respect Principle is apparent. Generally speaking, it seems wrong to impose serious costs on others in order to provide them with benefits, unless they consent to one's doing so or at least unless one has good reason to believe that they would or at least reasonably could regard the ratio of benefits to costs as acceptable. There are three basic grounds for this presumption. The first is a healthy appreciation of the fallibility of even the most sincere would-be benefactors and of the tendency for the insincere to disguise themselves as benefactors. The second is a more basic commitment to respecting individual autonomy. The third is instrumental: if popular support for democratization is lacking, then resistance to military occupation and forcible institution building will likely be greater and in consequence the project of democratization may involve unacceptably high human costs or may fail altogether.

The point of the Respect Principle is not that one may never act to secure human rights without the consent of all of those whom one's actions will affect. The claim is much narrower: to impose costly benefits on a people one should have credible evidence that they could reasonably regard this trade-off as acceptable.[19]

[19] Any attempt to determine whether the Antipaternalism Principle is satisfied is complicated by the fact that the costs of successful forcible democratization are likely to be disportionately borne by the present population, while the benefits largely will accrue to later generations. Notice, however, that this problem is not unique to forcible democratization from without. It also arises for revolution. Furthermore, support for democratic revolution is not likely to be anywhere near unanimous even among those now living. These reflections raise an interesting question whose exploration must await another occasion: Is forcible democratization from without significantly more morally problematic than democratic revolution? I am indebted to an editor of *Philosophy & Public Affairs* for prompting me to consider this issue.

It could be argued that another principle must be satisfied if forcible democratization is to be justified: the would-be forcible democratizer must reasonably believe that the benefits to the intended beneficiaries will significantly exceed the costs to them. Call this the Beneficiary Proportionality Principle. This principle seems reasonable, given that the purpose of the war is to bring the benefits of democracy to the people whose country is invaded. The assumption is that democracy will make them significantly better off. But if the process by which democracy is brought about is too costly to them, democracy will not make them better off. So unless the Beneficiary Proportionality Principle is satisfied, the war is futile on its own terms. However, the two principles could point in opposite directions. Suppose the would-be forcible democratizer judges that the expected costs to the intended beneficiaries would be excessive, but the intended beneficiaries find the costs acceptable. My inclination is to say that this is not a problem, because the Respect Principle is the appropriate criterion and that the Beneficiary Proportionality Principle should only be invoked as a proxy for the Respect Principle under conditions in which it is difficult to determine more directly what costs it would be reasonable for the intended beneficiaries to accept.[20] The idea would be that, in the absence of credible evidence of what sorts of costs they would find acceptable, imposing costly benefits on a people is morally permissible only if there is strong evidence that the expected costs to them will be exceeded significantly by the expected benefits to them.

Fortunately, it is not necessary for me to support this intuition here. Instead, I will proceed on the weaker, quite plausible assumption that forcible democratization would only be justified if either the Beneficiary Proportionality or the Respect Principles is satisfied. The next step is to explore the special risks of relying on the Forcible Democratization Justification, understood as

[20] An editor of *Philosophy & Public Affairs* suggested this idea to me.

including the requirement that at least one of these principles must be satisfied.

The Risks of Using the Forcible Democratization Justification

As with the Preventive Self-Defense Justification, the risks of this justification result from the interaction between its speculative character and the characteristics of the agents that are likely to employ it. To ensure that the Beneficiary Proportionality or Respect Principles are satisfied requires empirical predictions, under conditions of considerable uncertainty; and this creates considerable opportunities for error, bias, deception of others, and self-deception. To make a sound judgment that either principle is satisfied, one must have something like a causal theory of forcible democratization, although all the causal links need not be clearly specified. Unless one has at least a basic grasp of the conditions under which forcible democratization can succeed, one cannot make credible estimates either of what the costs of the effort to the beneficiaries are likely to be or whether those costs could be reasonably accepted by them.

Now it could be argued with considerable persuasiveness that at present no one is in possession of a causal theory of forcible democratization capable of grounding the predictions that are necessary for determining whether the Beneficiary Proportionality or Respect Principles are satisfied ex ante, that is, at the time when the would-be forcible democratizer is supposed to be determining whether they are satisfied. Nonetheless, let us suppose for the sake of argument that there is credible information about the circumstances in which forcible democratization is more likely to succeed. Even if this is so, there will clearly be considerable opportunity for honest errors of judgment, as well as deception, self-deception, and manipulation of evidence. Everything said earlier about the inherent risks of the speculative character of the Preventive Self-Defense Justification applies, perhaps with

even greater force here. When the would-be forcible democratizers have ulterior motives for going to war that they are loathe
to cite in public justifications, the possibility of motivated false
belief exacerbates these risks. This last factor should not be
underestimated. It is very likely that any state willing to incur
the human and material costs of going to war will have additional
motives beyond that of humanitarian concern for those upon
whom it proposes to bestow the blessings of democracy.

In addition, there is another feature of the Forcible
Democratization Justification that carries special risks. This justification is open-ended in a way that the Preventive Self-Defense
Justification is not. The end to be achieved in the case of the
Forcible Democratization Justification is less determinate in two
ways than the end to be achieved in the case of the Preventive Self-
Defense. First, 'democracy' refers to a range of governance institutions, whereas in the Preventive Self-Defense Justification the
end for which war is undertaken is the removal of a wrongfully
imposed risk of a dire harm. In the former case, the indeterminacy of the end facilitates what might be called *goal substitution*. If the forcible democratizer has congruent interests, then
she may be tempted to pursue their realization under the cover
of achieving democracy, and this is easier to accomplish, other
things being equal, if the end is indeterminate. In consequence,
it may be harder for third parties to detect that goals other than
democracy are driving, and in fact distorting or undercutting, the
putative democratization effort until very late in the game. The
would-be forcible democratizer, then, may have strong incentives
for not clarifying the nature of the goal ex ante. Furthermore,
failure to specify the goal may only increase the opportunities for
erroneously believing, or deceitfully saying that one believes, that
the Beneficiary Proportionality and Respect Principles are satisfied when in fact they are not.

Second, in the case of forcible democratization, the end is
temporally indeterminate. Given the lack of a serviceable causal
theory of how democracy is to be produced, no timetable can

be given for when the end will be achieved. If democracy is not achieved in three years, the forcible democratizer can say that it will likely take five or more, and so on. To put the same point differently, the use of the Preventive Self-Defense Justification, as we have explicated it, requires the justifier to identify a rather concrete harm to be averted, to link that future harm to something the target of preventive action has already done in such a way that the "wrongful imposition of a dire risk" condition is satisfied, and to say something determinate about how the harm would come about if preventive action were not taken. Unless all of this is done, the case for preventive self-defense is not made. But if it is done, then the agent invoking this justification has in effect created some of the conditions that are necessary for her being held accountable. The case of Iraq illustrates the point nicely: if the claim is that war is necessary to prevent WMDs from falling into the hands of terrorists, but no WMDs are found and there is no evidence that they were spirited away in the nick of time, then this counts toward discrediting the justification.

It is quite different in the case of going to war to create democracy. Failure to produce democracy is not evidence that the justification has failed, at least not for a very long time. Even after the non-democratic government is deposed, the would-be democratizer can argue that ongoing armed resistance comes from antidemocratic forces and that antidemocratic "wreckers" are impeding the development of new institutions. In that sense, the agent who uses the Forcible Democratization Justification incurs less risk of being exposed as insincere and less risk of being held accountable than an agent who uses the Preventive Self-Defense Justification. Furthermore, if democracy is never achieved, the agent who invoked the latter justification has a ready excuse that is likely to have considerable rhetorical appeal, especially if there is widespread prejudice toward the culture and character of the intended beneficiaries: she can blame the failure on the intended beneficiaries' lack of political will or ignorance or cultural backwardness.

The twin indeterminacy of the end in the Forcible Democratization Justification therefore diminishes the accountability of those who employ it and to that extent encourages goal substitution and other forms of self-deception or deception of others. To put the same point differently, the nature of the justification itself reduces the expected costs to the justifier of misusing the justification. This makes using the justification riskier, other things being equal.

This brief exploration of the risks of relying on the Forcible Democratization Justification is not intended to be exhaustive. However, it should suffice to establish that the risks of using the Forcible Democratization Justification are so great that its use would be morally permissible only if credible measures were taken to reduce them. Once these risks are understood, it seems clear that credible measures would have to include institutionalizing the decision-making process. As noted earlier, and Keohane and I have argued in detail, a necessary condition for justified preventive self-defense is that the decision to engage in preventive action must be made within an institutional framework aptly designed to reduce the special risks of this kind of justification. The institutionalist conclusion applies a fortiori to the Forcible Democratization Justification, because it is, if anything, even more subject to error and abuse than the Preventive War Justification. If this is the case, then the TJWN should not be abandoned in favor of a more permissive norm that allows forcible democratization unless the new norm would be embedded in a system of institutional safeguards.

The analysis thus far indicates that at minimum the needed institutional safeguards would have to do two things. First, they would have to cope with the risks associated with the indeterminancy of the goal of democratization. Second, they would have to ensure reliable predictions of the sort necessary for a credible effort to determine ex ante whether the Beneficiary Proportionality and Respect Principles are satisfied. I now want to show how an accountability regime for making use-of-force decisions that include decisions to make war to create democracy might achieve these two objectives.

Making the Goal More Determinate

In order to reduce the risks associated with the indeterminancy of the goal, an institution for making responsible decisions concerning forcible democratization would need to do at least three things: (1) specify benchmarks for progress toward democratization; (2) provide mechanisms for monitoring progress, according to the benchmarks; and (3) attach significant costs to failure to make appropriate progress. Furthermore, such an arrangement could only be expected to work if it were multilateral or at least included adequate provisions for independent and comparatively impartial monitoring of progress according to antecedently specified benchmarks.

To specify benchmarks for progress toward democratization, the vague concept of democracy would have to be made more determinate. The state or coalition proposing war for forcible democratization would be required to specify what sort of democracy they aim to help create. From a cosmopolitan standpoint the aim is presumably some form of constitutional democracy, with an independent judiciary and other institutions for protecting the rights of individuals and, where appropriate, ethno-national minorities as well. The task here is to steer a course between a conception of democracy that is so indeterminate as to create the risks of mere rationalization or goal substitution and one that is specified in such a narrow way as to invite the criticism that the forcible democratizers are imposing their own parochial conception of democracy on a people who may have good reason to reject it.[21]

---

[21] In particular, it would be important not to allow the goal of democratization to be replaced with that of creating a particular kind of democratic society that the forcible democratizer happens to favor, for example, one that features relatively unregulated markets or one that cooperates in the forcible

Institutionalizing the Beneficiary Proportionality and Respect Principles

Ensuring the reliability of the sorts of empirical predictions that one would have to make in order to do a credible job, ex ante, of determining whether the Beneficiary Proportionality and Respect Principles are satisfied would require two things. First, one would have to know enough about how forcible democratization works to formulate a set of conditions under which the prospects for successful forcible democratization are good. These conditions need not be understood as being either jointly sufficient or individually necessary for success. Instead, they might be more like what Rawls calls "counting principles": the more of them are satisfied and the greater the extent to which they are satisfied, the more likely the effort will succeed.[22]

Second, there would have to be a way of helping to ensure that the criteria were accurately applied to the assessment of the case at hand. Presumably this would require the application of the counting principles by a comparatively impartial body, that is, someone other than the state/(or states) that is/(are) proposing forcible democratization. There would have to be an accountability mechanism similar to the one Keohane and I propose for preventive war decisions, to create incentives for the would-be

---

democratizer's geopolitical projects or is willing to sell the forcible democratizer oil at favorable prices. The difficulty of specifying, without overspecifying, the notion of democracy should not be underestimated. The institutional arrangements would have to avoid two errors: making the goal of democracy so indeterminate as to invite goal substitution, on the one hand; and making it so determinate ex ante as to deprive the forcible democratizers of the ability to make reasonable revisions of their initial plans for how to achieve democracy during the process of implementation, on the other. I thank Christopher Griffin for this point. In addition, there is the thorny problem of how the democratization should take into account input from the people themselves as to what particular form of democracy they want, independently of whether what they want is in fact judged to be optimal by the democratizing force.

[22] John Rawls, *A Theory of Justice* (Cambridge, MA: Harvard University Press, 1971), 415–16.

forcible democratizer to make the case for action on the basis of reliable predictions concerning the costs and benefits. Similarly, whether relevant states would agree to participate in such an institution would depend upon a number of factors, including how much state leaders value the credibility that participation would bring and the extent to which politically effective domestic groups see their state's participation as worthwhile on prudential and/or moral grounds.

At present there is considerable controversy as to the conditions under which forcible democratization is likely to occur.[23] That it *can* occur is clear from the fact that it *has* occurred in at least three cases: Japan, Germany, and Italy after World War II.[24] Simply for purposes of illustration, let us consider a hypothesis about what a plausible list of counting principles would look like: the prospects for forcible democratization are greater the more of the following criteria are satisfied and the greater the degree to which they are satisfied, other things being equal.[25]

1. The current regime (that is, the despotism that is to be toppled and replaced by a democracy) is foreign.
2. There is a fairly recent history of democracy (Germany).

---

[23] The literature on democratization indicates that there is a great deal of uncertainty as to the conditions under which democracy is likely to occur. For contrasting prominent views, see the following works: Fareed Zakaria, *The Future of Freedom: Illiberal Democracy at Home and Abroad* (New York: W. W. Norton & Co., 2003); Samuel P. Huntington, *The Third Wave: Democratization in the Late Twentieth Century* (Norman: University of Oklahoma Press, 1993); Adam Przeworski, Michael E. Alvarez, Jose Antonio Cheibub, and Fernando Limongi, *Democracy and Development: Political Institutions and Well-Being in the World, 1950–1990* (Cambridge, UK: Cambridge University Press, 2000).

[24] Detlef Junker, Phillipp Gassert, Wilfried Mausbach, and David B. Morris eds., *The United States and Germany in the Era of the Cold War, 1945–1990, A Handbook, Vol. I: 1945–1968* (Cambridge: Cambridge University Press, 2004); John W. Dower, *Embracing Defeat: Japan in the Wake of World War II* (New York: W. W. Norton & Co./New Press, 1999).

[25] I am grateful to Robert O. Keohane for suggestions about what should be included in the list of "counting principles."

3. The current regime has just suffered a total defeat in a war caused by its own aggression (Germany, Japan, and Italy).
4. Economic development is sufficient for a substantial middle class and literacy rates are high (Germany, Japan, and Italy).

If the current regime is an alien imposition, the people in question presumably will be more likely to cooperate with, or at least not as vigorously resist, an invasion to topple it than if it were their "own" regime. If there is a history of democracy, then that is some reason to hope that it can take root again or at least to believe that there is no essential incompatibility between democracy and the dominant culture of the country. If the current regime has been totally defeated in a war caused by its own aggression, the population may be more receptive to fundamental political change, even if it is imposed from without. Some theorists have suggested that condition 4 may be more important for preventing a newly established democracy from deteriorating than for creating democracy in the first place. Perhaps the point is that high literacy rates enable more effective participation in democratic processes and that where there is a substantial middle class significant numbers of people will be economically secure enough to continue to support democratic processes even when short-term results are not optimal from their point of view. If this is the case, then condition 4 is relevant to the question of whether forcible democratization is likely to create a stable democracy.

At most, only one of these conditions, the fourth, was satisfied in the case of Iraq. In fact, it is not even clear that it was satisfied. By the time the war was launched, the level of economic development had declined seriously, due to a combination of a decade of sanctions and gross mismanagement on the part of the Baathist regime.

What is striking is that nothing in the actual decision-making process that led to the invasion of Iraq required US leaders to take a stand on what conditions improve the prospects for successful forcible democratization, much less to provide any evidence that such conditions were present in Iraq. Suppose, instead, that the decision to engage in forcible democratization had been made in an institutional framework that (1) required the public articulation of a plausible list of favorable conditions for forcible democratization and the marshalling of evidence that at least some of them were satisfied in the case at hand; and (2) facilitated a critical, impartial evaluation of the criteria and the evidence; and (3) attached significant costs to a negative evaluation. Such an arrangement would reduce the extraordinary risks of relying on the Forcible Democratization Justification.

My aim in this section has not been to develop either a comprehensive moral theory of forcible democratization or to advance an institutionalist solution to the risks that reliance on the Forcible Democratization Justification entails. Instead, I have tried to show that as in the case of preventive self-defense, the moral controversy cannot be resolved without a consideration of the ways in which institutional innovations might cope with the special risks of this type of justification, and to establish that appropriate institutionalization of the decision-making process is a necessary condition for justified forcible democratization.

Nor is my aim to show that the institutional approach outlined here is likely to be adapted by the most powerful states either at present or in the future. If it turns out that the institutional demands for morally permissible decisions to engage in preventive self-defense or forcible democratization will not be met, then my argument supports the conclusion that neither preventive self-defense nor forcible democratization are justifiable. If the institutions in question cannot be realized, then continued adherence to the TJWN's blanket prohibitions will be vindicated. And my fundamental point will have been made: whether a particular kind of justification for war is valid can depend upon its institutional context.

Institutions and the Ethics of Leadership

The institutionalist approach I have articulated in this chapter has important implications for how we ought to conceive of the ethics of leadership. A cogent theory of the ethics of leadership will include principles for evaluating the conduct of leaders that are grounded in reasonable assumptions about what we can expect of them. If a leadership role itself makes the individual who occupies it especially vulnerable to certain sorts of moral failings or cognitive errors, because of the social expectations that constitute the role, the requirements of staying in power, or specific features of the institutions within which leaders function, then our moral evaluations of leaders ought to take this into account. Otherwise, evaluations will be unrealistic and unfairly blaming.

It is a mistake, however, to assume that the special moral risks of the leadership role are fixed. Both the character and the gravity of these risks can vary, depending upon the institutional context in which the leader functions. Constitutional theory is grounded on this simple point. Appropriate institutional checks and balances can reduce the risks attendant on leadership roles in various branches of government.

More generally, properly designed institutions can reduce the moral risks of leadership by protecting leaders from moral lapses or cognitive errors that facilitate unethical decisions. This could be achieved in either or both of two ways. First, institutions that require leaders to justify their actions to the public; to parties in other branches of government; or in the case of multilateral institutions, to other leaders and their publics, and could simply prohibit appeals to certain types of justifications, on the grounds that they are too risky. (The idea that institutions can constrain the types of justifications that may be employed is not new, of course. Every legal system employs it. Only certain kinds of arguments, those that appeal to established legal principles, are permitted to be used in legal proceedings.) Second, especially risky types of justifications might be allowed, but only if they are deployed within a properly designed set of institutional safeguards to reduce these risks to acceptable levels. The ethics of leadership should take institutions seriously, then, not only in order to make fair evaluations of the performance of leaders in the light of the contributions institutions can make to the risks that leaders labor under, but also in considering how institutional arrangements can improve the performance of leaders.

A disturbing feature of the scholarly discussion of the justifiability of the US invasion of Iraq and of the more general issues of preventive war and forcible democratization the invasion raised is the absence of any serious consideration of the ethics of leadership. Justifications are treated more as abstract objects, as sets of propositions, than as actions performed by justifiers. One implication of my analysis here is that what might be called the *ethics of justification* ought to be central to moral theorizing about war. Decisions to go to war are made by state leaders, and state leaders are subject to incentives and motivations that can make their recourse to certain kinds of justifications for going to war extremely dangerous; and the dangers, at least to some extent, are knowable. So leaders should be judged not simply for their actions, but also for the sorts of justifications they invoke for them. Similarly, arguments intended to justify war ought to be evaluated not only according to the truth of their premises and the validity of their inferences, but also according to the epistemic and moral demands their proper use makes on the sorts of agents that are likely to employ them.

III. *The Limits of Just War Theory*

Through a critical examination of two challenges to the Traditional Just War Norm, I have made the case for rethinking the framing assumptions of traditional and contemporary thinking about the morality of war. I have argued that the validity of use-of-force norms can depend upon institutional context and that the validity of the TJWN, according to which war is only justified in response to an actual or imminent attack, is at best contingent. This highly constraining norm, which rules out preventive force and forcible democratization, may be quite plausible where institutional resources for constraining war are negligible. The attraction of the TJWN is that it avoids the extraordinary risks of the Preventive Self-Defense and Forcible Democratization Justifications by taking them off the table—excluding them from the set of legitimate justifications for going to war. However, here, as elsewhere, risk reduction is not costless. When circumstances change, costs that previously were tolerable may become excessive. The question then arises as to whether the old norm is still valid.

Whether it is, I have argued, cannot be determined without going beyond the noninstitutionalist framing assumption of just war theory. The proper question to ask is not whether the TJWN ought to be replaced with a more permissive one, but rather whether we should continue to adhere to the TJWN or create new institutions within which reliance on a more permissive norm would be morally responsible. The key point is that constraint can be achieved not only by narrowly drawn norms, but also by a combination of institutional safeguards and more permissive norms. Whether we should stick to the old norm or institutionalize a more permissive one depends upon two factors: whether the new norm-institution package would be morally better than the status quo and the feasibility and costs of creating the new institution. Among the costs to be considered is the possibility that the effort to create a new institution may weaken support for the old, more constraining norm without in fact producing an institution that adequately ameliorates the special risks of resort to preventive self-defense or forcible democratization justifications.

Once the interdependence of norms and institutions is understood, the inadequacy of just war theory becomes clear. If the domain of just war theory is limited to large-scale military conflict under conditions in which institutional resources are negligible, then it cannot tell us whether we should create new institutions for the sake of adopting better norms, and its approach to the morality of war is inherently and arbitrarily conservative. If the domain of just war theory is simply large-scale military conflict, then the TJWN, whose plausibility depends upon the assumption that constraint is to be achieved without reliance on institutions, is not adequately supported. To show that the TJWN is valid, it is necessary to engage in empirically grounded institutional reasoning. Philosophical argument, although necessary, is not enough. A defensible theory of the morality of war must integrate moral reasoning with institutional thinking.

In this chapter, I have argued that without a consideration of the possibility of institutional innovation, one cannot answer some of the most important questions that traditional and contemporary just war theorists address, including whether preventive war and war for democratization are permissible. In the next chapter I show that once the importance of institutions is appreciated, the scope of the questions that just war theory should answer expands dramatically.

Notes

I am indebted to Robert O. Keohane for many insights that helped stimulate me to write this article and to Keohane, Jeff McMahan, Christopher (Kit) Wellman, and the editors of *Philosophy & Public Affairs*, for valuable comments on earlier drafts.

CHAPTER 2

A Richer *Jus Ad Bellum*

I. *Narrow versus Wide* Jus Ad Bellum

The Dominant Understanding of the Scope of Just War Theory

The aim of most contemporary just war theorists appears to be simple: to provide an account of the necessary and sufficient conditions for war acts to be morally right—that is, to articulate *objective moral justifications* for war acts. In the case of the *jus ad bellum* part of just war theory, the goal is to determine objective justifications for acts of going to war. If one defines "just war theory" as an account of which war acts are right, then it is trivially true that articulating objective moral justifications of war acts is the aim of just war theory, indeed, by definition, its only aim. Correspondingly, the sole aim of *jus ad bellum* would be to articulate objective moral justifications for acts of going to war.

A Broader Scope

There is nothing wrong, per se, with opting for such a definition of "*jus ad bellum*" (or the corresponding definition of "just war theory"). Yet it is important to understand that the aim referenced in this definition is very limited, given the much greater potential scope of moral theorizing about recourse to war. Even if it is true that identifying sound objective justifications for going to war is the first task of *jus ad bellum*, it is not the only important task. The following list indicates a much more expansive conception of the domain of *jus ad bellum* theorizing.[1]

1. Providing objective justifications for recourse to war (identifying criteria for justified acts of going to war).

2. Determining which directly action-guiding rules leaders, combatants, and others faced with the decision whether to go to war or to support or oppose war morally ought to employ.[2] It cannot be assumed that they should treat the elements of objective justifications as directly action-guiding. In some cases it might be the case that they ought instead to use directly action-guiding norms whose content diverges from the elements of objective justifications. "Directly action-guiding norms" here covers but is not limited to heuristics. Heuristics can produce better decisions when they serve as shortcuts or reliable rules of thumb in situations (a) where there is insufficient time for more complex decision processes, (b) where the information required for an ideal decision-making process is not available or too complex to process adequately, or (c) where the decision-makers are subject to incentives or cognitive biases that tend to distort their decisions (and where heuristics can function like self-binding strategies to reduce the risk of distortion).[3]

---

[1] Most of what I say in this chapter about *jus ad bellum* will have obvious analogs for *jus in bello*.

[2] For discussion of the importance of just war theory developing applied moral principles alongside its objective justifications, see Seth Lazar, "Morality & Law of War," in Andrei Marmor, ed., *Companion to Philosophy of Law* (New York: Routledge, 2012), 364–79.

[3] In ideal circumstances, even the most basic moral principles may be action-guiding, but my focus here is on principles that are intended to be action-guiding in non-ideal circumstances in which attempting to guide action by direct appeal to basic principles would be counterproductive.

3. Providing guidance for the moral evaluation of the institutional processes within which leaders make decisions about going to war.[4]

4. Providing criteria for morally evaluating domestic or international laws regarding recourse to war. (This is distinct from 3, because the actual institutional processes through which decisions to go to war are made may or may not be effectively constrained by a commitment to law.[5])

---

[4] This could in principle include institutions that identify authorities on war-making, on the assumption that soldiers and civilians should defer to them in deciding how to act. For examples of those just war theorists who do not consider the possibility that different norms may be appropriate depending on the institutional context in which war-making decisions are made, see all of the essays except the ones by Allen Buchanan in the following anthologies: *Ethics and Foreign Intervention*, eds. Deen K. Chatterjee and Don E. Scheid (Cambridge, UK: Cambridge University Press, 2003); and *Humanitarian Intervention: Ethical, Legal and Political Dilemmas*, eds. Robert O. Keohane & J. L. Holzgrefe (Cambridge, UK: Cambridge University Press, 2003). The best explanation of these authors not considering the moral difference that alternative institutions can make may be that they either implicitly assume a purely instrumental view of the relationship between principles and institutions, that is, they assume that institutions are important only as mechanisms for realizing principles whose grounding does not take institutional capacities into account; or they assume that the institutional status quo is very unlikely to change. None of these authors defend either of these assumptions. Only a small minority of contemporary just war theorists place institutional considerations at the heart of their inquiries. For perhaps the most developed examples of institutional approaches, see Allen Buchanan and Robert O. Keohane, "Justifying Preventive War: A Cosmopolitan Institutional Proposal," *Ethics & International Affairs* 18, no.1 (2004): 1–22; and Allen Buchanan, "Institutionalizing the Just War," *Philosophy & Public Affairs* 34, no. 1 (2006): 2–38.

[5] Along with 1, this topic has received the most discussion on this list, in contemporary just war theory. See especially Lazar, "Morality & Law of War"; Jeff McMahan, "The Morality of War and the Law of War," in David Rodin and Henry Shue, eds., *Just and Unjust Warriors: The Moral and Legal Status of Soldiers* (Oxford: Oxford University Press, 2008), 19–43; Jeff McMahan, "Laws of War," in Samantha Besson and John Tasioulas, eds., *The Philosophy of International Law* (New York: Oxford University Press, 2010), 493–510; David Rodin, "Morality and Law in War," in Hew Strachan and Sibylle Scheipers, eds., *The Changing Character of War* (Oxford: Oxford University Press, 2011), 446–63; Henry Shue, "Do We Need a Morality of War?," in David Rodin and Henry Shue, eds., *Just and Unjust Warriors: The Moral and Legal Status*

5. Providing guidance for how to achieve a division of labor between directly action-guiding rules to be employed by leaders, on the one hand, and institutional processes, on the other, which is most conducive to morally sound recourse to war.
6. Providing criteria for morally evaluating the decisions of leaders regarding recourse to war. (Note that all of the preceding tasks, 1–5, are relevant to this one.)
7. Providing an account of the virtues of leaders, so far as their decision-making regarding recourse to war is concerned. (According to moral theories that give a prominent role to virtues, this will be a central element of task 6, for other types of theories it will be negligible or less important.)
8. Providing criteria for morally evaluating social practices regarding what counts as legitimate public justifications for recourse to war by leaders. Given the prominence of war in human life and the seriousness of its consequences, it is both unsurprising and appropriate that societies develop practices that include norms that identify some justifications for going to war as legitimate and others as illegitimate. For example, in the eighteenth century in Europe it was widely agreed that going to war to maintain or restore "the balance of power" was legitimate, but this is no longer the case. These practices and the corresponding norms can and should be evaluated from a moral standpoint. This item overlaps with but is distinct from item 4 above, because such social practices may rely more or less heavily on legal norms.
9. Providing criteria for morally evaluating leaders' public acts of justifying recourse to war. On some accounts, this evaluation will depend crucially on whether these public acts

of Soldiers (Oxford: Oxford University Press, 2008), 87–111; Henry Shue, "Laws of War," in Samantha Besson and John Tasioulas, eds., *The Philosophy of International Law* (New York: Oxford University Press, 2010), 511–30.

of justification count as legitimate according to the relevant social practice regarding public justifications for going to war. In some cases, a leader's public justification may tend to undermine a sound practice regarding legitimate types of justifications, as when the Bush administration attempted to make preventive war credible by mislabeling it as preemptive war in 2003.

Theory and Practice

Item 1 might be regarded as a purely theoretical aim. Item 2 is a practical aim, at least if it is assumed that there is some chance that the guidance provided may actually be followed. It is perfectly legitimate, of course, for a just war theorist to concentrate only on the theoretical aspects of *jus ad bellum* and leave the task of contributing to the achievement of practical aims to others. The point is simply that comprehensive moral theorizing about war should include theorizing about how best to achieve practical aims. Such theorizing will, of course, rely on empirical assumptions, but it will also be a normative enterprise and one to which moral philosophers should be able to contribute. Normative analysis is needed to determine what the proper aims are (or by what processes they should be determined) and to ascertain the morally sound ways of achieving them.

Moral philosophers may not be the most effective agents among all those who might contribute to the improvement of behavior regarding recourse to war, but they are best equipped to explore the possibility that systematic moral reasoning can play some role in that worthy endeavor. So there is good reason for some moral philosophers who think systematically about war to devote their energies to the practical aims.[6]

---

[6] For examples of some such reflection in philosophical outlets, see Jeff McMahan, "The Prevention of Unjust Wars," in Yitzhak Benbaji and Naomi Sussman, eds., *Reading Walzer* (New York: Routledge, 2013), 233–56; Henry Shue, "Targeting Civilian Infrastructure with Smart Bombs: The New

In Part II, I set out in greater detail the full set of topics that a comprehensive *jus ad bellum* should address and explain important connections among them. In Part III, I explore neglected relationships among moral principles, institutions, and law. I argue that *jus ad bellum* theory should take seriously the idea that the relationship between the morality and the law of recourse to war is not purely instrumental but also partly constitutive—that the law, when it is appropriately institutionalized, can alter the moral landscape in significant ways. In Part IV, I examine the practical roles that an enriched *jus ad bellum* could play.

II. *Elements of an Enriched Jus ad Bellum*

Objective versus Directly Action-Guiding Norms

This first task, the sole theoretical aim of the *jus ad bellum* part of just war theory narrowly construed, seems wholly uncontroversial. But the phrase "criteria for justified acts of going to war" is ambiguous between (i) objective justifications and (ii) directly action-guiding norms for leaders or other agents.[7] Suppose it is understood in the first way. Here is an example of an objective justification.

It is (morally) justifiable for a state to go to war in self-defense if and only if

   (i) the target of the war of self-defense has perpetrated a wrongful (unjustified) attack,

  (ii) war is a last resort (roughly, all reasonable alternatives have been exhausted),

---

Permissiveness," *Philosophy & Public Policy Quarterly* 30, no. 3/4 (2010): 2–8. Michael Walzer, David Luban, Jeff McMahan, David Rodin and others have also long sought to influence public opinion through popular outlets such as *Dissent, The New Republic, The Boston Review, The Guardian,* and *The New York Times.*

   [7] Of course, just war theory can and should also provide guidance for soldiers. For simplicity's sake, I will only discuss guidance for leaders, but what I say will also apply, with suitable adjustments, to guidance for soldiers.

(iii) the act of going to war satisfies the Proportionality Requirement (roughly, the good to be achieved by waging the war justifies the harms it will bring), and

(iv) the act of going to war satisfies the Discrimination Requirement (roughly, reasonable care is taken to minimize harm to those not morally liable to be harmed).

I am not assuming that these are the correct elements of an objective justification for going to war in self-defense. (In fact, I believe the case has been made by myself and Robert O. Keohane that (i) is too strong, because it rules out cases of justified preventive war, situations in which the target of military action poses a dire threat of wrongful harm but one which will only be realized at some temporally distant point.[8]) I make no effort in this chapter to contribute to theorizing about objective justifications; nor will I have much to say about the fourth task, the moral evaluation of laws regarding war.

My aim, rather, is to call attention to areas of just war theorizing that have been relatively neglected: items 2 and 3, and 5 through 9. The sample objective justification outlined above is only intended to help ground the distinction I wish to emphasize between objective justifications and directly action-guiding norms and to lay the groundwork for showing how much of the terrain of a comprehensive *jus ad bellum* remains unexplored after the task of identifying objective justifications has been successfully completed.

Directly Action-Guiding Norms

The best way for leaders to ensure that their actions conform to the requirements of sound objective justifications for recourse to war may *not* be for them to attempt to determine whether an act of war-making they are contemplating satisfies the conditions set

---

[8] Buchanan and Keohane, "Justifying Preventive War," n. 4, *supra*.

out in the relevant objective justification. State leaders are not ideal decision-makers who can be trusted to apply the conditions for objective justification directly. They are fallible agents laboring under all of the limitations common to human beings, including normal cognitive biases and errors, as well as weakness of the will. They are also subject to special incentives as a result of the institutional roles they occupy and the values that led them to come to occupy those roles, and these too can impair their decision-making. For example, given that her country has recently suffered a humiliating defeat, and in the context of a rival political leader's allegation that she is soft on national security, a leader may rightly conclude that her grip on power requires taking a hardline position in a current international crisis, and this in turn may bias her judgment toward recourse to war. To take another example: a leader may understandably conclude that the political consequences for her of not taking preventive action in the event of a terrorist act or surprise military attack that could have been prevented are far more serious than the error of taking preventive action that turns out to have been unnecessary. In sum, particular institutional roles, including that of commander in chief, can create powerful incentives that are often not well-aligned with the requirements of objective justification.

Further, even though leaders have access to information not available to ordinary people, they may nonetheless suffer serious epistemic liabilities. Their advisors may exaggerate their own expertise, in order to maintain or augment their own power; or may succumb to the temptation to slant the information in a direction they anticipate will please the leader, given what they know or believe they know about his preferences. And of course, advisors and leaders deliberating together are vulnerable to various other errors stemming from so-called group think. In particular, if sufficient care is not taken to distinguish expertise from loyalty, important corrective information may be excluded from the decision-making process and the phenomenon of polarization may occur: shared views or preferences may become intensified

in the absence of evidence to support making such a shift. Even
when none of these distorting influences is at work, limitations
on information may make attempts to apply objective justification criteria highly fallible.

The main point here should be familiar from discussions of
the distinction between direct and indirect consequentialism, but
it applies to both consequentialist and deontological varieties of
just war theory. Because of epistemic and/or motivational limitations, an agent may do better by not attempting to apply the
criteria for right action but instead relying on directly action-
guiding norms whose content is quite different.

Neglecting the Epistemic Predicament of Decision-Makers

Judgments of proportionality can be extremely difficult to make,
even if one assumes away uncertainty as to how the Principle of
Proportionality itself is to be understood. (A chief source of disagreement concerns which harms and benefits count and how they
are to be weighted.) Beyond uncertainty as to how the principle
itself is to be understood, the chief difficulty is that proportionality judgments are very epistemically demanding. Predictions
about the effects of various military operations must be made,
but usually on the bases of inadequate evidence. One source of
difficulty in making predictions is that the effects of a military
intervention—in particular, how much death and destruction
it will entail, as well as the distribution of harm—will depend
upon how the enemy reacts, how civilians in the area of operation
react, and how one's own troops will behave, all of which may be
difficult to predict.

Suppose that, either due to limitations of information or due
to the risk that her judgment will be distorted by incentives that
attach to her role in the situation at hand or other biases, a state
leader is likely to err if she tries to determine whether the act of war
she is contemplating satisfies the Proportionality Requirement,
in the case of a war of humanitarian intervention. In particular,

she may fail to give sufficient weight to the harmful effects of the intervention on noncombatants and give undue consideration to preventing harm to her own armed forces, because she is politically accountable for the latter but not the former.

Under these conditions, it may well be that the leader will be more likely to make the right decision if instead of trying to assess proportionality, she follows a heuristic that makes no reference to it: "Engage in humanitarian military intervention only in cases where the humanitarian crisis is extremely grave—a genocide or mass killing of comparable scale." In fact, most accounts of the "justification" (note the ambiguity) for humanitarian war include a high threshold of violence condition. The problem is that they seldom make it clear whether it is intended as a heuristic or an element of an objective justification.

Contemporary just war theorists have not ignored the epistemic obstacles to correct application of objective justification criteria.[9] Their focus, however, has been rather narrow: for the most part, theorists have discussed the epistemic issues in the context of a dispute over the moral symmetry thesis, the assertion, advanced by Michael Walzer but also reflected in international humanitarian law of war, that the rules of *jus in bello* should not discriminate between just and unjust combatants (those who fight in a just cause and those who do not).[10] Some have concluded that in many cases ordinary soldiers cannot be faulted for being unable to make accurate judgments as to whether the war in which they are called on to fight is just.

Some of the most prominent contemporary theorists, including most notably Jeff McMahan, have developed a theory of moral liability to be subjected to armed force according to which it is

---

[9] See, for example, Cécile Fabre, *Cosmopolitan War* (Oxford: Oxford University Press, 2012), 77; Seth Lazar, "The Responsibility Dilemma for Killing in War," *Philosophy & Public Affairs* 38, no. 2 (2010): 180–213; Jeff McMahan, *Killing in War* (Oxford: Oxford University Press, 2009), 119.

[10] Michael Walzer, *Just and Unjust Wars* (New York: Basic Books, 1977), 36.

morally impermissible for unjust combatants to kill just combatants, even if in doing so they adhere strictly to *jus in bello* principles in their war-making activity.[11] In order to render this claim consistent with the conviction that in many cases combatants cannot be expected to know whether the cause for which they fight is just, McMahan and others have emphasized the distinction between the morality of war and the law of war.[12] Their view is that even though, as a matter of the "deep" morality of war, Walzer's moral symmetry of combatants must be abandoned, the law regarding war should maintain symmetry. The clear assumption here is that the "deep" morality of war should be concerned only with objective justifications and the judgments of moral culpability that follow from applying their criteria to the behavior of agents, but that the law properly has other concerns, including satisfying the conditions for just punishment, in the light of the epistemic limitations that afflict actual agents.

This particular focus on epistemic obstacles is unduly narrow in two respects. First, it attends only to the implications of one sort of epistemic obstacle to morally sound acts or practices (whether legal or less formal) of holding combatants responsible for their war acts: the difficulty for ordinary soldiers of determining whether their side's war-making is just or not. It does not address the special epistemic obstacles leaders face; nor does it consider how epistemic obstacles can interact with the peculiar incentives under which leaders labor to distort decision-making. Second, it does not consider other morally defensible responses to the epistemic problem it does address. More precisely, it does not acknowledge the possibility that in some cases the use of

---

[11] Jeff McMahan, "On the Moral Equality of Combatants," *Journal of Political Philosophy* 14, no. 4 (2006): 377–93. For an in-depth treatment of the issue of the moral symmetry of combatants, see *Just and Unjust Warriors: The Moral and Legal Status of Soldiers*, eds. David Rodin and Henry Shue (Oxford: Oxford University Press, 2011).

[12] McMahan, "The Morality of War." See also Cécile Fabre, "Guns, Food, and Liability to Attack in War," *Ethics* 120, no. 1 (2009): 36–63.

heuristics might mitigate the risks of acting when the information needed to apply objective justification criteria is not available.

For example, in some cases—depending on the history of one's country's recourse to war—a reasonable heuristic for soldiers or potential soldiers might be "Proceed on the assumption that any given recourse to war by the leaders of one's country is unjust, unless there is very strong evidence that it is just." Such a heuristic might be eminently reasonable for a citizen of a country whose leaders have repeatedly shown themselves to be untrustworthy when it comes to their public justifications for going to war. In extreme cases, an individual might be morally culpable for not following it.

Clarity in theorizing *jus ad bellum* requires not only distinguishing between objective justifications and directly action-guiding principles and acknowledging that the latter are an important subject in theorizing the morality of war. It also requires a recognition of the fact that because heuristics serve to mitigate epistemic and/or motivational defects of decision-makers and because different decision-makers have different defects, it is a mistake to assume that there is only one correct set of heuristics. In order to make the case for a particular heuristic, one must first of all provide an accurate characterization of the decision-making agent and her situation.

To illustrate this point, consider Michael Walzer's assertion that leaders contemplating the use of armed force to intervene in a conflict in another state ought to proceed on the assumption that there is a "fit" between the political structure and the society there, unless the government is engaging in extreme violence, such as genocide.[13] Walzer could be interpreted here as proposing a heuristic designed to cope with the risk of error that a leader contemplating intervention would incur if she attempted to make more fine-grained judgments about the relationship between the

[13] Walzer, *Just and Unjust Wars*, 90, n. 7.

government and the people, and in particular, whether the government in some sense represents or expresses the values and will of the people. But Walzer does not consider the possibility that the information needed to make such judgments may vary across agents and that different agents may be subject to a greater or lesser degree to incentives that affect their willingness or ability to utilize relevant information effectively. It is likely that different heuristics would be appropriate, depending on whether a decision to go to war were being made by Dick Cheney, on the one hand; or Abraham Lincoln, on the other.

Which heuristics (if any) are appropriate will depend upon the characteristics of the agent and of the situation in which the decision will be made, because the function of heuristics is to mitigate the cognitive and motivational deficiencies of the agent who will apply them, and these will vary across agents and decision contexts. If, for example, a heuristic is an epistemic proxy, that is, designed to cope with an informational deficit, it will matter whether all agents suffer this deficit or only some.

Institutional Processes for Recourse to War Decisions

An argument to justify a heuristic is more complex and requires more empirical premises than a moral intuition-based argument to establish an element of an objective justification: one must first establish that there is a significant risk involved in the effort to use the objective justification as a direct guide to action. As I have just noted, this will require not only a description of the relevant epistemic and motivational features of the decision-maker but also a characterization of how features of the choice situation, when combined with these features of the agent, create the risk of bad decisions.

In the case of leaders, it will not be enough to include in the characterization the normal cognitive biases and errors to which people in general are liable. In addition, it will be necessary to note the special incentives that attach to the role of leader and these, of course, will vary depending upon how the role of leader is understood in a particular society and on contingent features of the role in its particular institutional setting. After providing this complex, highly contextual characterization of the agent, one must then show that the proposed heuristic significantly reduces that risk while producing an adequate degree of congruence between what the objective justification, if perfectly applied, would recommend; and what the heuristic tells one to do.

The theoretical domain of *jus ad bellum* is even more complicated than that, however. Once one takes seriously the potential effects of institutions on decision-making, it becomes clear that the only alternatives are not (i) decision-makers directly applying the elements of sound objective justifications, on the one hand; or (ii) employing heuristics, on the other. Relying on heuristics is only one way of coping with the epistemic and motivational limitations of decision-makers. Institutional procedures, including requirements of transparency, consultation with relevant experts, and accountability mechanisms, can also mitigate the distorting effects of both epistemic and motivational limitations. For example, as Keohane and I have argued, institutions capable of imposing costs on decision-makers who exaggerate the risk of potential, temporally distant harms can counteract incentives for making morally unjustifiable decisions.[14]

A Morally Sound Division of Labor between Directly Action-Guiding Principles and Institutional Processes

I have argued that focusing exclusively on identifying objective justifications does not address a major moral problem regarding war: bad recourse to war decisions may be due, not to ignorance of sound objective justifications, but rather to the epistemic and motivational liabilities of decision-makers. I have also argued that heuristics are one solution to this problem, but not the only

---

[14] Buchanan and Keohane, "Justifying Preventive War," n. 4, *supra*.

one and in some cases not the optimal one: there is also the institutional alternative. The distorting effects of decision-makers' epistemic and motivational limitations can be reduced, either by encouraging them to follow heuristics whose contents are more constraining than the requirements of sound objective justifications (as with the heuristics "Engage in humanitarian intervention only when killing has reached the level of genocide" or "Engage only in preemptive war, never preventive war"); or by embedding directly action-guiding rules that are more permissive than such heuristics within an institutional context that supplies the needed constraints. Alternatively, the best alternative might be some combination of heuristics and institutional constraints.

So, one important question for a comprehensive theory of *jus ad bellum* is this: What is the optimal division of labor between direct appeals to elements of objective justifications, the use of heuristics or other directly action-guiding principles, and reliance on institutional mechanisms, for improving the decision-making of fallible agents and in particular of leaders, given their pivotal role? The right answer will be grounded in the facts about institutional capacities, but it will require moral reasoning as well, since some institutional arrangements will be permissible, others will be impermissible, and among those that are permissible some may be morally better than others.

Recourse to War Justification as a Social Practice

It can be morally preferable or even morally obligatory for a society to avoid a practice of justification in which direct appeals to certain objective justifications by leaders are regarded as legitimate. Not only justifications, considered as abstract objects, but also justifications as public acts, are subject to moral assessment, and so is the public's response to such public acts.

In circumstances in which direct appeals to a particular kind of objective justification are highly likely to result in a leader making an erroneous judgment about whether to go to war, it is wrong for her to do so, at least if there is a sound heuristic and she either is aware of it or should be. Some types of justifications for going to war are *practically dangerous*: under the circumstances in which leaders typically find themselves when considering recourse to war, relying on them to determine how to act is very likely to produce a decision that is seriously morally defective. The public can also be morally blameworthy — either as individuals or even collectively if they ratify the leader's decision through some formal act of group decision-making — for accepting a particular practically dangerous justification as legitimate. A social practice regarding public justifications for recourse to war in which practically dangerous justifications are routinely regarded as legitimate is a morally defective practice.

Robert O. Keohane and I have argued that, under current conditions, even the best type of preventive war justification is practically dangerous.[15] We first argue that there is a sound objective justification for preventive war (under certain highly constrained circumstances) and then make the case that the preventive war justification is practically dangerous, due to the typical epistemic and motivational situation of those leaders who would be prone to have to rely on it. Because the harm to be averted is temporally distant, the prediction that it is likely to occur may be highly speculative, and this may provide the leader with opportunities to misrepresent or misinterpret ambiguous information in ways that serve his purposes — purposes the pursuit of which may undermine the integrity of the decision-making process. (In Chapter One, I argued that justifying war as necessary for forcible democratization is also practically dangerous, unless adequate provisions are made to reduce the special risks that this type of justification carries.)

In the light of these risks, the view that defensive war is justified only against an imminent attack looks more plausible — not

---

[15] Buchanan and Keohane, "Justifying Preventive War," n. 4, *supra*.

as an element of a superior objective justification, but as a valuable heuristic. Even if there are cases in which preventive war is justified, leaders may do better by following a heuristic that forbids preventive war and only allows preemptive war. In the absence of institutional processes aptly designed to reduce the special risks of deciding to go to war for preventive purposes, the most responsible course might be to rely on such a heuristic.

Whether or not leaders can be relied on to follow the heuristic "Avoid preventive war" (and do not use The Preventive War Justification) may depend upon whether they believe that the public to which they are responsible regards prevention as a legitimate justification for going to war. If the Preventive War Justification is very dangerous and if aptly designed institutional safeguards to guide and constrain its application are not presently available, then the best course may be to develop and sustain a social practice of regarding public justifications of war that rely on it as illegitimate.

Such a practice could be either more or less formal. A formal version would utilize a constitutional prohibition against leaders publicly justifying their decision to go to war by appealing to the preventive war justification (just as the post-World War II constitutions of both Germany and Japan included provisions against any form of war other than self-defense). A less formal version would be a widely accepted social norm serving the same purpose. The key point is that in addition to assessing moral justifications understood as abstract objects, the *jus ad bellum* theorist should provide reasoned evaluations of particular public acts of justification and public justificatory practices.

The Ethics of War Leadership

Once we recognize that the moral quality of recourse to war decisions can be affected both by the characteristics of the specific institutional processes within which such decisions are made and by social practices regarding what counts as a legitimate public justification for going to war, it becomes clear that it is a mistake to think that a moral assessment of the actions of leaders or of ordinary citizens is simply a scaled-up version of the moral assessment of acts of violence performed by non-situated, bare individuals, considered in abstraction from their institutional roles.[16] For example, whether a citizen is morally blameworthy for participating in her country's recourse to war (or for supporting or at least not opposing it) may depend on the moral qualities of the institutional process and broader social practice of justification within which her country's leader made the decision to go to war. If the institutional process and the practice of justification are sound, and known to be so, then it will be reasonable for the individual citizen to be more confident that recourse to war is justified, and, other things being equal, she will be less blameworthy if that turns out not to be the case. Similarly, if a leader operates within a highly defective institutional process for decision-making that is supported by a social practice of treating practically dangerous types of recourse-to-war justifications as legitimate, her blameworthiness for a bad decision may be less than it would be in other circumstances.

Contemporary just war theory has had surprisingly little to say about the morality of leadership regarding war. A leader might launch a war for which there is an objective justification and yet be morally blameworthy for doing so. This would be the case if she should have followed a heuristic that would have prohibited her from doing the (objectively) right thing. The leader would also be morally blameworthy for doing the right thing if she failed to follow institutional procedures that would have prevented her from doing the right thing or if she acted contrary to the norms of the most morally defensible practice regarding public justifications for going to war. Furthermore, an agent can be morally blameworthy for the decision-making process she

---

[16] Contra Jeff McMahan, "War as Self-Defense," *Ethics & International Affairs* 18, no. 1 (2004): 75–80.

actually engaged in, if it was shaped by bad motives or bad intentions or involved culpable reliance on defective or incomplete information, even if it resulted in her doing the right thing. For these reasons, sound moral evaluations of the actions of leaders in deciding to go to war may require investigations into the roles of heuristics, institutional processes, and practices regarding public justifications that have received virtually no attention in *jus ad bellum* theory.

Consider again the fact that a leader's public justification for going to war may have little to do with her actual decision-making process. One could argue, in fact, that this is precisely what happened in the case of the Iraq War that began in 2003. Suppose that preventive war is sometimes justified in the sense that there is an objective justification for going to war to avert the threat of a temporally distant harm. That is quite compatible with concluding that the Bush administration acted wrongly. Suppose, as appears likely, that the Bush administration invoked the plausibility of such a justification to rationalize to itself and to justify to the public the results of a deeply flawed decision-making process, one that was distorted by a willingness to overinterpret quite limited and conflicting information in the pursuit of geopolitical ends that had nothing to do with Saddam Hussein's capacity to inflict harm on the United States. If recourse to war resulted from such a flawed decision-making process, then it is correct to say that in going to war Bush acted wrongly, even if there is a sound objective justification for preventive war and even though Bush publicly justified the war as preventive. And he would have still acted wrongly, even if by some happy coincidence, all of the necessary and sufficient conditions specified in the objective justification had in fact been obtained in the case of Iraq at the time.

This is not to say that one is blameworthy for performing a right act whenever there is any defect whatsoever in the reasoning that led to the act if one's motives or intentions are in any way less than pure. The point, rather, is that some motivations and intentions and some errors of reasoning can be so seriously defective as to render an agent blameworthy for acting even though the act he performs is a right act.

The Virtues of War Leaders

So far, I have discussed the neglected topic of the morality of leadership in recourse to war from the standpoint of directly action-guiding principles and institutional processes and by reference to the idea of social practices regarding what counts as legitimate public justifications for going to war. But a comprehensive *jus ad bellum* would also consider the possibility that certain virtues are relevant to the ethics of leadership. There are two quite different ways in which an account of the virtues of leaders might figure in a comprehensive *jus ad bellum* theory. First, one might take what may be called an Extreme Virtue Ethics approach. According to this view, a sound account of the virtues of war-making decision-makers provides the full content of *jus ad bellum*: just wars are those that virtuous decision-makers engage in or approve and unjust wars are those they eschew. On this view, to try to articulate objective justifications in the form of a list of right-making conditions is either impossible or superfluous, and similarly for heuristics to be applied directly by decision-makers.

This approach is properly labeled "Extreme" because it denies any significant role either to objective justifications or to heuristics, and relies solely on an account of the decision-making virtues, understood as stable dispositions (to judge, to experience various moral sentiments, and to act). Right acts of war-making are then defined as those an agent with those virtues would engage in or approve of. Because I am convinced by the familiar criticism that such an Extreme Virtue Ethics view fails to show how one can identify the virtuous person without recourse to moral principles that can be stated independently of reference to the virtues, I will focus on the second way in which Virtue Ethics might function in *jus ad bellum* theorizing.

The more modest and plausible proposal is that a comprehensive theory of *jus ad bellum* will include an account of the virtues of leaders who decide on recourse to war, but without denying the importance of objective justifications, directly action-guiding principles, institutional processes, or practices of public justification. For example, it could be argued that leaders must possess certain virtues if they are to be counted on to follow appropriate heuristics (and to know when to disregard them) and to conform to appropriate institutional requirements designed to improve their decision-making (and to know when to disregard them). To the extent that (i) there are exceptional circumstances in which disregard of generally appropriate heuristics or other directly action-guiding principles or institutional procedures is either morally permissible or morally obligatory and; (ii) ascertaining them is a matter of judgment and cannot be achieved by following rules, the virtues of leaders, if they include the capacity for such judgments, may be crucial. At the very least, it might turn out to be the case that, unless decision-makers are free of certain vices, even the most commendable heuristics and institutional safeguards will prove ineffective.

Finally, which virtues leaders need may depend on how effective the institutional constraints on war-making decisions are. If institutional constraints are highly effective, less robust virtues will be required for acceptable leadership; and if leaders typically are not robustly virtuous, then greater institutional constraint will be needed. What this means is that the virtues of leaders and the institutional dimension must be theorized in a way that recognizes their interdependence.

III. *Moral Principles, Institutions, and Laws*

I have argued that an enriched *jus ad bellum* will attend to the fact that the quality of the institutional processes within which substantive norms regarding recourse to war are invoked can affect the soundness of decisions are made. I have not yet said anything about how the discussion thus far bears on the relationship between law and morality. To begin to fill this gap, I will first explore the relationship between the morality of law and existing institutions.

How Institutions Transform the Moral Scene

There are two fundamentally different conceptions of the role of institutions in a comprehensive theory of *jus ad bellum*. On the first, purely instrumental conception, institutions are simply mechanisms for implementing moral norms that are justified independently of any institutional considerations. On the second, partly constitutive conception, the validity of some moral norms depends upon the institutional context in which they will be applied. I suspect that the purely instrumental conception of institutions is prevalent in contemporary just war theory generally, and not just in its *jus ad bellum* part, and that the partly constitutive conception has not been adequately appreciated.

Of course, in many cases, institutions are purely instrumental and their usefulness as instruments is the sole source of their value. But in some cases, the relationship between moral norms and institutions is more intimate.

In discussing heuristics, I have already shown that which norms a leader should directly follow in deciding to go to war may depend on the institutional context within which she decides. Both heuristics and institutional processes can serve to mitigate biasing factors that would otherwise distort the agent's decision. But heuristics that would be justified in the absence of institutional resources for mitigating bias may be redundant or even counterproductive if the institutions within which decisions are made are well-designed. Conversely, institutional constraints may be an unnecessary cost if heuristics do an adequate job of mitigating biasing factors. So the relationship between heuristics and institutions can be constitutive, not merely instrumental.

The same is true for norms that are elements of objective justifications rather than heuristics. Consider the case of moral norms of individual self-defense. Contrast two different situations in which an individual might act in self-defense. In the first, the individual must rely solely on her own resources to defend herself against an unjust attack by a spouse or partner. In the second, the social context provides impressive resources for protection against unjust attacks: the police are trustworthy and can be relied on to respond very quickly, and one can count on one's fellow citizens intervening on one's behalf; in addition, there are easily accessible shelters that provide sanctuary for those fleeing unjust attacks. In the first context, there may be valid moral norms regarding self-defense that are more permissive—for example, it may be justifiable, under certain circumstances, for an individual to use preventive force, not merely to try to thwart an occurring or imminent attack. In the second context, where others can be relied on, preventive force may be unjustifiable.

An analogous point applies in the case of collective self-defense, a major topic of the theory of *jus ad bellum*. Which forcible acts of self-defense a country is morally permitted to undertake may depend upon whether there is an effective supranational security system. If this is the case, then a comprehensive *jus ad bellum* must take institutions seriously.

The Moral Evaluation of Legal Institutions for Constraining War

Law as an institution is both instrumental and partly constitutive in its relationship to morality. Some contemporary theorists have advanced moral assessments of some aspects of international law's treatment of group armed conflict, especially with respect to the offenses that fall within the writ of the International Criminal Court. But much more work remains to be done. A comprehensive theory of *jus ad bellum* would include a moral evaluation not only of legal doctrine but also of the institutions through which international law pertaining to recourse to war is created, interpreted, and implemented. Morally impeccable legal norms may lack legitimacy if the institutions through which they are created and applied lack legitimacy.

IV. *Practical Aims*

In the current just war literature, there is surprisingly little discussion of whether *jus ad bellum* theory has practical aims and, if so, what precisely they are—and how achievement of the theoretical aim of providing objective justifications would contribute to them. First consider the practical aim of aiding the development of a more morally defensible international law regarding recourse to war. Even if it is true that just war thinking has in fact influenced international law in the past, it would be unjustified to assume that new advances in theory will produce further changes, in the absence of an account of the causal pathways by which theoretical work can find its way into law. Providing such an account would require social science expertise that philosophers lack. If it turned out that there are serious obstacles to the theory of *jus ad bellum* influencing the international law of war, then recourse to the theory of institutional design and to work in social epistemology might be needed to propose feasible remedies, along with moral reasoning to determine whether what is feasible is also morally permissible.

How Can Contemporary Jus ad Bellum *Theory Influence the Law of Recourse to War?*

One way to begin this formidable task would be to undertake a critical examination of recent or current cases in which there is systematic deliberation by public bodies (whether civilian or military) or judges concerning the adequacy of the current international law of war, to see whether there are adequate opportunities for "up-take" of the results of philosophical theorizing. For example, there are a number of groups now working on the question of whether changes in the law of war are needed to accommodate the peculiar problems raised by the use of weaponized drones. Eventually, these deliberations might result in proposals for new treaties or amendments of existing treaties regarding permissible weapons of war. If that transpired, it would be interesting to know if moral theorizing played any role.

If it turned out that those agents who can actually influence the interpretation or development of international law regarding recourse to war are not benefiting from philosophical work, then steps might be proposed for correcting this deficiency. One option would be to try to introduce a new institutional epistemic practice: a formal recognition that *jus ad bellum* theorists constitute an important "epistemic community" whose expertise should be utilized in evaluating the existing law of war. Something analogous has already occurred in a different domain of practical ethics: the institutionalization of high-level (in the US, presidential) commissions on bioethics, which operate on the understanding that the interdisciplinary membership of such groups should include a prominent role for moral philosophers. This epistemic institutional innovation is now employed in a number of countries. Bioethics commissions have several purposes, including providing systematic moral thinking as an input into the process of developing new law.

The point is that it is one thing to say that *jus ad bellum* theory provides potentially valuable insights for shaping what law has to say about recourse to war, but quite another to ensure that these insights are understood, much less utilized by those who are in a position to influence the character of the law. Similarly, from the fact that a comprehensive *jus ad bellum* theory provides guidance for leaders, combatants, or ordinary citizens regarding their decisions whether to make war or to support or oppose it, nothing whatsoever can be inferred about whether anyone's behavior will actually be influenced by it. In both cases, providing valuable guidance—or, more properly, guidance that would (only) improve matters *if* it were heeded—is in itself a practical benefit only in a very anemic sense.

From Theory to Practice

Some prominent contemporary just war theorists are to be commended for taking this problem seriously. They have taken on the important but difficult role of public intellectual by publishing in nonspecialist outlets their thoughtful responses to actual armed conflicts—from the NATO intervention in Kosovo in 1999, to the US-led invasion of Iraq in 2003, to the 2014 Israeli incursion into Gaza. Some philosophers have also provided formal instruction in various military academies to those who will actually fight wars. In addition, several universities have standing academic units or long-term grant-funded centers that bring together just war theorists, military personnel, and government officials, and philosophically trained just war theorists seem to be playing an increasingly important role in their activities.

Nevertheless, I think it is fair to say that both the practical aims of *jus ad bellum* and the alternatives for realizing them in a morally sound and effective way have been undertheorized. As long as the focus is on *jus ad bellum* theory narrowly construed—as a quest for objective justifications for recourse-to-war acts—the task of theorizing practical aims is likely to be neglected, in part because the gap between knowledge of which acts are right and the achievement of right behavior, as I have argued, is so wide.

In contrast, the more comprehensive conception of *jus ad bellum* that I am recommending would provide more resources for addressing the most important practical concerns. For example, by exploring the possibility of a fruitful division of labor between heuristics and institutional processes for decision-making regarding recourse to war, a more comprehensive theory of *jus ad bellum* can inform strategies for increasing the probability that leaders will actually make decisions that conform to the requirements of sound justifications rather than merely appeal to them as cover for wrongful acts.

Conclusion

There are two different ways to conceive of a richer *jus ad bellum*: in a purely *theoretically* comprehensive way, that is, as an attempt to illuminate all of the morally significant aspects of recourse to war, but with no pretensions to practical efficacy; or in a way that also takes seriously the idea that theory can be a valuable resource for helping to achieve morally better behavior regarding recourse to war. So far, contemporary *jus ad bellum* theory has not succeeded in either task; and in that sense it is doubly impoverished. By focusing chiefly on determining the elements of objective justifications for recourse to war, it has neglected other important aspects of the morality of recourse to war, including the moral evaluation of the actual decision-making of leaders, of the institutional processes through which decisions to go to war are made, of leaders' public justifications for going to war, and of social practices regarding what counts as legitimate public justifications. Further, the role of both directly action-guiding principles and institutional processes in correcting for distortions of decision-making needs to be systematically explored. Just as important, more must be done to develop an account of the virtues of war leaders and of the partly constitutive relationship between morality and the law.

From the standpoint of reasonable practical aims, contemporary *jus ad bellum* theory also comes up short, to the extent that it tends to ignore the question of practical aims entirely or proceeds as if determining the elements of objective justifications for recourse to war will somehow have good practical effects. The *jus ad bellum* part of the ethics of group armed conflict is theoretically more complex, of potentially greater practical value, and certainly more difficult than many contemporary theorists have assumed.[17] A richer *jus ad bellum* would use a cogent account of objective justifications for recourse to war as a solid foundation on which to address a much more comprehensive set of subjects for systematic moral thinking.

[17] I am indebted to Cécile Fabre, Helen Frowe, Jeff Holzgrefe, Robert O. Keohane, Seth Lazar, Jeff McMahan, Kit Wellman, Chad Van Schoelandt, and Bas van der Vossen for their helpful comments on drafts of this chapter.

CHAPTER 3

Institutional Legitimacy

This chapter offers a general theory of institutional legitimacy grounded in an account of the distinctive practical function of legitimacy assessments. Such a theory is vitally necessary for any approach to the morality of war that takes institutions seriously. Without a sound theory of institutional legitimacy, one cannot achieve a comprehensive evaluation of existing institutions that affect war-making or responsibly propose institutional innovations. Part I lays out the account of the distinctive practical function, the Metacoordination View. On this account, legitimacy assessments are part of a social practice that aims at achieving consensus on whether an institution is worthy of our moral reason-based support—support that does not depend on the fear of coercion or on a perfect fit between our own interests and what the institution demands of us. Part II makes two main points. First, it uses the Metacoordination View's account of the practical function of legitimacy assessments to identify criteria of legitimacy that apply to a wide range of institutions, while at the same time allowing for differences in criteria depending upon the special function of the institution and also allowing for variations in the stringency of the criteria depending upon how badly we need the institution in question. Second, it shows that, for institutions that rule in the strict sense—those that back their rules with coercion—conformity to the requirements of the rule of law is a presumptive necessary condition of legitimacy. Part III explores the role of the virtue of law-abidingness in a viable social practice of making legitimacy assessments and shows how understanding this role explains features of legitimacy assessments that cannot be accounted for without it. Part IV uses the theory of legitimacy thus far developed to identify the inadequacies of two widely influential views about legitimacy: the attempt to employ Raz's Service conception of authority as an account of institutional legitimacy and the assumption that a legitimate institution (of the sort that rules) has a claim-right to compliance with its rules. The Conclusion sets out the attractions of the theory of institutional legitimacy developed in the chapter.

I. *The Metacoordination View of Institutional Legitimacy*

Institutional Legitimacy Assessments as a Solution to a Practical Problem

What is at stake when questions are asked or assertions are made regarding the legitimacy of an institution? What is the point of engaging in such discourse? The term "legitimacy" is used in a number of different senses and the point of legitimacy discourse can vary, depending upon the context. The focus of this chapter is on the legitimacy of institutions. Even with this restriction, it would be a mistake to assume that there is a single, unified practice regarding the use of the term "legitimate." In some cases, for example, the term "legitimate," as applied to institutions, is used to mean legal or justified or just. Such usage is unfortunate, because it obscures any distinctive value that legitimacy discourse may possess. In this chapter, I offer an account of institutional legitimacy that makes it clear that the term "legitimacy" can have a distinctive sense and refer to something of distinctive value. Without claiming that the concept of institutional legitimacy I articulate provides the only valid sense for the term, I identify an important function that legitimacy discourse can have, define a concept of legitimacy whose employment best serves that function, and then develop general criteria for determining whether an institution is legitimate according to that concept of legitimacy.

My hypothesis is that institutional legitimacy discourse can serve an important function: the achievement of a consensus on whether an institution is worthy of our *moral reason-based support*, that is, this discourse can help us ascertain whether we should accord the institution a certain kind of respect independently of the fear that it will coerce us and independently of whether there happens to be a congruence of our own interests with its demands. This is a crucial question, because our predicament would be dire if the threat of coercion or the promise of congruence with self-interest were the only resources available for marshaling support for institutions—support they must have if they are to provide the benefits that make them valuable. Relying solely on a perfect fit between self-interest and institutional demands is unworkable, because institutions often rightly require one to act contrary to one's interests. Relying solely on the threat of coercion would be unacceptable, because the amount of coercive power required would make the institution too costly and too dangerous. Reasons that appeal to moral values or principles can provide a basis for supporting an institution that is independent of fear of coercion and appeals to self-interest. Let us call this sort of support "moral reason-based support." The key point is that moral reason-based support enables institutions to function without undue reliance on the threat of coercion or the inducements of self-interest.

An institution may function well enough if a sufficient number of people who are able to facilitate or hinder its operations simply support it through unreflective habit. Under these circumstances the discourse of legitimacy may be absent. The concept of legitimacy tends to perform a distinctive and valuable function when something has occurred that raises the question of how we ought to orient ourselves vis-à-vis an institution. The perception that the institution is failing to perform its functions or a challenge from a rival institution can make the question of support salient, thereby prompting legitimacy discourse.

Empowering an institution with our moral reason-based support can carry great risks: the institution may abuse or squander its power or it may operate in such a way as to cause discoordination, including interference with valuable activities of individuals and with the operation of other valuable institutions and social practices. So we need to determine what an institution must be like if it is to warrant such support. Whether it does will depend on whether the benefits of supporting it outweigh the risks. *According to the Metacoordination View, an institution is legitimate if and only if it is morally worthy of our support and an institution is morally worthy of our support only if the benefits of empowering it outweigh the risks of doing so.* On this view, the assertion that an institution is legitimate represents an all-things-considered judgment regarding the moral reasons for supporting it, namely, that those reasons weigh in favor of supporting the institution, in spite of the risks that such support entail.

With this understanding of the practical problem that legitimacy assessments address, the basic elements of the Metacoordination View can be outlined as follows. First, at least under reasonably favorable conditions, we should expect more of an institution than that it makes us somewhat better off than the noninstitutional alternative; yet we should not be so demanding as to expect it to be fully just. Full justice is usually too demanding, for two reasons: (i) in our world, it may simply be unattainable; and (ii) we often need institutions to help us make further progress in justice, so refusing to regard an institution as legitimate unless it is fully just would be self-defeating from the standpoint of justice. The best would be the enemy of the better.

Second, generally speaking, for an institution to deliver the goods that render it valuable, there must be *sufficient moral reason-based support* for it: enough of those who are in a position either to facilitate or hinder its operation must regard it as worthy of respect, as having the special standing that is generally required if it is to deliver the goods that make it valuable *and do so without excessive recourse to coercion.* In other words, for the distinctive practical function of institutional legitimacy assessments to be successful in any particular instance, what might be called a workable consensus, not unanimity, is required. What is needed is that enough people support the institution, on the basis of moral reasons, sufficiently to empower the institution to supply its distinctive benefits. Sufficient moral reason-based support reduces the need to rely on coercion and thereby lowers the material costs and the threats to freedom that a massive enforcement apparatus poses. A workable consensus that the institution is morally worthy of support need not be grounded in a thorough-going and deep agreement on all relevant moral values or principles. For example, persons who have different views about what justice requires may still converge in their assessments as to whether an institution is morally worthy of support, if they agree that the institution has certain characteristics and believe that those characteristics count in favor of supporting the institution, even if they hold different views about why those characteristics matter.

Third, although different institutions supply different goods, they all facilitate coordination and their value depends on their doing so. But if they are to play this coordinating role, we need to solve a prior coordination problem: we need to be able to converge in our moral reason-based support on some particular institution. It is not enough that we all recognize that we need an institution; we must coordinate our support on one institution among the alternatives. We need to achieve convergence on judgments that *this* institution deserves our support, is worthy of our respect. Thus the title "Metacoordination View."

Fourth, a proper showing of respect—the appropriate response when an institution is judged to be legitimate—involves different behaviors for different parties, depending upon their relationship to the institution. For those to whom the institution addresses its rules, it involves a presumption of compliance that operates independently of an assessment of the content of any particular directive. The disposition to comply is defeasible, because some rules might be so patently and egregiously unjust or so at odds with achieving the proper goals of the institution that they give addressees no reason whatsoever for acting, regardless of how admirable the institution is that issues them. For other parties, respect will simply be a matter of not interfering with the institution's operations, of according its agents a kind of impersonal respect, and of proceeding on the assumption that if the institution is flawed then the proper initial response is to try to reform it rather than to destroy or bypass it.

In the case of rule-addressees, an institution's legitimacy does *not* imply that addressees owe to the institution a moral duty of compliance. In other words, on this view, a legitimate institution need not have a claim-right to our obedience—we need not owe obedience to it. All that is necessary is that rule-addressees have a defeasible, content-independent reason to comply.

Content-Independent, Exclusionary Reasons

If the point of the practice is to achieve convergence on moral reason-based support for the institution and if what support requires in the case of those to whom the institution's rules are addressed is that they operate on the presumption that the rules as such are to be complied with, then the fact that the institution is worthy of support constitutes a content-independent reason for those individuals to comply with its directives. The content-independent reasons feature, then, is explained by the Metacoordination View's characterization of the nature and point of the practice of making legitimacy assessments.

Further, this content-independent reason is "exclusionary" in the sense that the judgment that the institution is worthy of our moral reason-based support implies that some reasons for not complying with its directives are inappropriate, that is, that they have no weight at all. In particular, the fact that it would be in one's best interest not to comply and the fact that one would not be coerced for failing to comply are excluded reasons, and the Metacoordination View explains why they are. The fact that in this particular instance I would do better, from the standpoint of my own interests, by ignoring its rules or can avoid being penalized for noncompliance is not a reason for noncompliance, because the point of securing moral reason-based compliance is to enable a valuable institution to function without excessive coercion and without the unsatisfiable demand of a perfect congruence between self-interest and what the institution demands. The Metacoordination View not only accommodates the idea of exclusionary reasons, but also explains why certain reasons are excluded, and this is a point in its favor. As with the content-independent reasons feature, the exclusionary reasons feature is explained, on the Metacoordination View, by its account of the nature and point of the practice of making legitimacy assessments.

Fifth, well-founded legitimacy assessments reflect a reasonable balancing of the benefits and risks of empowering an institution by giving it our moral reason-based support. By granting institutions the special standing that legitimacy connotes, we empower them so that they can provide us with benefits we could not otherwise obtain. Such empowerment carries the risk that the power will be abused or squandered or will have unacceptably deleterious effects on the activities of individuals or the operation of other valuable institutions. The practical problem is that we need to develop a *shared* conception of what an institution must be like to warrant our moral reason-based support, one that reflects a reasonable balancing of the benefits of having a functioning institution and the risks that empowering it to perform its functions entails. Without a shared conception, normative coordination will not be achieved and without normative coordination, the institution will not provide the coordination that makes it valuable.

Preserving the Distinction between
Sociological and Normative Legitimacy

Although the Metacoordination View takes sociological legitimacy (the widespread belief that an institution is legitimate)
seriously and explains why it is important, it is an account of legitimacy in the normative sense. According to the Metacoordination
View, an institution is legitimate if and only if it *is* worthy of
our moral reason-based support. It recognizes the importance
of achieving sociological legitimacy, but does not confuse it with
normative legitimacy.

II. *General Criteria for Institutional Legitimacy*

Suppose we succeed in coming to a shared understanding of
what normative standards an institution should meet if we are to
run the risks of empowering it through our moral reason-based
support. If more than one feasible institution satisfies those
standards, then we face two alternatives: we can either allow that
each is legitimate, though neither enjoys exclusive legitimacy,
that is, neither has the right to prohibit the other from operating
in the domain; or, if allowing two institutions to operate in the
same domain would cause serious problems, we can choose to
support one over the other on the basis of something other than
a legitimacy assessment (for example, tossing a coin or throwing
our support behind the temporally first institutional proposal
or choosing on grounds of comparative efficiency or transition
costs).

   If only one institution is already operating in a certain domain,
we need to know whether it measures up—whether it is worthy
of the standing that it needs to have to deliver the goods, keeping
in mind that thus empowering it carries risks. Yet, as I said earlier,
often we cannot reasonably expect it to be fully just.

   As was already noted, institutions are typically valuable because they enable coordination. Yet in anything other than the
most unfavorable circumstances, to decide whether an institution

is worthy of support we need to look to other considerations—not merely whether, *were* it to be accorded the standing that a judgment of legitimacy implies, it would achieve coordination. So the question arises: Are there general criteria whose satisfaction warrants our according institutions forms of respect that they need to have if they are to provide their distinctive benefits and do so without excessive reliance on coercion? Can anything general be said about what features are likely to make such support a good bargain, given the risks of empowering institutions with our support?

A Complex Standard for Institutional Legitimacy

In an earlier work, I argued for an affirmative answer to those questions: across a broad range of different kinds of institutions, including those that attempt to rule and those that do not, certain criteria are typically especially relevant to legitimacy assessments, because satisfaction of these criteria is generally a reasonable requirement for an institution to warrant the various forms of support that I noted above.[1] None of them is strictly necessary for legitimacy, but the more of them that are satisfied, and the greater the extent to which they are satisfied, the stronger the case for concluding that the institution is legitimate.

1. Comparative benefit: the institution provides significantly better benefits than the noninstitutional alternative.
2. Institutional integrity: there is not a large disparity between the institution's most important professed goals and procedures, on the one hand, and its actual performance on the other; or if there is such a disparity there is an explanation of it that shows it to be beyond the institutional agents' control and allows for a significant prospect that the disparity will be reduced over time.

[1] Allen Buchanan and Robert O. Keohane, "The Legitimacy of Global Governance Institutions," *Ethics and International Affairs* 20, no. 4 (2006): 405–37.

3. Minimal moral acceptability: the institution does not engage in violations of basic rights (or at least violations are not pervasive and there is good reason to believe that effective efforts to reduce violations are underway).
4. Acceptable origination (or sound pedigree): the institution came to be in a morally acceptable fashion, through an appropriate process.
5. Sound procedures: especially in cases where there is likely to be serious disagreement about outcomes or where outcomes will significantly advantage some and disadvantage others, an institution's procedures should be sound—that is, reliably apt for achieving the institution's aims—and in particular should be sufficiently fair that those who disagree with an outcome can reasonably conclude that the procedures did not stack the deck against them.
6. Minimal substantive fairness: the outcomes produced by the institution should at least avoid seriously and uncontroversially unfair results. (Fairness in procedures is covered by 5 above.)

Generally speaking, only when an institution satisfies these criteria is empowering it likely to be a good bargain, that is, to be worth the risks. These general criteria of institutional legitimacy make good sense, then, from the standpoint of the Metacoordination View.

It would be wrong, however, to construe these criteria as strictly necessary conditions for institutional legitimacy, for one simple reason: how demanding we should be in setting the conditions for empowering an institution by granting it our support will depend upon how bad the noninstitutional alternative is. If the noninstitutional alternative is awful, it will be reasonable to be less demanding: the expected benefits of the institution will outweigh risks of empowering it that would be unacceptable under more favorable conditions. At least in circumstances that are less than utterly grim, the six criteria above are presumptively necessary for institutional legitimacy.

The acceptable origination criterion may not satisfied by some institutions that many would deem legitimate. This might be true, for example of some of the first democratic, rights-respecting states if they originated from violent political changes or without democratic constitutional foundings. Relaxing this requirement in such cases makes sense because states are so vitally important that it would be unacceptable to withhold our support simply because, at some point in the remote past, they came to be through unjust actions. Moreover, constitutional democracies have sufficient virtues to offset the worry about their tainted origins; in other words, we have reason to expect that their sullied pedigree will not seriously affect their current performance. Nonetheless, it may be reasonable to expect the creation of new states to be a cleaner process than that by which even the best existing states came to be, and in some cases, extremely unsavory origination may rob a new institution of legitimacy.

For some institutions it is not enough that they merely refrain from violating human rights. Given their distinctive roles, they must also act affirmatively to promote human rights. This would be true, presumably, not just of the state, assuming that one of its primary justifying functions is to protect human rights, but also constitutional courts in domestic systems, supranational tribunals that are explicitly designated as human rights courts (like the European Court of Human Rights), international criminal courts, and the International Court of Justice. For other international courts or quasi-judicial institutions, depending upon their distinctive domain of competency, legitimacy might require only non-violation, not active promotion of human rights. Over time, if human rights concerns come to penetrate such a domain, as may already be beginning to occur in the case with international commercial law and environmental law, then the legitimacy of the institution may come to require active promotion of human rights, not merely non-violation.

Legality, Lawfulness, and the Legitimacy of Institutions That Attempt to Rule

The six general criteria apply to a wide range of institutions, including those that attempt to rule and those that do not (such as international institutions that merely issue guidelines that serve as coordination devices for states). But in the case of institutions that attempt to rule—that issue rules and attempt to secure compliance with them through the use or threat of coercion—something else is required, namely, reasonable satisfaction of the requirements of the rule of law. To see why this is so, let us begin with the paradigmatic case of an institution that attempts to rule: the state.

Because a distinctive feature of states is that they create and sustain public order *through law*, their conformity with the requirements of the rule of law is of critical importance for their legitimacy. When backed by coercive power, as in the case of the state, law is profoundly dangerous—unless it is constrained within the requirements of the rule of law. Satisfying the requirements of the rule of law does not guarantee that the power of institutions that attempt to rule will not be abused or squandered, but it significantly reduces the risk that it will be.

Further, the protections it provides can be effective across a wide range of types of legal systems and across substantively quite different types of laws within a given system. The general applicability of the requirements of the rule of law is a reflection of the fact that they are tailored to reducing risks that are common to law generally. Some of the requirements (see (ii) and (vi) below) are also valuable because they enable law-like systems of rules to facilitate coordination.

Lawfulness (conformity to the requirements of the rule of law) is important not just for the legitimacy states, but also for any institution that wields significant power through ruling. Satisfaction of the requirements of the rule of law helps to prevent institutional power from being misused and in so doing it makes more acceptable the risk of empowering such institutions with our support. The more state-like an institution is—that is the more closely its activities approximate ruling in the strictest sense—the greater the peculiar risks that arise from attempts to wield power through rules and hence the more relevant lawfulness is as a requirement of its legitimacy.

The requirements of the rule of law can be satisfied to a greater or lesser degree. The more state-like an institution is—the more comprehensive its sphere of operation is and the greater the coercive power it wields—the more fully it should satisfy the requirements, other things being equal.

There is considerable consensus that the requirements for the rule of law include the following.

(i) Rules are to be sufficiently general to reduce the risk that they will be weapons for discrimination or tools for favoritism.

(ii) Rules are to be sufficiently long-standing to facilitate the predictability required for rational planning on the part of individuals and groups.

At least in the case of rules that specify criminal offenses, there is a strong presumption if not an outright prohibition against retroactivity.

(iii) Rules are to be interpreted and applied impartially, with like cases being treated alike.

(iv) All who are subject to the rules are to have effective access to them for the protection and advancement of their interests.

(v) No one is to be a judge in his own case and all are to be accountable under the rules.

(vi) Rules are to be public, that is, widely available and understandable, without undue costs, to all who will be held accountable under them.

Where these requirements are satisfied, the risks of living within an order in which power is exercised through coercively backed rules are significantly lessened. Accordingly, whether these requirements are satisfied is relevant to determining whether an institution that rules is worthy of our empowering it with our moral reason-based support, given the extraordinary risks that such institutions pose. The Metacoordination View helps to explain why satisfaction of the requirements of the rule of law is presumptively necessary for the legitimacy of state-like institutions.

III. *Legitimacy and the Virtue of Law-Abidingness*

William Edmundson has suggested that an appreciation of the virtue of law-abidingness is important for understanding the authority of law.[2] I want to suggest that the notion of law-abidingness, if this virtue is understood as *a disposition to value the rule of law*, is crucial both for understanding the legitimacy of institutions that attempt to rule and for the actual achievement of moral reason-based support for such institutions. I will show that the virtue of law-abidingness is important for both normative and sociological legitimacy.

Law-Abidingness

A person who has the virtue of law-abidingness has a deep and stable recognition of the importance of the rule of law and is thereby disposed to respect institutions that conform to and promote it, and this recognition is motivationally potent for her. She is committed to living in public order that satisfies the various requirements of the rule of law listed above, though she may not be able to articulate them precisely. At the deepest level of conviction, she is convinced that human beings ought to live together

---

[2] William A. Edmundson, "The Virtue of Law-Abidance," *Philosophers Imprint* 6, no. 4 (2006): 1–21.

in a way that recognizes and promotes their responsible agency and the important role that plans play in their lives, on terms of equality and mutual accountability, and that law is crucial for achieving this form of association. But she also understands that if the law is to enable this form of association, it must meet certain standards. That is why her commitment is ultimately to lawfulness, not mere legality. Under conditions in which a legal order is either absent or underdeveloped, this commitment will be expressed by her willingness to cooperate with others to create institutions that will achieve the rule of law. Where there is a legal system but it systematically violates the requirements of the rule of law, she will not regard it as worthy of respect. Its laws will not activate her disposition to comply with law.

Law and Law-Abidingness

What distinguishes law is not simply that it achieves coordination through norms that are presented as authoritative nor that it is in principle enforceable, but that it achieves coordination by appealing to the virtue of law-abidingness. This claim is not circular, because the virtue of law-abidingness can be characterized, as I have done above, without reference to the law. All that is necessary is the idea of a public order under rules, along with the notion that the rules must satisfy certain criteria if they are to enable a form of association that publicly acknowledges that we are all reason-responsive, plan-making agents who are accountable under those rules on terms of equality.

Courts and Legitimacy

This understanding of the intimate connection between lawfulness and legitimacy in the case of state-like institutions also sheds light on the distinctive contribution that courts can make to the legitimacy of states. In political discourse, the legitimacy of a state is often thought to depend, inter alia, on whether it includes an independent judiciary. The judiciary is independent when it is sufficiently immune to political influence, especially influence exercised by the state itself, to achieve a reasonable approximation of the requirement that the law is to be interpreted and applied impartially and, above all, that no one (including especially the state) is to be above the law or a judge in her own case.

Courts facilitate coordination in a special way: by appealing to the virtue of law-abidingness while protecting and exemplifying it; not just by specifying certain rules that may be liable to enforcement (which any mechanism of unprincipled, predictable coercion could do), but by helping to ensure that those rules, and the judicial processes through which they are identified, conform to the requirements of the rule of law and are publicly shown to do so. When they operate properly, courts play the crucial role of authoritatively identifying the proper object of the disposition to law-abidingness, while at the same time exemplifying, in their own conduct, what it is to be law-abiding.

This last point merits elaboration. To be law-abiding is to recognize the moral importance of living together in a social order that satisfies the requirements of the rule of law. It is also to understand that actual legal systems and their constituents, including courts, can conform well enough to the requirements of the rule of law to be regarded as legitimate, and hence to be accorded the standing that legitimacy implies, without their being able to close the gap between morality and legality—that is, without having the power to create moral duties simply by issuing rulings. Because law-abidingness is a *moral* virtue, a disposition to expect the law to satisfy certain standards whose ultimate importance is grounded in moral values; those who possess this virtue can never fully cede their capacity to ascertain how they ought to act, morally speaking, to a court or to any other legal institution. The law-abiding person recognizes the importance of the law for morality, but does not conflate legal obligation and moral obligation. Her disposition to comply with law (or more generally with rules) is constrained by her sense of justice. When law-abidingness is not thus constrained, it becomes the vice of unreflective obedience and can result complicity with, or even participation in, grave injustices.

The virtue of law-abidingness and the distinctive role of courts in a legitimate state are in a kind of symbiosis. Courts, when they operate as they should, aid individuals in their exercise of the virtue of law-abidingness by helping them to understand what being law-abiding requires in particular circumstances; and individuals, to the extent that they have this virtue and therefore possess an independent sense of what it is to be law-abiding, are in a position to evaluate the legitimacy of courts, to determine whether they are doing well enough in protecting, promoting, and exemplifying the rule of law to warrant our moral reason-based support.

If an institution is a court, then the proper way of showing respect—of acknowledging the legitimacy of the institution— is to view its decisions as *legally* binding. If one possesses the disposition to law-abidingness, one's recognition that one has a legal duty will create a presumption that one is to comply, independently of the content of the particular legal duty, at least if one assumes that the law that imposes the legal duty is part of a system of law that approximates the rule of law sufficiently to be worthy of respect—*and* if the particular law is not egregiously unjust. For example, if a law arbitrarily stated that certain parties were to be immune to accountability under the criminal law or that a certain group of people have no legal right against enslavement, no law-abiding person would have any reason whatsoever to comply with it, even if it issued from a legitimate legislative process and was approved by a hitherto legitimate court. If the particular law were sufficiently unjust, the fact that the legislature had passed it and the court had approved it would count heavily against either institution being legitimate (in both cases one of the six general criteria for institutional legitimacy, minimal moral acceptability, would be violated).

I have suggested that accounts of the legitimacy of states or state-like institutions that make no mention of law much less of lawfulness are incomplete because such institutions must at least seriously approximate the rule of law if they are to be legitimate. An adequate account of state legitimacy should also capture the intuition that the lack of an independent judiciary is usually a serious challenge to the legitimacy of a state and should accordingly include an account of the distinctive contribution that courts make to the legitimacy of the state. The present account does this by linking the importance for state legitimacy of lawfulness and the distinctive role of courts in helping to ensure that states rule lawfully, that is, in conformity to the requirements of the rule of law.

My account's emphasis on the connection between legitimacy and the virtue of law-abidingness is also attractive for another reason. It shows how important the virtue of law-abidingness is for the viability of a sound social practice of legitimacy assessments in the case of institutions that rule. Unless this virtue is widespread, it may not be possible to secure sufficient moral reason-based support for valuable institutions.

Focusing on the virtue of law-abidingness has yet another benefit. It shows why foreigners ought to regard themselves as presumptively bound to comply with the laws of a legitimate state. A presumption of compliance grounded in the virtue of law-abidingness does not depend upon consent or upon any associative ties or any special relationship whatsoever between the individual and the institution. In contrast, consent or associativist theories cannot explain (at least not in any direct and plausible way) why foreigners should feel obligated to comply with the laws of a state that we intuitively regard as clearly legitimate. A theory of legitimacy that includes a role for the virtue of law-abidingness can explain why those who have no special relationship to an institution that rules can nonetheless have a defeasible, content-independent, prima facie obligation to comply with its rules.

Democracy and Legitimacy

In an earlier article, I suggested that in democratic states citizens owe each other a defeasible duty of compliance with democratically created laws.[3] Thomas Christiano holds a similar view and fleshes it out more fully. He argues that people living together under a legal order that determines the basic terms of their association owe one another a public recognition of their equal status and that democracy is the only form of government that can enable them to fulfill this obligation. He then concludes that in a democracy each citizen owes the people of the democracy as a collectivity a duty of compliance with the laws.[4] To evaluate this argument adequately would require probing the theory of equality that Christiano develops at length. For present purposes, it will suffice to say that the Metacoordination View is consistent with the thesis that in democracies citizens can owe each other or the people as a collectivity compliance with the laws, while still maintaining that institutions, including the state, can be legitimate in the absence of any claim-right on its part to obedience—that is, without any moral duty of compliance being owed to it. They are consistent because, on my account, even if it is true that democracy is a necessary condition of legitimacy in the case of state-like institutions, it is only a necessary condition *where democracy is feasible.* If democracy is not presently feasible for international institutions that in some significant sense rule, they may nonetheless be legitimate, if they satisfy other relevant

---

[3] Allen Buchanan, "Political Legitimacy and Democracy," *Ethics* 112, no. 4 (2002): 689–719.
[4] Thomas Christiano, *The Constitution of Equality* (Oxford: Oxford University Press, 2008), 76–130, 231–59.

legitimacy criteria sufficiently well to realize the basic values that make democracy valuable.

Two of the most important of these values are physical security and nondiscrimination. As Amartya Sen,[5] Thomas Christiano,[6] and others have argued, human rights to physical security tend to be better realized in developed democracies due to the fact that democratic accountability, achieved through elections and competition among political parties, makes governments more responsive to the basic interests of citizens. Democracies publicly manifest a recognition of equal basic status by according all citizens the right to participate as equals in the most important political processes.

Satisfaction of the six general criteria of legitimacy listed earlier—especially the minimal moral acceptability condition—helps to ensure that governments are responsive to the basic interests of citizens, in the absence of democratic accountability *stricto senso*, that is, even if there is no accountability through elections under conditions of competition among parties. Satisfaction of the requirements of the rule of law, even in the absence of democracy, contributes to physical security by preventing the most dangerous misuses of the law, while at the same time affirming basic equal status at least so far as it erects barriers against discrimination and favoritism and ensures that all are accountable under the law and all have access to its resources.

The theory of institutional legitimacy advanced here explains how, under conditions in which democracy is not feasible, states and state-like institutions can be legitimate though not democratic, if they sufficiently realize the values that underlie democracy to warrant our noncoerced support. So, even if democratic institutions—and they alone—feature a claim-right to obedience,

---

[5] Amartya Sen, *On Famines: An Essay on Entitlement and Deprivation* (Oxford: Oxford University Press, 1981).

[6] Thomas Christiano, "An Instrumental Argument for a Human Right to Democracy," *Philosophy & Public Affairs* 39, no. 2 (2011): 142–76.

this does not in itself impugn the legitimacy of non-democratic institutions. That is an important conclusion, because it shows that my account can accommodate three intuitions: first, that for state-like institutions democracy is only a necessary condition of legitimacy where it is feasible; second, that democracies are a unique form of political association in which citizens stand in thick moral relations to one another (having a claim-right on each other or owing obedience to the democratic collective); and third, that even when there is agreement that democracy is infeasible for international institutions, it still makes sense to argue about whether they are legitimate.

Finally, my account explains why, even if democracy is a necessary condition for the legitimacy of state-like institutions where it is feasible, it is not sufficient. In principle, a state could be democratic, in the sense of having competition among political parties and majoritarian electoral processes in which all can participate, and even in the extended sense of also featuring constitutional individual rights, but still fall short in satisfying the requirements of the rule of law. This would be the case, for example, if the actual effectiveness of individual constitutional rights for some citizens were undercut by discriminatory interpretation or enforcement of the law. Given the importance of the rule of law in making the formidable power of states morally acceptable, significant departures from the rule of law can undercut the legitimacy of even a democratic state.

IV. *Two Rival Accounts of Legitimacy*

With the main ideas of the Metacoordination View and its application to the case of institutions that attempt to rule on the table, we can now begin to see why this approach is superior to two influential alternative accounts of legitimacy, the Claim-Right View and the Razian View. The former holds that an institution (of the sort that attempts to rule) is legitimate vis-à-vis those to whom it addresses its rules only if they have a moral duty, owed to the institution, to comply with those rules, independently of their particular content.[7] The latter holds that an institution (of the sort that attempts to rule) is legitimate vis-à-vis an individual A if and only A would do better, according to the best reasons that apply to her, by complying with the institution's rules than she would if she did not (that is, than if she determined how to act in any other way).[8] Both of these alternative views are presented as accounts of the concept of legitimacy, on the understanding that this concept applies to institutions. My aim here is to evaluate them as alternatives to the practical concept of legitimacy that I have articulated, the Metacoordination View. My goal is to determine whether they illuminate what I have identified as a distinctive practical function or point of institutional legitimacy assessments. My assessment will also proceed on the assumption that although there is a distinction between the concept of institutional legitimacy and the criteria an institution must satisfy to instantiate the concept, an account of the concept ought to provide some guidance as to what the criteria are.

Against the Claim-Right View

It may be that state officials sometimes *say* that we owe a duty of obedience to the state, but the Metacoordination View shows that the truth of such a claim is not necessary for states being legitimate. The state may garner the moral reason-based support it needs in order to provide the coordination and other benefits that make it valuable and do so without excessive reliance on coercion, even if no one has or believes she has a duty, owed to the state, to obey the laws. Sufficient support may be achieved if

---

[7] John A. Simmons, *Moral Principles and Political Obligations* (Princeton, NJ: Princeton University Press, 1981), 29–56.

[8] John Tasioulas, "The Legitimacy of International Law," in *The Philosophy of International Law*, eds. Samantha Besson and John Tasioulas (Oxford: Oxford University Press, 2010), 97–118.

enough people generally believe they should refrain from interfering with the state's operations and if addressees of the state's
laws believe they have a (non-directed) defeasible, prima facie,
exclusionary, content-independent reason to comply. In fact, all
that may be required is that enough addressees have a disposition
to comply, grounded in the virtue of law-abidingness.

There are many reasons for compliance with the law, and taken
together they can motivate sufficient support for institutions even
if no one has or believes she has a moral duty owed to the state.
In some cases, there are straightforward moral reasons to comply,
as when the law mirrors moral norms. (The chief reason for complying with a legal prohibition against murder, for example, is
that murder is morally wrong.) In other cases, the prospect of
penalty may suffice, if the costs of compliance are sufficiently
low. Further, if one has the virtue of law-abidingness and believes
that the system of law under which one lives meets certain moral
requirements, and in particular that it reasonably approximates
the requirements of the rule of law, one will have a strong moti-
vation to obey the law, without believing that one is morally obligated to obey it simply because it is the law. Exercise of the virtue
of law-abidingness does not require the belief that any institution
has a moral claim-right to obedience, but it can nonetheless contribute to moral reason-based support for institutions.

There are two other reasons for thinking that the Claim-Right
View is too demanding to be of much use in real-world disputes
about legitimacy. First, the claim-right requirement is only satisfied (if at all) in the case of democratic institutions, and if (under
present conditions) it is infeasible to require international institutions to be democratic, then it follows that no international institution can be legitimate, no matter how well it satisfies what are
generally thought to be relevant criteria for legitimacy (such as
the six criteria listed above) and no matter how substantively just
its actions are. This conclusion should give one pause, because
it conflicts with the intuition that one can still argue meaning-
fully about what international institutions would have to be like

in order to be legitimate after acknowledging that they cannot presently be democratic. Given how valuable some international institutions are, one should be reluctant to accept a view that rules out the possibility of their being legitimate, simply on the grounds that they are not democratic. One should suspect that the Claim-Right View is not of or for this world.

Second, if the standard for legitimacy is set so high as to be unsatisfiable in our world, the concept of legitimacy will be incapable of performing its valuable and distinctive practical role. That role is to achieve moral reason-based metacoordination—convergence of support, grounded in moral reasons, capable of empowering institutions to function effectively without excessive reliance on coercion. A conception of legitimacy that is unsatisfiable cannot perform this function.

Of course, as a matter of linguistic stipulation, one may say that an institution that attempts to rule is legitimate only if it can create duties merely by issuing directives or for some other reason has a claim-right to compliance. As far as I can ascertain, however, no one who opts for this usage, including Simmons, has shown why this understanding of legitimacy is most important for Political Philosophy. In contrast, I have an explanation of why it is *not* the conception of legitimacy that is of most philosophical interest: it is incapable of guiding a social practice of legitimacy assessments in which the concept of legitimacy can play its distinctive role, the role that distinguishes it from conceptions of justice, on the one hand, and of mere advantage relative to the noninstitutional *status quo*, on the other.

Nor have proponents of the Claim-Right View given us any reason to think that it is often at stake in real-world disputes about the legitimacy of institutions that rule. On the contrary, what seems to matter in real-world disputes is whether an institution ought to be accorded a certain standing—whether it is worthy of respect, based on moral reasons. What respect amounts to will vary, as I have already noted, depending upon which parties are involved. For those to whom the institution addresses its rules, the proper mode of showing respect will be to presume that the institution's directives are to be complied with, unless they are patently unjust. This falls short of taking oneself to have a directed duty to comply, but there is no reason to think that more is required for institutions to garner the support they need to function effectively without undue reliance on coercion.

Against the Razian View

According to Raz, A has authority over B just in case B does better, according to the reasons that independently apply to her, by complying with A's directives than she would by determining on her own how to act.[9] Tasioulas asserts that the Razian View provides the best general conception of institutional legitimacy.

There are two main problems with the attempt to deploy Raz's understanding of authority as an account of institutional legitimacy: (1) it is unilluminating, because it yields scant insight about the features that make institutions legitimate in the absence of intuitions about those features that we have independently of accepting the Razian View; and (2) it is ill-suited for the practical task for which a notion of legitimacy is distinctively valuable (solving the metacoordination problem) because of its individualistic understanding of legitimacy: an institution whose directives may enable me to act better according to the best reasons that apply to me need not perform the same service for you, and vice versa.

To appreciate objection (1) we need only ask: How does the Razian View help us identify the features of institutions that are relevant to assessments of their legitimacy? If we did not already have an idea of what those features are, how would the Razian View enlighten us?

---

[9] Joseph Raz, *The Morality of Freedom* (Oxford: Oxford University Press, 1986), 53–57.

In the absence of a comprehensive account of what the reasons are for all agents (an account which, I suspect, no one possesses), we must rely on speculation as to which reasons are relevant to the assessment of institutional legitimacy. But to the extent that such speculation yields plausible results, it relies implicitly on intuitions about what makes for institutional legitimacy that we have independently of and prior to our introduction to the Razian View, not upon the Razian View. In other words, we must already have some idea of which sorts of reasons are relevant to assessments of institutional legitimacy. The problem is that the idea of "best reasons" does no work in helping us to determine what we should require of an institution if we are to confer that standing on it that legitimacy connotes; it sheds no light on what an institution should be like if the risks that empowering it with our uncoerced support are acceptable. It does not even indicate that what is at issue is whether the benefits of empowering the institution are worth the risks.

Whenever someone proposes an alternative account of institutional legitimacy which, like the Metacoordination View as I have fleshed it out here, specifies some intuitively plausible substantive criteria for institutional legitimacy, the proponent of the Razian View may say "Well, if those are the proper criteria, then one will in fact do better, according to the best reasons that apply independently to one, by complying with the directives of an institution that satisfies those criteria. For example, if acceptable origination or institutional integrity or minimal moral acceptability are criteria of institutional legitimacy generally or if conformity to rule of law requirements is a criterion of legitimacy for state-like institutions, that is because one does best, according to the reasons that independently apply to one, if one complies with the rules of institutions that satisfy those criteria. One's best reasons will reflect the importance of those criteria for determining whether the institution is legitimate. So the Razian View is vindicated."

Rather than rebutting my claim that the Razian View provides little guidance, this reply confirms it. Criteria of legitimacy are identified independently of any consideration of the Razian View and then, if they are deemed acceptable on independent grounds, or enjoy strong intuitive plausibility, the Razian View simply puts the stamp of approval on them and claims them for its own. In other words, the notion of applicable reasons is an empty shell that provides no guidance as to what makes an institution legitimate. If one has an independent notion of what the legitimacy-making features of an institution are, then one can fill the shell, but the shell adds no value. It contributes nothing of substance to an account of legitimacy to say "such and such makes an institution (of the state-like type) legitimate and, oh, by the way, if it is legitimate, then one will do better according to all the reasons that independently apply to one if one takes its directives as content-independent reasons for acting." Most of us, if we are honest, will admit that we don't know what all the reasons are that apply to us across the board, though we are likely have some idea of what sorts of reasons are relevant to assessing the legitimacy of institutions before we ever encounter the Razian View. The good news is that we don't have to know what reasons apply to us across the board; all we have to know is what sorts of characteristics institutions need to have if they are to be worthy of our moral reason-based support, given the point of the practice of making legitimacy assessments.

Suppose the Razian replied as follows: "Your first objection trades on a failure to distinguish between the concept of legitimacy and the criteria for legitimacy. The Razian View characterizes the concept, not the criteria".[10] Perhaps, but the problem is that the Razian characterization of the concept provides no guidance for what to look for in criteria. In contrast, the Metacoordination View characterizes the concept in a way that helps us identify the criteria: it tells us to look for criteria which, if satisfied, would make the institution worthy of

---

[10] Tasioulas, *The Legitimacy of International Law*, 99.

our moral reason-based support, given that we must balance the benefits of empowering it with such support against the risks of thus empowering it. Given that we know (through bitter experience) a good deal about what the risks of empowering various types of institutions are, this tells us quite a lot. For example, it tells us that for state-like institutions, those that wield substantial power through coercively backed rules, the criteria for legitimacy should be more demanding than for institutions that do not wield coercive power. And in directing us to identify the peculiar risks of empowering that type of institution, it points toward the conclusion that satisfaction of the requirements of the rule of law is required for their legitimacy. Once we understand the practical function of legitimacy assessments, the problem of identifying the criteria for legitimate institutions is (thankfully) different from and much more manageable than the problem of determining what one's best reasons are.

Now for objection (2): the Razian View does not capture the point of the social practice of making public legitimacy assessments, namely, to try to come to some shared standards that institutions are to satisfy if they are to receive the kind of morally based, widespread support that they need to have to achieve coordination and produce other benefits, without excessive reliance on coercion. On the Razian View, legitimacy is a strictly individual matter. Therefore, there is no reason to think that if complying with an institution's directives will enable me to do best according to the reasons that independently apply to me the same will be true for you or for others.

The Razian might nonetheless say that her view is compatible with a recognition that the practical importance of legitimacy assessments lies in the possibility that a social practice of assessments can yield sufficient consensus to achieve moral reason-based coordinated support for valuable institutions. She could say that whether a particular individual should regard an institution's directives as authoritative will depend, in part, on whether it is likely that enough others will do so, because the achievement of coordination is of great practical importance for all of us and because coordination requires that most of us, at least, regard the institution's directives as authoritative. Notice, however, that if enough others take the institution's rules as authoritative to enable the institution to deliver the relevant goods, then the individual may plausibly conclude that this will occur regardless of whether she takes the rules as authoritative or not. Whether the individual's decision is determined by the desire to free-ride or simply by an impartial desire to avoid costs of compliance that would contribute nothing to successful coordination, she will conclude that, according to her own best reasons for acting, it is not the case that she should regard the institution's rules as authoritative. So, it appears that the individualistic character of the Razian account of legitimacy cannot accommodate the idea that legitimacy judgments function to achieve principled, coordinated support of institutions. One final difference counts in favor of the Metacoordination View: it can explain the exclusionary reasons feature; Raz's view assumes it without explaining it.

Conclusion

The Metacoordination View of institutional legitimacy has several advantages.

1. It explains how legitimacy assessments can play a vital practical role—that of achieving the coordinated moral reason-based support that is needed to allow institutions to facilitate beneficial coordination without excessive recourse to coercion. In so doing, the Metacoordination View (i) explains what sociological legitimacy is (namely, widespread moral reason-based support, as opposed to support based solely on the fear of coercion or on self-interest) and (ii) why sociological legitimacy is so important (it enables us to reap the benefits of institutions without excessive reliance on coercion), but (iii) it does both of these things without conflating sociological and normative legitimacy.

2. It explains why the ability to facilitate coordination is an important contributor to an institution's legitimacy without suggesting that coordination is sufficient for legitimacy. It emphasizes that, except in the bleakest of circumstances, we can often reasonably demand more of an institution than that it achieves coordination and the benefits that depend on coordination.

3. It provides a unified account of legitimacy that applies to a wide range of institutions, including those that rule and those that do not, but in such a way as to acknowledge that the full set of criteria for legitimacy will vary depending upon the function of the institution.

4. It explains the intuition that legality is important for legitimacy, at least in the case of state-like institutions, but without making the mistake of thinking that mere legality confers legitimacy. Unlike some other recent philosophical accounts of legitimacy, it does not ignore the role that lawfulness and hence the law plays in legitimacy, but at the same time does not reduce legitimacy to mere legality, that is, to conformity to whatever the law happens to be, because it acknowledges that it is important for the law to satisfy the requirements of the rule of law.

5. It explains the intuition that whether a state is legitimate can depend, not just on whether it is democratic, but also upon whether it has an independent judiciary, because it illuminates the distinctive role of courts as guardians of the rule of law and recognizes the importance of the rule of law for state legitimacy.

6. It explains why we should take the directives of legitimate institutions seriously; that is, why we should presume that they are to be complied with (unless their content is patently unjust or patently at odds with the proper functioning of the institution). More specifically, it explains why the rule-addressees of a legitimate institution have a (defeasible) content-independent, exclusionary reason to comply with

its rules—but without assuming that they have a content-independent directed moral duty to comply, owed to the institution. It can also accommodate the view, however, that in democratic states citizens morally owe one another, or the people as a collectivity, obedience to the laws.

7. It shows that the Claim-Right View, as a general requirement of legitimacy for institutions that rule, ought to be rejected for two reasons: because, at least for institutions for which democracy is not feasible, it makes a successful practice of legitimacy assessments impossible under realistic conditions; and because such a practice can get along quite well without such a demanding notion of legitimacy.

8. It shows what is unsatisfying about the attempt to construe the Razian understanding of authority as an account of institutional legitimacy: it provides no independent insight into what the substantive criteria for legitimacy are because it offers no account of the point of the practice of making legitimacy assessments; and its individualistic character does not acknowledge the distinctive social role of legitimacy assessments as attempts to converge on shared understandings of what institutions must be like if they are to warrant *our* uncoerced support. Without bringing in the notion of the point of the practice, there is no guarantee that an institution that satisfies Raz's criterion for legitimacy for *me* or for *you* will be worthy of *our* support. But if the notion of the practice and its point are available, the Razian criterion adds nothing of substance to our understanding of how to make legitimacy assessments.

9. In emphasizing the role of the virtue of law-abidingness in assessments of institutional legitimacy, the Metacoordination View has a significant advantage over any theory that defines legitimacy in terms of a special relationship, such as consent or associative ties, between individuals and institutions that rule. Unlike such theories, the theory provided here explains the intuition that foreigners should regard the laws

of a legitimate institution as presumptively to be complied with. If an institution is worthy of moral reason-based support, then anyone capable of complying with its rules has a defeasible, content-independent reason to comply, regardless of any special relationship. Individuals who possess the virtue of law-abidingness will acknowledge this reason and act accordingly.

10. It accommodates the fact that the legitimacy of an institution sometimes depends upon its relationships to other institutions, including relationships of reciprocal legitimation, because those relationships can be relevant to whether the institution warrants our moral reason-based support. In contrast, theories that understand legitimacy solely in terms of the relationship between an institution and those within its sphere of operation cannot account for the phenomenon of reciprocal legitimation. For example, it has been argued that states contribute to the legitimacy of international courts by creating them through treaty-making (one way of satisfying the acceptable pedigree criterion of legitimacy) while international courts in turn contribute to the legitimacy of states by providing an impartial determination of the law that binds them, thus preventing a situation in which states would be judges in their own case.[11] Nor, consequently, can theories that understand legitimacy solely in terms of how institutions relate to individuals subject to them explain the fact that institutional legitimacy is often an ecological affair, that is, that in many cases the legitimacy of an institution cannot be assessed without understanding its relationship with other institutions.[12]

[11] Allen Buchanan, "The Legitimacy of International Courts," unpublished paper (2016).
[12] Allen Buchanan, *The Heart of Human Rights* (Oxford: Oxford University Press, 2013), 173–223.

11. It accommodates the intuition that, where democracy is feasible, institutions that rule must be democratic to be legitimate, while also accommodating the institution that even though it is not currently feasible for international institutions to be democratic, it still makes sense to argue about whether they are legitimate.

I will conclude with three final points about the highly practical, thoroughly social conception of legitimacy I have outlined in this chapter. First, on this view, the legitimacy-making features of an institution are not, as it were, out there, to be discovered by normative analysis that pays no attention to the requirements of achieving sociological legitimacy. Instead, it explains why achieving *sociological* legitimacy is important *from a normative standpoint*, namely, because it enables us to empower institutions so that they can provide their distinctive benefits without giving them dangerous levels of coercive power. Accordingly, the proper task of the philosopher who theorizes institutional legitimacy is not to ignore the importance of achieving sociological legitimacy concerning valuable institutions, but to articulate the distinctive practical role and social character of legitimacy assessments and help clarify and render more accurate our intuitions about how demanding we should be in determining whether to accord an institution the various forms of respect that it must enjoy if it is to deliver the benefits we believe we cannot achieve noninstitutionally and do so without excessive reliance on coercion.

Second, my view lies between two extreme views of the legitimacy of state-like institutions: on the one hand, a very weak notion that identifies legitimacy with merely being justified in wielding power, where being justified means simply not acting wrongly (having a mere Hohfeldian liberty-right); and on the other, the very strong Claim-Right View. Elsewhere I have noted that the Weak View fits some uses of the term "legitimacy".[13] The Weak View, however, does not attach any *uptake condition* to legitimacy: it does not imply that when an institution is legitimate, we are morally required to show it respect, for example, by not interfering with it or by presuming that its directives are to be complied with, or by first trying to reform it if it is flawed, rather than destroying or abandoning it. The Weak View only tells us that if an institution is legitimate, its agents are justified in attempting to rule; it says nothing about how others should respond. Yet surely in many cases when the term "legitimacy" is used, an uptake condition is implied. In fact, as I have argued, legitimacy assessments can only function as part of a social practice that can solve the practical problem that makes the concept of legitimacy distinctively valuable if it implies an uptake condition, because moral reason-based support is a kind of uptake. The Weak View cannot accommodate such uses of the term. Thus my account of the practical function of legitimacy assessments explains exactly why the Weak View is unsatisfactory. The Claim-Right View remedies this deficiency of the Weak View, but at a prohibitive cost: it holds that if an institution is legitimate, then it is not only justified in ruling but also that a very robust uptake is required on the part of those it addresses, namely, they ought to regard themselves as having a moral duty to obey its rules, owed to the institution, regardless of their particular contents. I have suggested that at most there is only one kind of institution that satisfies the claim-right requirement: democracy, if Christiano's account is correct. If this is so, then the Claim-Right View entails that no non-democratic institutions, no matter how just they otherwise are and no matter how well they satisfy other criteria for legitimacy, can be legitimate. That is an unpalatable conclusion, at least in the case of institutions we desperately need and for which democracy is not presently feasible.

[13] Buchanan, "Political Legitimacy and Democracy."

My view lies between these extremes. Unlike the Weak View it includes an uptake condition, specifying a range of respectful behaviors whose appropriateness depends the relationship between the individuals in question and the institution. But unlike the Claim-Right View, it does not hold that the only proper uptake on the part of rule-addressees is to regard themselves as having a moral duty to comply, owed to the institution, independent of content.

Third, the view of institutional legitimacy offered here is both variable and dynamic. It is variable in the sense that it allows that less-demanding criteria for legitimacy may be appropriate if we need an institution very badly, because in those circumstances the risks of empowering the institution with our uncoerced support may be lower than the risks we face if we withhold our support because the institution does not measure up to some higher standard. It is dynamic in the sense that as conditions improve, it will be appropriate to demand more of an institution, if it is to be worthy of our uncoerced support.

Acknowledgments

I am grateful to Samantha Besson, Thomas Christiano, Julian Culp, Andrea Sangiovanni, Bas van der Vossen, and Christopher Wellman for valuable comments on a draft of this paper.

CHAPTER 4

Reciprocal Institutional Legitimation

The international landscape has changed dramatically. Despite the absence of a world government, there is now an expanding mélange of global governance institutions, including the World Trade Organization (WTO); various environmental regimes; judicial and regulatory networks; a more assertive UN Security Council that has authorized armed humanitarian intervention and intervention to restore democratic regimes; a permanent International Criminal Court authorized to prosecute state leaders; and a collection of legal and quasi-legal human rights institutions that link domestic legal systems, regional human rights regimes, UN human rights treaty bodies, and human rights nongovernmental organizations (NGOs).

As international institutions have proliferated and become more powerful, the question of their legitimacy has naturally become more salient. The traditional international lawyer's answer to the question "Are international institutions legitimate?" is that they are rendered legitimate by state consent. That answer is no longer satisfying, however. It is now widely believed that for states to be legitimate they must be minimally democratic and rights respecting. But since many states fail to meet this standard, it is hard to see how their consent could legitimate anything. If we revise the traditional international lawyer's answer to say that international institutions are rendered legitimate by the consent of legitimate states, there is still the problem of "bureaucratic distance": the supposed chains of delegation between democratic publics, their state officials, and the agents of international institutions are so complex and tenuous that it is hard to see how the consent of states, even democratic and rights-respecting ones, can render international institutions legitimate. This problem is exacerbated by the fact that some international institutions, though created by state consent, have developed a legislative life of their own, making important decisions that are neither plausibly subsumed under the "general consent" that created them nor subject to "specific consent" on an ongoing basis. Finally, worries about the legitimacy of international institutions are exacerbated by the fact that democracy is becoming the gold standard for the legitimacy of the state. International institutions are not democratic, in either a "state-majoritarian" or an "individual-majoritarian" sense of democracy. Power over international institutions is very unequally distributed among states, and individuals have nothing approaching the influence on them that they have in democratic states. As the power of international institutions grows, it is not surprising that their "democratic deficit" increasingly calls their legitimacy into question.

Elsewhere I have written on the legitimacy of international law and Robert O. Keohane and I have offered the outlines of a theory of the legitimacy of international institutions.[1] In the preceding chapter, I developed much more fully a theory of institutional legitimacy designed to encompass both domestic and international institutions. In the present chapter, after briefly recapitulating some of the main features of the theory of legitimacy laid out in Chapter Three, I focus on the question of how issues concerning the legitimacy of international institutions should

---

[1] Allen Buchanan, "The Legitimacy of International Law," in *The Philosophy of International Law*, eds. Samantha Besson and John Tasioulas (Oxford: Oxford University Press, 2010), 79–96.

be framed. My chief conclusions can be previewed as follows. First, the autonomy of state legitimacy view (ASLV), according to which the *internal* legitimacy of a state (its legitimacy vis-à-vis its own citizens) depends solely on the relationship between the state and those citizens, is false, because whether a state is internally legitimate can depend in part upon whether its exercise of power respects the human rights of people in other states. Second, a state's participation in international institutions can contribute to its legitimacy, by helping to ensure that (1) it does not treat its own citizens with excessive partiality at the expense of the rights of noncitizens, that (2) it provides its own citizens with the goods and protections against harms that they rightly demand, and that (3) it provides reliable protection of the constitutional rights of its own citizens. Participation in the right sort of international institutions can prevent a state from acting in ways that undermine its legitimacy and also can provide its citizens with assurance that their state is legitimate. Third, when international institutions contribute to the legitimacy of states, their doing so can contribute to their own legitimacy. So, fourth, a theory of international legitimacy ought to recognize *reciprocal legitimation* between states and international institutions.

In other words, the legitimating arrows in a picture of the international order go in both directions, from states to international institutions and from international institutions to states. Once it is seen that participation in international institutions can enhance the state's legitimacy (and in extreme cases be crucial for it), the relationship between the state and international institutions looks quite different. It is wrong to think of international institutions merely as limitations on state sovereignty that must be tolerated for the sake of the "practical" goods (such as economic coordination and the amelioration of negative externalities that damage the environment) that they provide. Instead, we should recognize that international institutions can also supply an important normative good: they can contribute to the state's legitimacy. And limitations on sovereignty that contribute to legitimacy are, other things being equal, more palatable.

To make the case for this reframing of the issue of the legitimacy of international institutions, I must first supply at least a rough account of what legitimacy means in this context. Rather than trying to make a thorough case for the conception of legitimacy upon which my reciprocal legitimation view rests, however, I will only try to say enough to make it plausible, relying on the fuller treatment I have given the topic elsewhere, including, most recently, in Chapter Three of this book. The next paragraphs summarize that fuller discussion.

Before we proceed further, it is important to recognize the ambiguity of the term "legitimacy." Legitimacy in the normative sense is usually understood, at least in the case of the state, to be *the right to rule*. (Agreement that legitimacy is the right to rule turns out to be compatible, of course, with disagreements about how strongly or weakly "right" in "the right to rule" is to be understood.) In the international legal and political science literatures, the term "legitimacy" is often used to refer to the widespread *belief* that an institution has the right to rule. In this chapter, the focus is on legitimacy in the normative sense.

I. *Legitimacy*

In political contexts, legitimacy usually implies agent justification: whatever else is involved, a legitimate institution is one that is justified in wielding power. Often, however, legitimacy is understood to mean more than that—to convey, in addition, the idea of authoritativeness. That is, when an institution is legitimate those to whom it addresses, its rules ought to regard them as content-independent reasons for acting.[2]

---

[2] Thomas Christiano, "Authority," in *Stanford Encyclopedia of Philosophy* (Stanford, CA: Stanford University, 2006), http://www.plato.stanford.edu/entries/authority (accessed March 2010).

Content-Independent Reasons

The notion of content-independent reasons seems to capture the central idea that a legitimate institution's rules are in a significant sense *authoritative*, without buying into the extremely demanding requirement that legitimate institutions create content-independent *moral duties* simply by issuing rules. To make plausible the claim that legitimate institutions impose moral duties, not just content-independent reasons, one must not only provide an account of how one goes from having a reason to having a duty, one must also explain what makes a duty a moral duty. If one takes it to be a mark of moral duties that they supply *exclusionary* reasons, then one also needs a plausible account of exclusionary reasons, something which, in my judgment, no one has yet succeeded in doing.[3] Apart from these difficulties, there seems to be something odd about the assumption that the authoritativeness of legitimate institutions is (necessarily) *moral* authoritativeness. To a large extent, the legitimacy of institutions depends upon their instrumental value, and the goods they enable us to attain are not limited to moral goods. They include things such as better economic coordination, for example. Moreover, whether institutions are instrumentally effective seems to depend on relevant actors treating their rules as content-independent reasons for acting, not on their regarding them as imposing moral duties. This seems especially plausible in the case of international institutions: the notion that legitimate international institutions create *moral duties* on states or that they *need* to do so (or even need to

---

[3] One difficulty of providing such an account is that it is hard to think of any duty that completely excludes considerations of any kind, including considerations of self-interest. The standard example of an exclusionary reason is that one has promised something. But the fact that one has promised something (under even the best conditions for generating special duties by promising) does not imply that reasons of interest are literally excluded from consideration. If the cost to oneself of keeping the promise is great enough, and the promise is trivial enough, then a consideration of one's own interest is not excluded.

be believed to do so) if they are to function effectively is counterintuitive. For institutions, including international institutions, to work, what is crucial is that relevant actors be in the habit of taking their rules as content-independent reasons for acting, not that they view them as imposing moral duties.

The Practical Implications of Legitimacy Assessments

Legitimacy assessments are importantly relevant to the *practical stances* we take toward institutions. For those to whom the institution addresses its rules, the primary relevant practical stance, if they judge the institution to be legitimate, is that of counting those directives as content-independent reasons for acting—taking them as authoritative. But in many contexts in which the legitimacy of an institution is affirmed or challenged, the question is not how rule-addressees ought to respond to them, but rather what practical stance *others* ought to take toward the institution's agents and operations. The legitimacy of institutions is often not just a matter of concern for rule-addressees, but for others as well.

International institutions typically address their rules to states, not individuals. Yet individuals who are not addressed by the rules can rightly regard the legitimacy of the institution as an important matter, and not just because they are interested in determining whether those to whom it addresses its rules ought to take them as authoritative. Political movements sometimes call on individuals to disrupt (or even try to destroy) institutions, and surely one relevant consideration in determining whether it is permissible to participate in such efforts is whether the institution is legitimate.

Legitimacy as a Kind of Standing

Legitimate institutions enjoy a certain *standing* and, generally speaking, deliberately setting about to try to destroy or disable them is incompatible with acknowledging that standing.[4] Similarly, if one judges an institution to be legitimate, then the presumption is that its agents, in their official capacities, ought to be treated with a certain respect, distinct from the respect we owe them as individuals.

The judgment that an institution is legitimate can influence our practical stance toward it in yet another way, again independently of whether we happen to be addressees of its rules: the presumptively appropriate response to the flaws of a legitimate institution is generally to try to reform it, not to destroy it or to try to convince others to transfer their allegiance to a rival institution. An institution that is legitimate warrants respect, and taking its rules to be authoritative is only one aspect of respect.

So, an account of legitimacy should take into account at least three features of the application of the term in political contexts: first, that agent justification (being justified in wielding political power) is necessary (though not sufficient) for legitimacy; second, that legitimacy implies authoritativeness (rule-addressees ought to regard the institution's rules as supplying content-independent reasons for acting); and third, that legitimacy assessments can have implications for the practical stances to be taken toward the institution, not only for those to whom the institution addresses rules, but for others as well. Now it may turn out that the same kinds of considerations that count in favor of addressees regarding the institution's rules as authoritative or in favor of concluding that the entity is justified in wielding

---

[4] This is not to say in all contexts that acknowledging an entity's legitimacy is incompatible with saying that it is permissible to try to destroy it. In cases of economic competition, for example, one might say that a rival firm is legitimate (a legitimate business), meaning only that it is not shady or does not operate illegally, and yet one might try to destroy it by outcompeting it in the market. In the case of political entities, however, in most cases acknowledgment of legitimacy implies recognition of standing in the sense described above. Legitimate political institutions are presumptively not to be destroyed, though it may be permissible to replace or dismantle them if appropriate procedures are followed. I am grateful to Jerry Gaus for pressing me to make this point clearer.

political power also give others reasons to adopt respectful practical stances toward the institution. In other words, the same institutional virtues that contribute to authoritativeness and justification may also ground the other positive practical stances that various parties may take toward the institution, including respect for institutional agents, refraining from interference, and a presumption in favor of reform. Later, I will suggest that this is the case, when I sketch some of the sorts of considerations that are relevant to judging an institution to be legitimate.

Of course, rule-addressees may have additional, special reasons for treating the rules of an institution as authoritative, over and above the reasons that others have for adopting respectful stances toward it. In particular, government officials may have fiduciary obligations as agents of states that have ratified the treaty that created an international institution. But because of the problems indicated earlier about the normative force of agreements by illegitimate states and the attenuated chains of delegation in democratic ones, other considerations, having to do with the virtues of the institution itself, may be preponderant among an official's reasons for treating the rules as authoritative. Nevertheless, although the practical stances of rule-addressees and others toward an institution deemed to be legitimate are different, and may be grounded to some extent in different reasons, there are some reasons common to both.[5]

---

[5] John Tasioulas has adapted Joseph Raz's normal justification criterion (NJC) to provide an alternative conception of legitimacy that he believes works for both states and international institutions. See John Tasioulas, "The Legitimacy of International Law," in *The Philosophy of International Law*, eds. Samantha Besson and John Tasioulas (Oxford: Oxford University Press, 2010), 97–118. An agent or entity A satisfies the NJC relative to an individual B if and only if B does better, according to the reasons that apply to her (independently of A's directives), by intending to act in accordance with A's directives. On Raz's view (and Tasioulas's), an institution satisfies the NJC when its rules constitute content-independent, exclusionary reasons for acting for those to whom it addresses them, so this conception of legitimacy, like mine, features a respondent aspect. However, the Razian View recognizes only one kind of response: the acknowledgment of authoritativeness on the part of rule addressees. For example,

II. *The Grounds of Legitimacy Assessments*

With this conception of legitimacy in mind, we can now ask the following question: What features of institutions confer legitimacy? Alternatively, *what kinds of considerations* are relevant to determining whether an institution is legitimate, given the implications of legitimacy assessments for what our practical stances

---

the Razian View does not acknowledge that there are contexts in which what is at issue is whether the institution is entitled to noninterference by parties other than rule addressees, a question that is of central importance for individuals and non-state groups in the case of international institutions, since the latter typically address their rules only to states. The Razian View is also silent on other practical stances that outsiders, as opposed to rule addressees, associate with legitimacy assessments. It would be implausible for Raz or Tasioulas to reply that their notion of authoritativeness subsumes the issue of practical stances for non-addressees. It may be true that one consideration a citizen should take into account in determining what her practical stance toward the WTO ought to be is whether states ought to take that institution's rules as authoritative, but it is not the only consideration. Such an individual might reasonably conclude that the fact that states have ratified the WTO Treaty and not formally de-ratified it gives the agents of those states a content-independent reason to comply with its rules, but that need not settle the issue of whether she ought to refrain from efforts to disrupt or even destroy the institution. This would most obviously be the case if her state was non-democratic, but it might be so in other circumstances as well. The point is that a conception of legitimacy such as Raz's explicitly takes into account only the perspective of rule addressees and the perspectives of others cannot be reduced to that. Bas van der Vossen and Thomas Christiano have pointed out that the Razian View has another, more serious drawback: it does not capture the fact that justification is a necessary condition of legitimacy. The NJC has to do only with the reasons of rule-addressees, not with the adequacy of the institutional agents' reasons for acting. It is conceivable that one could have content-independent, exclusionary reasons for complying with the rules an institution addresses to one, even if the institution was created and controlled by usurpers, who, for that reason, were not justified in exercising power. So, if justification is a necessary condition of legitimacy and being authoritative in the Razian sense does not guarantee justification, then the Razian conception of legitimacy is inadequate; at most, satisfaction of the NJC is a necessary, not a sufficient condition for legitimacy. See Bas van der Vossen, "On Legitimacy and Authority: A Response to Krehoff," *Res Publica* 14, no. 4 (2008): 299–302; Thomas Christiano, "The Authority of Democracy," *Journal of Political Philosophy* 12, no. 3 (2004): 278–79. To meet this objection, Tasioulas makes a desperate move, arguing (or asserting) that among "the reasons that apply to us" considerations of justification have such

toward institutions should be? Broadly speaking, there are two kinds of considerations: those that have to do with the fact that institutions have instrumental value for securing public goods whose value can be characterized independently of their connection to justice and those that are grounded in considerations of justice. Let us begin with the case of international institutions and then see if the analysis extends to the state.

International institutions typically develop as a result of the perception that states are incapable of solving certain problems unilaterally, through bilateral arrangements, or through multilateral treaties unsupported by permanent organizations. The clearest cases are those of international security (including coping with global crime and terrorism, as well as reducing the incidence and severity of war) and environmental problems (in particular, those involving negative externalities that spill across state borders). The next subsections set out the least controversial of the more comprehensive set of criteria for institutional legitimacy set out and elaborated in more detail in Chapter Three.

Comparative Benefit

Although legitimacy is not to be confused with efficiency, an institution's patent failure to deliver the goods for which it was created can impugn its legitimacy. That this is so is not hard to understand, from the perspective of the account of legitimacy I have offered: if, for example, an environmental regime fails miserably

---

great weight that it will never be true that one does best in acting in accordance with all the reasons that apply to oneself, if one takes as authoritative the rules of an institution that is not justified in exercising political power. In my judgment, this move is utterly unpersuasive. But for the sake of argument, let us not take exception to it. There is still a problem with the Razian analysis thus understood: it buries the justification condition, hiding it from sight, as it were. It appears to be much more analytically perspicacious to exhibit the justification condition along with authoritativeness, rather than subsuming it under authoritativeness (via a dubious claim about the preponderance of considerations of justification among the various "reasons that apply to us").

to ameliorate the particular problems (such as depletion of the ozone layer) it was created to address, then interfering with its efforts may be justifiable (it may be appropriate to try to dismantle it and replace it with a more effective arrangement) and the fact that it issues certain rules may not give anyone reason to comply. Moreover, if an important part of the justification for having an institution with certain powers is that it is needed to do a certain job, then its patent failure to do that job can undermine the claim that it is justified in wielding power. In brief, gross incompetence undermines legitimacy. Put more positively, efficacy contributes to legitimacy, at least in the case of institutions whose justification is primarily instrumental.

Institutional Integrity

If an institution persistently acts in ways that are clearly inconsistent with the functions it publicly cites in justifying its existence, then this undermines its legitimacy, especially if the agents in charge give no credible evidence that things are going to change.[6]

Respect for Human Rights (Minimal Moral Acceptability)

Among the most important moral considerations relevant to determining an international institution's legitimacy is its posture regarding human rights. An institution whose operations predictably or persistently violate the most basic human rights on a significant scale is presumptively illegitimate. By "basic human rights" here, I mean the least controversial candidates for inclusion in lists of human rights: the right against torture, the right against slavery, the right to physical security and bodily integrity, and so on. Of course, some international institutions are expected to do more than simply not violate basic human rights;

---

[6] Allen Buchanan and Robert O. Keohane, "The Legitimacy of Global Governance Institutions," *Ethics & International Affairs* 20, no. 4 (2006): 405–37.

they should also make credible efforts to promote human rights if the promotion of human rights is among the institutional goals that justify their existence or necessary for the attainment of those goals.

In some cases (the WTO may be the most obvious example), there is heated controversy about whether the promotion of human rights (as distinct from their non-violation) should be an institutional goal. Such disagreement is not surprising, given two facts. First, many international institutions are quite new and their identities are still evolving in response to a rapidly changing institutional landscape in which new problems are constantly emerging. Second, given the absence of international institutions with the power to enforce human rights norms (in the ways that states enforce their laws), there is an understandable impulse to commandeer existing institutional resources to promote human rights, even in the case of institutions that were created for quite different purposes (such as the liberalization of trade in the case of the WTO). To the extent that there is uncertainty about what the fundamental goals of an institution are, there is likely also to be uncertainty about whether it is legitimate.

(Minimal) Fairness

Another obvious moral consideration of relevance to legitimacy is fairness, or, more accurately, the avoidance of egregious unfairness. Even if an institution does not violate human rights, its operations may be disproportionately controlled by more powerful states, without any justification for this asymmetry of power that is consistent with the institution's publicly avowed goals and principles. There may be unfairness in its procedures, in their substantive outcomes, or both. An institution can exhibit some degree of unfairness, yet still be legitimate; in that sense, fairness or, more generally, justice are more demanding standards than legitimacy. But in extreme cases, unfairness can deprive an institution of legitimacy, especially if unfairness is, as it were, built into its very structure, as opposed to being an occasional consequence of aberrant policies.

It should be clear that all of these instrumental and moral considerations apply to the state as well as to international institutions. At least in the broadly liberal tradition, the state is justified not because it is good in itself, but because it solves problems we cannot solve without it, and whether a particular state is legitimate vis-à-vis its own citizens depends in part upon whether it does a credible job of solving those problems for them. Further, a legitimate state is not only instrumentally effective, it must perform its functions in ways that do not involve persistent or predicable violations of basic human rights. (Of course, we now also expect the state to do more than that—to promote human rights, at least among its own citizens.) A state that systematically and persistently treats some of its citizens in grossly unfair ways (and gives no credible assurance that it is striving to correct this fundamental flaw) is also presumptively illegitimate. Finally, a state that is fundamentally lacking in integrity, one that regularly functions in such a way as to thwart its own core public commitments (as was true of the USA during the Jim Crow period) is also presumptively illegitimate.

All of these considerations are intuitively relevant to determining what our practical stance toward an institution should be, regardless of whether we are rule-addressees or others. All are also intuitively plausible candidates for inclusion in a standard for assessing the legitimacy of institutions. This convergence is some indication that the conception of legitimate sketched above is correct.

In the next section, I argue that, given this conception of legitimacy and this sketch of the sorts of considerations that are relevant to legitimacy assessments, *international institutions contribute to the legitimacy of states in this sense: through participation in international institutions, states are better able to satisfy the instrumental and moral criteria that confer legitimacy.* I also explain how the contribution that international institutions make to the legitimacy of states contributes to *their own* legitimacy.

III. *How International Institutions Contribute to the Legitimacy of States*

More Reliable Protection of Citizens' Rights

Even the most democratic, rights-respecting states sometimes fail to protect the rights that their own constitutions accord to their citizens.[7] This is especially true with respect to women, racial and national minorities, gays, lesbians, transgender people, and immigrants; but virtually all citizens are vulnerable to rights violations in cases of perceived national emergencies, such as war and terrorism. To the extent that there is congruence between international human rights and the civil and political rights that are recognized in a particular state, the state's participation in international human rights regimes can provide a "backup" for domestic rights protection. Because the protection of citizens' rights is one of the key justifying functions of the state and because justification is a necessary condition for legitimacy, the adequacy of that protection is an important consideration in assessments of the legitimacy of the state. Whether a state does a creditable job of protecting its citizens' rights is relevant to whether those citizens should regard its laws as authoritative, to whether others should refrain from interfering with its operation and adopt other respectful stances toward it, and indeed to whether it is justified in wielding political power. International institutions therefore

---

[7] This section draws on Allen Buchanan and Russell Powell, "Survey Article: Constitutional Democracy and the Rule of International Law: Are They Compatible?," *Journal of Political Philosophy* 16, no. 3 (2008): 326–49. For another account of the benefits that participation in international institutions can provide for states, see Robert O. Keohane, Stephen Macedo, and Andrew Moravcsik, "Democracy-Enhancing Multilateralism," *International Organization* 63, no. 1 (2009): 1–31.

contribute to the legitimacy of the state when they help ensure the adequacy of its protection of citizens' rights.

Whether participation in international human rights institutions merely *enhances a state's legitimacy* or is critical to its *being legitimate* will vary from state to state. If a state has domestic legal institutions that generally do a creditable job of protecting the rights of all its citizens, then its abstention from international institutions that provide a backup for that protection would not render it illegitimate. Thus, Switzerland's refusal to join the UN until quite recently almost certainly did not impugn its legitimacy. In contrast, in the case of new states emerging in conditions in which there are powerful threats to the rights of national minorities and there are as yet no domestic institutions capable of providing adequate protections against such threats, refusal to participate in international human rights institutions could deprive a state of legitimacy, not just make it less legitimate than it would be if it participated. This was arguably the case with some of the new states emerging from the breakup of the Soviet Union and Yugoslavia. Participation in the Council of Europe, in particular, appears to have resulted in several newly independent European countries abandoning policies that grossly violated the rights of national minorities within their borders.[8]

Helping to Secure the Goods and Protections from Harms Citizens Rightly Demand of Their States

As with international institutions, the primary justification for the state is instrumental: states provide benefits and protections from harms we cannot reliably achieve without them. In some instances, the harms are so important that the state's failure to see that they are prevented impugns its legitimacy. This would be the case, for example, if states refused to construct and support

---

[8] Judith Kelley, *Ethnic Politics in Europe: The Power of Norms and Incentives* (Princeton, NJ: Princeton University Press, 2006).

international environmental regimes that took reasonable steps to mitigate the effects of global warming or to curb large-scale terrorism. For example, suppose it is true, as seems likely, that an effective global, institutional response to global warming will not occur without the support of the USA. If the USA staunchly refused to cooperate in global institutions that were needed to cope effectively with the problem of global warming, this could undermine its legitimacy.[9] A state that persisted in acting in this grossly irresponsible way (one that predictably thwarted all reasonable efforts to prevent very serious harms to its own citizens) would forfeit legitimacy. There would be good reason to conclude that it was not fit to wield political power and that it did not warrant the respect we associate with legitimacy.

The citizens of democracies rightly expect their states to do more than avert serious harms, however. They are also supposed to help achieve the goods that citizens choose to pursue through democratic processes. In some cases, these goods, including economic growth and scientific advancement, cannot be achieved without participation in international institutions. When this is the case, international institutions contribute to the legitimacy of states.

Helping to Prevent Excessive Partiality

So far, I have argued that a state's participation in international institutions can enhance or, in extreme cases, be critical for its legitimacy by virtue of the effective that participation has on that state's own citizens. Now I want to argue for a more ambitious conclusion: participation in international institutions can have an

---

[9] Whether such behavior would undermine not only the legitimacy of the US government, but also of the US state itself would depend upon the duration of the refusal to participate (its persistence through changes of government) and also, perhaps, whether the best explanation of the persistence of the refusal invoked features of the US constitutional order or what might be regarded as the character of the US state as a historical entity.

impact on a state's legitimacy by virtue of the effect of participation on the interests of foreigners.

All but the most extreme cosmopolitans acknowledge that it is appropriate, if not obligatory, for the state to show partiality toward its own citizens. But anyone who takes the idea of human rights seriously must acknowledge that there are limits to partiality. Constitutional democracies are designed so as to ensure that government officials are accountable to their fellow citizens. The democratic commitment to the accountability of government to citizens tends to produce not just accountability, but near exclusive accountability: democratic processes and the constitutional structure of checks and balances create formidable obstacles to government taking into account the legitimate interests of anyone else. In other words, there is an inherent structural bias in democracy toward excessive partiality. This is most evidently true with regard to accountability through periodic elections: foreigners have no votes. Participation in international institutions can force domestic government officials to take the rights of foreigners into account and to that extent curb the structural bias toward *excessive* partiality. This is another way in which international institutions contribute to the legitimacy of states.

Whether an institution is legitimate depends in part, as I noted earlier, on whether its agents are justified in wielding political power. A state does not merit the sort of respect that legitimacy implies if its agents are not justified in exercising power. Modern states, especially the more powerful ones, wield power not just over their own citizens, but also over others who have no standing whatsoever in domestic political processes. They do so not only in explicit foreign policy, but also through their domestic policies, especially in economic matters. Human rights (everyone's human rights, not just those of citizens) constrain the justifiable exercise of political power; so whether a state's agents are justified in wielding political power, and hence whether the state is legitimate, depends in part on whether power is wielded in ways that are consistent with respect for the human rights of foreigners.[10] Participation in international institutions can contribute to the legitimacy of states (and in extreme cases can even be critical for legitimacy) by preventing them from wielding political power in ways that egregiously violate the human rights of foreigners.

Earlier, I suggested that "legitimacy" connotes a kind of standing and I also argued that, in most political contexts, being justified in wielding political power is a necessary condition for legitimacy. I now want to connect these two points in such a way as to add support to my claim that how a state treats foreigners can make a difference to its internal legitimacy, its legitimacy vis-à-vis its own citizens. The state, at least if it pretends to be anything other than a gunman writ large, claims to act in the name of its people, and this is true for all of its actions, whether they are directed toward foreigners or not. What a state does in the name of its citizens (whatever it does in their name, not just what it does to them) can affect whether it is justified in wielding power and whether its citizens ought to treat its laws as authoritative. If a state persistently acts in ways that grossly violate the basic human rights of foreigners, whether through aggressive war or as a predictable result of its "domestic" economic policies, it imputes these actions and hence the responsibility for them to its citizens. By perpetrating gross injustices against foreigners and imputing them to its citizens, the state undermines its standing as a justified wielder of political power *tout court* and the authoritativeness of its laws (all of its law) for them. Its citizens

---

[10] Here is it important to distinguish carefully between an institution being illegitimate and a particular action of that institution being illegitimate. An institution may perform actions whose wrongness undermines the legitimacy of those actions, without the legitimacy of the institution itself being called into question. But when there is a pattern of sufficiently egregious wrongful action, this can undermine the institution's claim to be a justified wielder of political power and hence can impugn its legitimacy.

may still have good reasons to comply with those of its laws that do not violate the human rights of foreigners (for example, because those laws replicate the requirements of morality), but they no longer have content-independent reasons to comply with the state's laws as such. In other words, if the injustice to foreigners is sufficiently severe and long-lasting, it can undermine the legitimacy of the government across the board, as it were, not just with respect to the particular domain of action in which it perpetrates the injustice. If the injustices are a function of the basic constitutional structure, they can even undermine the legitimacy of the state, not just the government.

Given the potential for violating the basic human rights of foreigners entailed by the state's ability to use armed force across borders, participation in international institutions that constrain the use of force can be critical for the legitimacy of the state. States that have powerful militaries and a propensity to use force beyond their own borders and that do not participate in available and effective international institutions to constrain their recourse to military action across borders run a serious risk of illegitimacy, given that, as I have already noted, domestic institutions exhibit a structural bias against taking the rights of foreigners seriously. Failure to participate in international security institutions can detract from a state's legitimacy; participation can bolster it.[11]

----

[11] David Estlund and others have argued that democracy has important epistemic virtues. It is important to understand, however, that the epistemic virtues of democratic institutions are chiefly relative to the good of the citizenry; in other words, democratic processes, including the right sort of deliberative procedures, can be distinctively valuable for producing and helping to ensure a utilization of information that is relevant to the pursuit of the good of the public. But the crucial thing to note here is that "the public" means only the citizens of the democracy in question. The epistemic virtues of democratic institutions are much less impressive with regard to the good of foreigners. On this point, see Kristen Hessler, "Democratic Government and International Justice," *The Monist* 89, no. 2 (2006): 259–73; David Estlund, *Democratic Authority* (Princeton, NJ: Princeton University Press, 2007).

Whether such participation is critical for a state's legitimacy (whether the failure to participate would deprive a state of legitimacy, as opposed merely to rendering it less legitimate than it would be if it did participate) will depend upon how dangerous the state's unrestrained behavior toward foreigners is. In the case of a single superpower, the potential for excessive partiality to result in egregious harms to foreigners is great indeed.

Publicity and Legitimacy

At the outset of this chapter, I noted a distinction between the normative and sociological senses of "legitimacy." I have focused on the normative sense of the term. However, it is worth pointing out that there are important connections between the two senses. On some accounts of legitimacy, as on some accounts of justice, a publicity condition must be satisfied: an institution is legitimate (or just) only if it is possible for competent individuals who are subject to its exercise of power to be able to make a reasonable judgment that it satisfies at least the more basic requirements for being legitimate (or just). One barrier to any such publicity condition being satisfied is the marked asymmetry of information about the actual performance of the state that typically exists between the agents of the state and its citizens. To the extent that participation in international institutions can reduce this asymmetry with respect to knowledge that is relevant to making reasonable judgments about the legitimacy of the state, such participation can provide assurance to citizens that their state is legitimate. For example, participation in human rights regimes can provide relatively independent and objective monitoring of the state's behavior regarding human rights and make this information available to citizens.

The Need for Empirical Research

I have argued that participation in international institutions *can* contribute to the legitimacy of states. Whether it actually does so is obviously an empirical matter. So far, relevant empirical studies are scanty and the results appear to be mixed. On the one hand, as I noted earlier, there is evidence that participation in international institutions has led newly independent European countries to abandon policies that undermined their legitimacy; on the other hand, some studies indicate that ratification of human rights treaties may not improve the human rights performance of states that systematically violate their citizens' human rights.[12] The latter studies indicate the complexity of the empirical issues, including the question of what counts as participation (surely ratification by itself is not sufficient). Participation is often not all or nothing; there can be degrees or levels of participation and these may have different effects; participation may have different effects on different kinds of states; the effects of participation may be direct or indirect and may occur either fairly soon after participation begins or only after a long time period. Further, if the most important effect of participation is to *prevent* state behavior that undermines legitimacy, then it may be difficult to provide strong evidence under conditions in which most states do in fact participate; carefully designed empirical studies to confirm complex counterfactual causal claims will be needed. My goal in this chapter is not to try to set a detailed agenda for empirical research, much less to sift through existing research, but rather to stimulate research that takes the possibility of reciprocal legitimacy seriously.

IV. *The Legitimacy of International Institutions*

I have argued that international institutions can contribute in several distinct ways to the legitimacy of states and that failure to participate can detract from legitimacy. I have also noted that, in extreme cases, whether a particular state is legitimate

---

[12] Beth Simmons, *Mobilizing for Human Rights: International Law in Domestic Politics* (Cambridge, UK: Cambridge University Press, 2009).

could depend upon whether it participates in particular international institutions. I now want to suggest that an international institution's performing the function of contributing to the legitimacy of states can contribute to its own legitimacy.

Consider an analogy. Within the state, a particular institution can contribute to the state's legitimacy by improving or safeguarding the functioning of other institutions. For example, an independent judiciary, with the power to review legislation, can help ensure that the legislative branch does not violate individual rights, and its performing of this function can contribute to the state's legitimacy. The fact that the judiciary functions in this way is part of what makes the state legitimate, because having a judiciary that functions in this way contributes to the justification of the state's exercise of political power.

In addition, the fact that the judiciary contributes to the state's legitimacy is surely a relevant consideration in assessments of the judiciary's *own* legitimacy. If the judiciary's exercise of its review powers did not constrain the legislature, its exercise of this power might be unjustified. From either of two respondent perspectives, legislators and ordinary citizens, the judiciary's contribution to the legitimacy of the state is a relevant consideration in determining what one's practical stance toward the judiciary should be.

The fact that the relationship between the judiciary and the legislative branch exists *within* the state is irrelevant. The point is that the contribution that an institution makes to the legitimacy of another institution can be among the considerations upon which its own legitimacy depends, and this holds for international as well as domestic institutions.

The "Extended Constitution"

Before summing up the conclusions of this chapter, I want to make a suggestion that I hope to pursue in depth on another occasion: once we see that participation in international institutions can contribute to the legitimacy of states, we should revise our conception of the bounds of the constitution of a state. If participation in an international institution is long-standing enough and makes a sufficiently important contribution to the legitimacy of a state, even if only by effectively preventing the state from engaging in behavior that would rob it of legitimacy, then it may make sense to include such participation in a characterization of the constitution of the state in question. The analogy here is with the extended mind hypothesis advanced by Andy Clark and others.[13] According to the extended mind hypothesis, an individual's mind is not confined to his brain. If one's interaction with a computer plays a large enough role in one's cognitive life, then it can be said that one's mind is "extended" to include the computer. The extended mind hypothesis is obviously based on an understanding of cognition that puts more weight on the integration of functionings than on the similarity or physical continuity of structures. Similarly, a characterization of constitutions that focuses on function will find it arbitrary to restrict the constitution of a state to those institutions that happen to exist within its borders. At present, the role of institutions within the state's borders is so much more central to its functioning that an extended constitution view may not be very illuminating. But that is a contingent matter and one that may be subject to change. If international institutions come to play the kind of role I have shown that they can in principle play, then the extended constitution view might turn out to give us a better understanding of political reality. In a world in which a state's constitution included its participation in certain international institutions, the worry that participation in international institutions as such undermines sovereignty would have to be reformulated in a more subtle way, if it could be coherently articulated at all.

---

[13] Andy Clark, *Supersizing the Mind: Embodiment, Action, and Cognitive Extension* (Oxford: Oxford University Press, 2008).

Conclusion

Theorizing about the legitimacy of international institutions tends to be framed in a way that privileges the legitimacy of the state. It is widely assumed that so far as its internal legitimacy is concerned, the state is self-sufficient—that its internal legitimacy depends entirely on how it relates to its own citizens. On some views, the state is internally legitimate if it respects its citizens' rights and is democratic; on others, the consent of the citizens is also required. To the extent that it is acknowledged that legitimacy requires the justified exercise of political power, justification is understood solely by reference to the relationship between the state and its citizens, in spite of the fact that the state exerts power over noncitizens as well.

Given this picture, it is not surprising that there is a tendency to think either that the legitimacy of international institutions must be transferred via consent to them from legitimate states or, if that is not possible, that their legitimacy must consist in their mimicking those features of the state's relationship to its own citizens that confer legitimacy on it. For those who think that legitimacy is conferred on the state by democratic processes, the natural assumption is that international institutions must be democratic to be legitimate.

I have argued that this picture is deeply flawed. The internal legitimacy of a state does not depend solely on how it relates to its own citizens; international institutions, not just domestic political arrangements, can contribute to the state's internal legitimacy. It is true that the legitimacy of international institutions depends in part on their being endorsed by states—it could not be otherwise in a world in which global democratic institutions are lacking and individuals' and groups' interests are represented, if they are represented at all, chiefly through their membership of states. But this should not blind us to the fact that legitimation can be bidirectional. International institutions can contribute to the legitimacy of states, even though they are the creations of states. Bearing that in mind may help break the hold of another distorted picture, one according to which international institutions are a growing threat to domestic political institutions, rather than a resource for enhancing their legitimacy.

The next three chapters elaborate the theme of reciprocal legitimacy, demonstrating how states' participation in various kinds of international institutions can enhance their legitimacy as entities that wield military force across borders.

Notes

I am grateful to Thomas Christiano, Gerald Gaus, Robert O. Keohane, Stephen Macedo, and Bas van der Vossen for helpful comments on an earlier draft of this article that was presented at a workshop on the ethics of international institutions in New Orleans in February 2009. I am especially indebted to Gillian Brock for her insightful and constructive contributions as the commentator on my conference paper.

CHAPTER 5

The Internal Legitimacy of Humanitarian Intervention

The preceding chapter made the case that a state's engagement with the right sort of international institutions can enhance its legitimacy and that participation by well-ordered states can enhance the legitimacy of international institutions. In the final two chapters of this volume, I will offer detailed accounts of how a state's participation in either of two different kinds of multilateral institutions—one designed to legitimize humanitarian intervention, the other to legitimize military support against the overthrow of democratic states—can enhance the legitimacy of a state's recourse to war. In this chapter, I argue that legitimate humanitarian intervention may require more than engagement with the right sort of multilateral institutions; it may also require institutional change within the state.

I. *The Neglected Problem of Internal Legitimacy*

Humanitarian intervention is often defined as infringement of a state sovereignty by an external agent or agents for the sake of preventing human rights violations.[1] The term "infringement"

---

[1] See, for example, Jack Donnelly, "Human Rights, Humanitarian Intervention and American Foreign Policy: Law, Morality, and Politics," *Journal of International Affairs* 37, no. 2 (1984): 311.

in this definition is carefully chosen: the implied contrast is between infringements and violations; not all infringements are unjust, so the definition remains neutral as to whether, or under what conditions, intervention is justified. Another implication is that humanitarian intervention is *nonconsensual* intervention by a country or group of countries; for if the state that is the target of the intervention consented, the intervention would not be an infringement of its sovereignty.

On a stricter definition, humanitarian intervention is limited to the use of force, as distinguished from economic sanctions. Some writers add the stipulation that humanitarian intervention must be purely humanitarian in intent, that the sole or at least the primary goal of the intervention must be to protect the welfare and freedom of those in another state, rather than some advantage to the intervening state or its citizens.[2] In my judgment, this further qualification is not helpful, because in our world many instances of what are reasonably called humanitarian interventions involve the pursuit of a mixed bag of goals, or the attempt to realize more than one intention.

The Problems of Humanitarian Intervention

The ethics of humanitarian intervention is a complex and passionately disputed topic. Familiar issues include the following. (1) Given the centrality of state sovereignty in international law, when, if ever, is humanitarian intervention legal, and under what conditions is it morally permissible to engage in illegal humanitarian intervention? (2) When, if ever, is unilateral, as opposed to collective, humanitarian intervention morally justified? (3) Does any persistent violation of human rights justify intervention, or only extreme violations, such as genocide? (4) Even if persistent human rights violations (or violations of certain basic human

---

[2] See, for example, Fernando Tesón, *Humanitarian Intervention*, 2nd ed. (Irvington-on-Hudson, NY: Transnational Publishers, 1992), 1–6.

rights) constitute a prima facie justification for intervention, what other conditions must be satisfied? (Proposals include a requirement of proportionality, such that the human rights violations that result from the intervention should be considerably less than those it is designed to prevent, and requirements of procedural justice for impartially identifying targets of intervention and for selecting disinterested agents of intervention.)

The Internal Legitimacy of Humanitarian Intervention

There is another fundamental issue of the ethics of humanitarian intervention that seems largely to have gone unnoticed in the contemporary scholarly debate: the problem of the internal legitimacy of humanitarian intervention.[3] This problem remains after all the familiar questions are answered satisfactorily; yet it precedes them all because, unless it can be answered affirmatively, the other questions do not arise. It is this problem that is the focus of this chapter.

The problem is this: How can the government of a state morally justify humanitarian intervention to its own citizens? Like the questions listed above, this is a question about moral justification, but unlike them it directs the question of justification inward. The other, more familiar questions concerning humanitarian intervention are questions about external legitimacy: they assume that there is no problem of internal legitimacy or, if there is, that it has been solved; they concentrate on whether intervention by one state or by a collection of states can be justified to the state that is the object of intervention, or to the community of states as a whole.

[3] I borrow the term internal legitimacy from Ronald Sanders. In an unpublished paper Sanders distinguishes between internal and external legitimacy. On his view, a state is internally legitimate if its citizens (or the majority of them) accept it as having rightful political authority. My use of the term does not follow his, however. I only use it to focus on which party the justification for humanitarian intervention is directed toward.

The failure to address the problem of the internal legitimacy of humanitarian intervention is a major deficiency, not only in the moral theory of intervention, but in the doctrine of human rights as well. Evolving human rights thinking specifies the conditions under which it is legally permissible for states to intervene to protect human rights when they choose to do so. In addition, under the basic principle that agreements are to be kept (*pacta sunt servanda*), international law recognizes that states that have signed human rights treaties have obligations under those treaties. Yet such treaties (including the International Covenant on Civil and Political Rights) only impose on signatories duties to protect the human rights of their own citizens and merely encourage states to promote human rights in other states.[4]

In other words, existing international human rights law does not establish clear obligations of humanitarian intervention on the part of states.[5] Human rights activists and some international legal scholars have advocated that international law should be modified so that it imposes clear obligations to engage in humanitarian intervention on states. However, it can be argued that unless humanitarian intervention is internally legitimate, the imposition of a duty of humanitarian intervention would itself be a moral wrong. Like the ethical literature on humanitarian intervention, international legal doctrine for the most part slides over the problem of internal legitimacy.

At this juncture a cautionary word is in order. The problem of the internal legitimacy of humanitarian intervention, as I have defined it, is a problem about the morality, not the legality, of humanitarian intervention. International legal writers have rightly noted that at least for some states the legality of participation in

---

[4] Article 2, Part II, International Covenant on Civil and Political Rights (1966), in James Nickel, *Making Sense of Human Rights* (Berkeley: University of California Press, 1987), 212.

[5] As opposed to those that might be generated by other more specific treaties into which states have entered.

some aspects of international human rights enforcement efforts is questionable. In some cases, as with Japan and Germany, the constitution of a state prohibits the use of military force abroad, even for humanitarian intervention. It has also been argued that participation in some international efforts to implement human rights norms, including war crimes trials, may be incompatible with the stringent demands of the equal protection and due process provisions of the US Constitution.[6] The question I shall focus on here, however, is not whether humanitarian intervention is internally legal (that is, according to the legal system of the state that intervenes) but whether the government can provide an adequate moral justification to its own citizens when it intervenes on humanitarian grounds and whether citizens have at least a prima facie obligation to comply with what the government demands of them in undertaking the intervention or at least not to interfere with their government's actions. An immediate response may well be this: there is no problem here; if the intervening state is legitimate, then its legitimacy justifies its interventions to its people, at least if those interventions are justifiable externally (that is, to the target of intervention and the world community). However, this response begs the question. It assumes, without argument, that among the legitimate activities of a state are undertakings whose primary aim is to protect the rights of persons who are not its citizens, when doing so is not needed for protecting the rights or furthering the interests of its own citizens. I shall argue that this assumption is unjustifiable from the perspective of what is arguably the dominant understanding of the nature of the state and the role of government in liberal political thought: the idea that the state is an association for the mutual advantage of its members and that the government is simply an agent whose fiduciary duty is to serve the interests or protect the rights of those citizens.

[6] Alfred Rubin, *Ethics and Authority in International Law* (Cambridge, UK: Cambridge University Press, 1997), 93.

Exploring the problem of the internal legitimacy of humanitarian intervention leads us back, then, to what is perhaps the most basic question of political philosophy: What are states for? I shall argue that the dominant understanding of the nature of the state and the role of government, what I shall refer to as the Discretionary Association View, makes internally legitimate humanitarian intervention impossible (except, perhaps, in the special case where it is explicitly authorized by robustly democratic processes). And I will suggest that the dominant way of thinking about justice—the view that justice is a matter of relations among members of a cooperative scheme—reinforces the Discretionary Association View's inability to account for the internal legitimacy of humanitarian intervention. I will also articulate the features of the Discretionary Association View that explain its perennial attraction.

However, I will then argue that humanitarian intervention nonetheless can be internally legitimate. First, I will raise several serious objections to the Discretionary Association View that makes the internal legitimacy of humanitarian intervention problematic. Second, I will show that the attractions of the Discretionary Association View can be preserved in an alternative understanding of the state as an instrument for justice in such a way as to provide a solution to the problem of the internal legitimacy of humanitarian intervention, while preserving the intuition that it is proper and indeed obligatory for a state to show some partiality toward its own citizens.

II. *The Discretionary Association View of the State*

What States Are For

The internal legitimacy of humanitarian intervention is an intelligible problem regardless of what view of the state one takes, but within the dominant view of the state in liberal political thought it is an especially daunting problem. According to the dominant view, the state is a discretionary association for the mutual advantage of its members. The government is simply the agent of the associated individuals, an instrument to further *their* interests and protect their rights. Or, on a more sophisticated, democratic variant of that dominant view, the state is a framework not simply for serving the interests and protecting the rights of the citizens but also for articulating their will, through democratic processes, and the role of the government is not only to serve the citizens' interests and protect their rights but also to realize their will (or rather the will of the majority of the citizens).

Perhaps the clearest proponent of the Discretionary Association View is Locke. For him the state is a discretionary association in this sense: although there is no moral obligation to enter into political society, it is permissible and even advisable for individuals who interact together in a state of nature to avoid its "inconveniences"—especially those attendant on private enforcement of the moral rules—by forming a political society and authorizing a group of individuals to be the government, to serve as the agent of the people.[7] For Locke political association is discretionary, not only in the sense that there is no moral obligation to form a state, but also in that individuals may choose with whom they wish to associate politically. There is no suggestion of what I have referred to elsewhere as an "obligation of inclusion"— a moral duty to help ensure that all persons have access to institutions that will protect their basic rights.[8]

The very idea of a social contract so central to liberal theorizing about justice suggests the Discretionary Association View. The state is understood as the creation of a hypothetical contract among those who are to be its citizens, and the terms of the contract they agree on are justified by showing how observance

---

[7] John Locke, *Second Treatise of Civil Government*, ed. C. B. Macpherson (Indianapolis, IN: Hackett, 1980), 1–2.

[8] Allen Buchanan, "The Morality of Inclusion," *Social Philosophy & Policy* 10, no. 2 (1993): 242–7.

of those terms serves *their* interests. No one else's interests are represented, so legitimate political authority is naturally defined as authority exercised for the good of the parties to the contract, the citizens of this state. Even in variants of the contract doctrine that view the parties as representatives of future generations, such as Rawls's, it is only insofar as future generations are presumed to be citizens of *this* state that their interests are considered in the making of the contract. The state is understood to be the enforcer of principles of justice, and principles of justice are thought of as specifying the terms of cooperation among those who are bound together in one political society, rather than as specifying how persons generally must be treated.

The Discretionary Association View usually includes a distinction between the state and the government. The justifying function of the state—what justifies the interference with liberty that it entails—is the well-being and freedom of its members. There is no suggestion that the state must do anything to serve the cause of justice in the world at large. What makes a government legitimate is that it acts as the faithful agent of its own citizens. And to that extent, government acts legitimately only when it occupies itself exclusively with the interests and rights of the citizens of the state of which it is the government.

The Attractions of the Discretionary Association View

The enduring popularity of the Discretionary Association View is no accident. It has several signal attractions, at least from the standpoint of a liberal political philosophy. First, it puts government in its place. It makes it clear who is master, namely, the people. Thus the Discretionary Association View is a powerful expression of the idea of popular sovereignty: the government, being the instrument of the people, serves at their pleasure. The government has no independent moral status, no rights on its own account. Second, the Discretionary Association View implies the equal freedom of the citizens. Individuals freely decide whether to enter into association with one another. Third, the state itself—the structure of institutions that create and sustain political society—is justified because it serves the interests of the people and for no other reason. Especially at a time when states (and even subjects) were seen as the property of dynastic families whose interests they were to serve, and when rulers used their power to uphold a hierarchy of rank among subjects, these features of the Discretionary Association View represented a profound moral revolution in political thought.

According to the simpler version of the Discretionary Association View, a government that engages in what I referred to earlier as pure humanitarian intervention violates its fiduciary obligation: by definition it fails to act in the best interest of its citizens and does not act so as to protect their rights. According to the Discretionary Association View, this failure is momentous: it is a violation of the fundamental fiduciary duty of the government, which in turn is founded on the justifying function of the state—the fact that the state serves the interests and protects the rights of its citizens.

On the more sophisticated democratic version of the Discretionary Association View, the mere fact that a government engages in humanitarian intervention by definition shows that it acts contrary to the best interests of its citizens, but it is apparently a further question as to whether the government acts illegitimately. For the citizens might democratically authorize pure humanitarian intervention even though they are aware that it is not in their best interest and is not needed for the protection of their rights. Such would be the case if the majority gave higher priority to justice than to their good.

Democratic Authority and Humanitarian Intervention

One should not be too quick to assume, however, that pure humanitarian intervention is within the sphere of legitimate democratic authorization allowed by the Discretionary Association

View. For according to this view, the state is not an instrument for moral progress. It has a much more limited purpose: the advancement of the interests and the protection of the rights of its citizens. Hence a proponent of the Discretionary Association View might hold that the function that justifies the state places an antecedent constraint on what may be authorized by democratic processes, just as a list of individual rights does. On this interpretation of the democratic variant of the Discretionary Association View, the majority is sovereign only over choices concerning which interests and rights of the citizens are to be given priority and how they are to be realized. At least so long is there is one citizen who votes against it, humanitarian intervention is illegitimate, because the purpose of the state (the goal that unites all citizens in one political association) is limited to the advantage of those citizens, and the effective pursuit of this goal limits the sphere of legitimate democratic decision-making.

It will do no good to say that democratic processes define the citizens' interests—that if the majority votes for humanitarian intervention, then ipso facto humanitarian intervention is in the citizens' interest, and that therefore humanitarian intervention democratically approved lies within the proper sphere of state action according to the Discretionary Association View. Such a claim is nothing more than verbal sleight of hand. At most, democratic endorsement of humanitarian intervention establishes that the majority of citizens, not even all citizens, prefer such intervention. It does not establish that it is in the interest of all citizens or even that the majority of the citizens believe it is in their interest. Furthermore, our question is whether humanitarian intervention—intervention that is not in the interests of the citizens (or even in the interests of a majority of them)—can be internally justified. At the very least, the assumption that democratic authorization legitimizes pure humanitarian intervention requires a departure from a strict interpretation of the

Discretionary Association View's central tenet, which is that the state is an arrangement for the mutual advantage of its citizens. Instead the Discretionary Association View would have to be reformulated as follows: the state is first and foremost an arrangement for the mutual advantage of its members; however, once the basic interests and rights of all the citizens are secured, it is permissible, through democratic processes, to authorize actions that do not serve the best interests of the citizens and are not needed to protect their rights.

Suppose that this modification is acceptable. Suppose, that is, that the Discretionary Association View can be reasonably interpreted to include an understanding of democratic authorization according to which legitimate democratic decisions are not limited to those that serve the best interests of the citizens or protect their rights. This only means that there are conditions under which pure humanitarian intervention is permissible. There is still nothing in the democratic variant of the Discretionary Association View that requires citizens ever to forego their own advantage for the sake of preventing even the most horrific human rights violations abroad. This is part of what is meant by calling it the Discretionary Association View.

If the citizens' will, duly expressed through democratic processes, is that their government should refrain from pure humanitarian intervention, then this is permissible, according to the democratic variant of the Discretionary Association View. However, once democratic processes have expressed the people's desire not to engage in humanitarian intervention, humanitarian intervention by the government is illegitimate. From the standpoint of the Discretionary Association View, humanitarian intervention is not only non-obligatory. It is in fact morally impermissible, unless there is a clear democratic mandate.

A consistent policy of avoiding humanitarian intervention would, of course, require that the state in question refrain from signing any human rights conventions or other agreements that create obligations of pure humanitarian intervention. Call this mode of state practice "the Swiss model."[9] From the standpoint of the Discretionary Association View, even on its democratic variant, there would be nothing morally defective about a world in which *every* state adopted the Swiss model.

Political Realism and Humanitarian Intervention

I noted earlier that an awareness of the problem of the internal legitimacy of humanitarian intervention is conspicuously absent in much of the contemporary scholarly literature on the ethics of intervention. However, so-called political realists, of which Hans J. Morgenthau and George F. Kennan are perhaps the most influential modern examples, have typically opposed humanitarian intervention.[10]

The realists have not fared well at the hands of recent moral theorists of international relations. They present easy targets, in great part because they often fail to give rigorous arguments in favor of their views and sometimes even appear muddled in their thinking.[11] My aim here is not to untangle the various threads of realist thinking in a systematic way, but only to indicate that there is one strand that is securely anchored in the Discretionary Association View of the nature of the state and the role of government. If this is so, then at least some realist arguments against

---

[9] This label is not intended to suggest that Switzerland actually pursues a purely self-interested foreign policy (all the time). The point rather is that this country, whether rightly or wrongly, has the reputation of sufficiently approximating such a policy to make the label a handy one.

[10] George F. Kennan, *Realities of American Foreign Policy* (Princeton, NJ: Princeton University Press, 1954). Hans J. Morgenthau, *In Defense of the National Interest* (New York: Knopf, 1952), and *Politics Among Nations*, 5th ed. (New York: Knopf, 1973).

[11] For excellent critiques of realist thinking, see Marshall Cohen, "Moral Skepticism and International Relations," *Philosophy & Public Affairs* 13, no. 4 (1984): 299–346; and Charles Beitz, *Political Theory & International Relations* (Princeton, NJ: Princeton University Press, 1979), 15–50.

pure humanitarian intervention cannot be convincingly re-
futed without rejecting a dominant paradigm of liberal political
thought.

There are two quite different ways to understand the realist's
antipathy to pure humanitarian intervention. According to the
first, what might be called the moral nihilist view, all moral action
in international relations is irrational, because the conditions for
moral behavior being rational do not obtain in the international
sphere.

According to the second realist view, which might be called the
"fiduciary obligation" position, there is at least one moral concept that is applicable to international relations: the concept of an
overriding fiduciary obligation on the part of the leaders of states
to serve the interests of their peoples, even when doing so violates
other putative moral principles. On this second realist view, the
ruthless leader is not a stranger to morality. He is the dedicated
servant of a higher morality.

Unlike the international moral nihilist or Hobbesian, the fiduciary realist does not make the mistake of assuming that there
is no room for moral concepts or for rational moral behavior at
all in international relations. However, the fiduciary realist view
constricts the morality of international relations almost to the
vanishing point. Government officials not only may, but ought
to transgress any moral principle for the sake of fulfilling their
fiduciary obligations.

Critics of this variety of realism have been quick to point out
that it is vulnerable to two serious objections. First, fiduciary
obligations are not absolute. By undertaking fiduciary duties
government officials do not thereby wipe the slate clean of all
preexisting obligations they may have as individuals, including
obligations not to violate human rights. So the fact that government officials have fiduciary obligations to their own citizens
does not show that it is permissible for them to violate other
moral principles, much less that they act wrongly if they act on
other moral principles. Second, at least for some states some of

the time, survival is not at stake in international relations. At least the more powerful states can engage in pure humanitarian intervention without risking their survival.

These objections are telling against the fiduciary realist position as it is usually presented. But they leave one important element of the fiduciary realist position untouched—its opposition to humanitarian intervention. The fiduciary realist can argue as follows: it is true that fiduciary obligations are not absolute; they can be overridden by weightier obligations. From this it follows that government leaders do not have moral carte blanche to do whatever is necessary to further the interests of their citizens. But that is not to say that they may use the resources of the state to further the interests of individuals who are not citizens of the state, and the Discretionary Association View provides no explanation of why they should be allowed to do so. (Similarly, if I hire you to be my agent, it is true that you do not thereby escape other obligations you may have, but the mere fact that you have other obligations does not entitle you to use my resources to fulfill them.) Yes, the realist continues, it is quite correct to point out that not all humanitarian interventions put the state's survival interests at risk. But this is irrelevant to the question of pure humanitarian intervention. The fact remains that government officials ought only to serve the interests and protect the rights of their own states.

Fiduciary realism, stripped of the implausible assumptions to which critics have rightly objected, has the merit of taking seriously the idea that the government is the agent of the people—the people of its state—and that the fact that it is their agent that makes a difference to what it may do. It is crucial to understand that this strand of realist thought is not a muddled aberration, a sui generis confusion or a free-floating anomaly in Western political thought. It is nurtured by the dominant discretionary association paradigm, which includes the idea that the government is only an agent, fundamentally bound by a fiduciary obligation. Unless we are willing to reject or modify the Discretionary Association View, there will be no convincing reply to the fiduciary normative realist's objection to humanitarian intervention.

III. *A Critique of the Discretionary Association View*

Objections to the Discretionary Association View

Despite its several attractions, noted above, the Discretionary Association View is subject to four serious problems. Two have already been mentioned. It not only leaves us without a convincing reply to the fiduciary normative realist, but also implies that there would be nothing morally wrong with a world in which every state adopted "the Swiss model." In such a world, the enforcement of human rights standards abroad would be regarded as purely optional. The language of moral obligation would be out of place in debates about humanitarian intervention.

A third, perhaps more serious problem is that the Discretionary Association View is afflicted by a deep incoherence, if not an outright inconsistency. It justifies the state as a coercive apparatus by appeal to the need to protect *universal* interests, while at the same time limiting the right of the state to use its coercive power to the protection of a particular group of persons, identified by the purely contingent characteristic of happening to be members of the same political society.

According to the most plausible version of the Discretionary Association View, the most important interests that states are to serve are basic human interests, not special interests that citizens of this or that particular state have but that the citizens of other states might not have. Thus for Locke, for example, government best serves the interests of its citizens by protecting life, liberty, and property. If the interests whose protection justifies the state are human interests, common to all persons, then surely a way of thinking about the nature of states and the role of government that provides no basis for *any* obligations, no matter how attenuated, to help ensure that the interests of all persons are protected is fundamentally flawed.

The Half-Hearted Universalist Basis of the Discretionary Association View

This point can be put even more forcefully if it is framed in terms of individuals' rights. According to the more influential examples of the Discretionary Association View such as Locke's and Rawls's, the state is to ensure that the cooperative framework it supplies works to the mutual advantage of all citizens by protecting every citizen's basic human rights. And it is the fact that the state protects all citizens' basic human rights that is supposed to justify its use of coercion: it is only because these rights are so important for all persons as persons, the interferences with liberty that this coercion involves are justified. So on the one hand the Discretionary Association View bases its conception of the nature of the state and the role of government on a universalist conception of which kinds of interests (or which rights) are worth protecting by the coercive power of the state, while on the other hand it provides no basis for imputing any obligation to use the resources of the state to implement this universalist conception beyond the boundaries of the state. The Discretionary Association View rules out obligations of humanitarian intervention in principle at the same time that it implicitly embraces a universalist conception of the worth of the individual that recognizes no boundaries.

A fourth problem with the Discretionary Association View takes the form of a dilemma. Either that view must deny that states have any obligations toward citizens of other states, including negative duties not to kill or injure them wantonly, in which case it is in stark conflict both with some of our most basic and widely held moral intuitions and with one of the most basic principles of international law; or else that view must acknowledge that states have such negative duties, making it then vulnerable to the charge that it provides no reasonable basis for not recognizing some positive duties as well. Let us consider each alternative in turn.

An Unacceptable Implication of the Discretionary Association View

Taken literally, the Discretionary Association View holds that the state may not legitimately do anything except serve the best interests of its citizens. This would mean that if it were the case that an unprovoked attack on another state would promote its citizens' interests, then the state may undertake such an attack—indeed that it ought to do so. Such an implication is squarely at odds with what is perhaps one of our most confident and widely shared moral intuitions, namely, that it is wrong to harm the innocent. It is also in conflict with one of the most basic principles of international law, namely, that wars of aggression are prohibited. Not surprisingly, most proponents of the Discretionary Association View would acknowledge that a state's efforts to serve the interests of its citizens must be constrained by certain basic negative duties toward others. Let us call this the Softened Discretionary Association View.

The difficulty is that once the Discretionary Association View makes this concession, it is hard to see how it can avoid going further, toward the recognition of at least some positive duties toward noncitizens. The most plausible reasons for holding that states have negative duties toward noncitizens appeal to the moral importance of human beings as such, and to the role which the fulfillment of the negative duties in question plays in protecting certain fundamental interests in liberty and well-being that human beings as such have. But, as has been convincingly argued in many other contexts, the protection of those fundamental interests also requires the fulfillment of positive duties as well, including duties to ensure that all have access to resources for subsistence and to basic educational opportunities. Libertarian attempts to limit duties to those that are negative either fail to appreciate that the same considerations that ground negative rights also ground positive ones or implausibly assume that the only morally significant sort of liberty is freedom from coercion. In brief, the same arguments that show that the state has positive as well as negative duties to its own citizens show that it is arbitrary to soften the harsh implications of the Discretionary Association View by admitting negative duties to noncitizens while denying any positive duties whatsoever to noncitizens.

Suppose that the proponent of the Discretionary Association View could somehow avoid the objection that acknowledging negative duties to noncitizens while denying positive ones is arbitrary. The Softened Discretionary Association View would still conflict with some rather basic moral intuitions. For example, it cannot explain what is wrong with a rich and powerful state refusing to exert even the most minimal efforts, at virtually no risk to itself, to prevent genocide in a neighboring state. In a world in which the Discretionary Association View were taken seriously no one could appeal to an obligation to engage in humanitarian intervention even as a prima facie obligation that might be overridden by practical considerations.

Distinguishing the Moral from the Legal Issue

Whether or not the international legal system should impose legal obligations to cooperate in humanitarian interventions upon states that democratically decide not to engage in humanitarian interventions is another matter. There might be sound reasons for refraining from efforts to impose such international legal obligations. My point is that the Discretionary Association View, even in its democratic and softened variants, makes it impossible to argue that even the most powerful and rich state has any moral obligation, no matter how limited, to cooperate in humanitarian intervention efforts, even when doing so is necessary to stop the most egregious violations of human rights and even when the costs of doing so are minimal.

Indeed, the Discretionary Association View cannot make sense of the fact that we experience the question of humanitarian intervention as a moral conflict. We experience a moral conflict because we feel the pull not only of moral reasons against humanitarian intervention, but in favor of it as well. On the Discretionary Association View, there are not two sides to the matter and hence there can be no conflict, because there can be no moral obligation to engage in humanitarian intervention.

One can, of course, construct practical arguments for why states generally should only attend to the interests of their own citizens and the fulfillment of negative duties toward noncitizens. One could argue that, even though there is a prima facie obligation to engage in humanitarian intervention, such intervention is never justifiable all things considered because any serious effort at humanitarian intervention would be excessively costly to the citizens of the intervening state; or because it is doomed to failure for lack of the resources and knowledge required for success; or because it is likely to be a disguised imperialist adventure, and not a genuine humanitarian intervention at all. But we are not concerned here with whether humanitarian intervention meets standards of practicality. We are asking whether it can even in principle be internally justified, given the dominant liberal model of what states are for and what the role of government is. Even if all the foregoing practical problems disappeared, our question would remain.

In addition, the same features of the Discretionary Association View that preclude it from recognizing that the people of one state sometimes have at least a prima facie obligation to intervene on humanitarian grounds in another state also make it unable to account for what I take to be a relatively uncontroversial moral intuition about the ethics of immigration. According to the Discretionary Association View, it is simply a confusion to argue that the people of a very rich and secure state have even a prima facie moral obligation to accept even a small number of refugees from genocide occurring just across the border, even when their acceptance carries no risks to the people of the state. It is one thing to say that the obligation to accept political refugees is limited—for example, that a people need not accept refugees if doing so will embroil them in a war or will create ethnic conflict within their state or will undermine the dominant culture of the state or erode its constitutional order. But it is quite another to say that there is no obligation at all. Yet, on the Discretionary Association View, there is no such obligation.

IV. *The State as an Instrument for Justice*

For all of these reasons it is worth asking whether the attractions of the Discretionary Association View can be preserved while avoiding its costs. The chief moral cost of the Discretionary Association View is not that it implies that *governments* should not undertake humanitarian intervention except (perhaps) when explicitly authorized to do so by democratic processes. The more basic problem is that it provides no basis for believing that the *people* of any particular state have any obligation to use the resources of their state to undertake pure humanitarian intervention or to accept refugees even under the least painful circumstances. On the contrary, the Discretionary Association View portrays pure humanitarian intervention and the acceptance of refugees as aberrations, as inexplicable departures from what political action ought to be. Even on the democratic variant of the Discretionary Association View there is still a problem, as we have seen: How can a majority voting in favor of pure humanitarian intervention justify their decision to a dissenting minority, given that the justifying function of the state is to serve the interests of its citizens, not to protect the rights of others?

The Natural Duty of Justice

There is a radically different conception of the nature of the state and the role of government that avoids the moral and theoretical costs of the Discretionary Association View while at the same time preserving its attractions. We may call it the "State as Instrument for Justice" view. It rests upon the premise that there is a natural duty of justice that requires us to help ensure that all persons have access to institutions for the protection of their basic moral rights.[12]

In *A Theory of Justice* Rawls articulates a natural duty of justice as having two parts: first, we are to comply with and do our fair share in just institutions when they exist and apply to us; and second, we are to assist in the establishment of just arrangements when they do not exist, at least when this can be done with little cost to ourselves.[13] The duty is said to be natural in the sense that individuals have it independently of any special undertakings and independently of the institutional roles they may occupy.

The scope of the second clause is perhaps not altogether clear. It could mean that we are to help establish just institutions that will apply to us, where no just institutions now apply to us. Or it could mean that we are to help establish just institutions for all persons.

In fact, three different understandings of the second clause can be distinguished. In each case the qualifier "if one can do so without excessive costs" is to be understood as being included (for brevity I will not repeat it each time).

NDJ1: Each person has a duty to contribute to the creation of just arrangements to include himself and his fellow citizens.

[12] The remainder of this section of the paper draws on my paper "Political Legitimacy and the Natural Duty of Justice" (unpublished).

[13] John Rawls, *A Theory of Justice* (Cambridge, MA: Harvard University Press, 1971), 334.

NDJ2: Each person has a duty to contribute to the creation of just arrangements to include himself and all those with whom he will interact (which may include some who are not his fellow citizens).

NDJ3: Each person has a duty to contribute to the inclusion of all persons in just arrangements.

It is the third, most demanding understanding of the "natural duty of justice" upon which I will focus. It alone provides a secure foundation for an obligation of humanitarian intervention, and only it provides a convincing solution to the problem of the internal legitimacy of humanitarian intervention.

The natural duty of justice (hereafter understood as NDJ3) is such a fundamental principle that it may seem impossible to provide an argument for it that does not assume at least one premise that is more controversial than the principle itself. However, even if no convincing argument can be presented for it, it has considerable intuitive appeal, at least if, as I have suggested, it is understood as imposing a limited obligation, not an obligation to help ensure that all have access to just institutions regardless of cost. Given its intuitive appeal, showing that the natural duty of justice thus understood provides the basis for a view of the nature of the state and the role of government that avoids the costs of the Discretionary Association View while preserving its attractions would be a valuable exercise, even if no argument for it could be supplied. Nevertheless, although I cannot attempt to provide a conclusive case for the natural duty NDJ3 here, I will indicate one plausible line of argument in support of it.

Before doing so, however, I would like to emphasize that proponents of the Discretionary Association View typically do not provide explicit arguments to support it. Instead, support for the Discretionary Association View is indirect. Its plausibility appears to depend solely upon what it implies: namely, that citizens are free and equal; that the state is to serve their interests, rather than the interests of the ruler or the citizens of some other state; and that the government is merely their agent, with no rights or moral standing of its own. Yet these attractive implications, I shall argue, also follow from what I have referred to as the Instrument for Justice View.

In Support of the Natural Duty

Perhaps the best way to argue for the natural duty of justice (NDJ3) is to tease out the incoherence of denying that this duty exists while at the same time affirming that persons as such have rights. I take it that the assertion that persons as such have rights means that we all have a duty to treat persons in certain ways, and that this duty is owed to persons because it is grounded in morally significant features that all persons possess. Different moral theories may provide different accounts of what it is about persons that is the source of their rights and hence of our duties toward them (Kantian theories, for instance, hold that it is the capacity for moral agency). But what is important is that the duties that correlate with the rights of persons as such are *owed* to persons simply as persons. They are not merely duties *regarding* persons (such as we would have if, for example, the sole basis for moral constraints on the way we may treat people were the commands of God or the relationships we happen to have toward persons).

To say that persons as such have certain rights, then, means that because of certain characteristics that all persons have they are entitled to certain treatment. But if this is so, then surely one ought not only to respect persons' rights by not violating them. One ought also to contribute to creating arrangements that will ensure that persons' rights are not violated. To put the same point somewhat differently, respect for persons requires doing something to ensure that they are treated respectfully.

Consider the alternative. Suppose that the ground of our duties regarding persons were external to them—that we are required to treat them in certain ways only because God commands us to do so, for example. We would have duties regarding persons but not owed to them. In this case there would be no incoherence or oddness at all about acknowledging that we are obligated to treat persons in certain ways while at the same time denying that we have any obligation whatsoever, no matter how limited, to help ensure that others treat them similarly. For although God *might* command us to see that our fellows treat persons as he commands us to treat them, he also might not.

Alternatively, suppose that the ground of one's duty not to violate persons' rights lay only in some relationship one happens to bear to them, such as being a fellow citizen or being co-participants in some international economic arrangement for our mutual advantage. If some such relationship were the sole basis of the duty, then one would not have a duty to persons as such to respect their rights, and there would be no presumption that there is a duty to help ensure that all persons' rights are respected.

In contrast, if the basic moral rights of persons are grounded in the morally important characteristics that all persons possess, then it is difficult to maintain a separation between respecting persons' rights and making some effort to see that their rights are respected. At the very least, the same appreciation for the nature of persons that is supposed to ground their most basic rights and hence our duty to respect those rights carries a presumptive duty to help ensure that all persons can live in conditions in which their basic rights are respected, at least if we can do so without excessive costs to ourselves.

I would not presume to assert that these considerations provide an unassailable foundation for the natural duty of justice. But let us suppose, for the sake of drawing out the implications of this duty for how we conceive of the nature of the state and the role of government, that each of us has an obligation to help ensure that all persons have access to rights-protecting institutions. The extent of what we are actually required to do to fulfill that obligation will vary with the costs of fulfilling it. If this is the case, then those individuals who are politically organized, who can collectively command the resources of a state, will have greater capacity to help ensure that others have access to a justice-protecting regime, without excessive costs.

With this greater capacity comes greater responsibility for alleviating the condition of other persons whose rights are imperiled. As individuals commanding only our own private resources, there may be little that any of us can do to help ensure that all persons can live in a rights-protecting regime. But when we are organized in a state our collective capacity for promoting just institutions abroad is greatly enhanced. And if we live in a powerful and rich state, there will surely be cases in which our collective resources can be used to further the cause of justice in the world, without excessive costs to us.

The Nature of the State, in Light of the Natural Duty of Justice

Because it is a natural duty, NDJ3 places a constraint on how we may use our institutional resources, upon what we may do with the state, and hence what our government, our agent, may do. Given the fact that having a state of our own enables us to act on the natural duty, we are not morally free to use our state merely as a framework for *our* mutual advantage. Thus if we were to adopt the "Swiss model," we would fail to acknowledge the natural duty of justice and ignore the fact that in our world at present states are the chief instrumentalities by which individuals can help ensure that all persons have access to institutions that protect their rights.

This is not to say that the sole legitimate purpose, or even the primary legitimate purpose of particular political associations is to promote justice for all of humanity. Because the natural duty includes an excessive cost proviso, it can accommodate the idea that citizens may rightly show partiality to their own interests. (Moreover, there are sound practical reasons for first seeking to establish justice locally, within the boundaries of existing states, working from within them.[14]) But what the natural duty does

[14] For an illuminating and systematic elaboration of this important point, see Jeremy Waldron, "Special Ties and Natural Duties," *Philosophy & Public Affairs* 22, no. 1 (1993): 22–30.

imply is that the state cannot be viewed simply as an arrangement for the mutual benefit of its members alone. And this suffices to rebut the fiduciary realist's claim that humanitarian intervention is in principle illegitimate.

The assumption that there is a natural duty of justice (NDJ3) allows us to develop a view of the state that preserves the attractive implications of the Discretionary Association View, while avoiding its moral and theoretical costs. If we suppose that there is a natural duty of justice (NDJ3), then we must acknowledge that those who collectively control effective political institutions have responsibilities to others and that consequently the state is not merely an association for the mutual advantage of its members, but a resource for ensuring that all persons rights are protected. Given this view of the state, we can explain the moral conflict we feel when we consider the pros and cons of pure humanitarian intervention.

A view of the state as an instrument for justice is clearly compatible with what is probably the single most attractive feature of the Discretionary Association View: a proper understanding of the status of government—that government is simply an agent, not a moral being with rights of its own. It also captures the idea that citizens are free and equal by affirming that all persons' rights matter. For even though the State as Instrument of Justice View places some constraints on the use of state resources for enhancing the condition of the citizens, it does not do so in the name of any assumption of unequal worth. On the contrary, the constraints it imposes follow from the assumption that all persons are of equal moral worth and that consequently all are entitled to protection of their rights. Finally, the State as Instrument of Justice View, like the Discretionary Association View, rules out any arrangements that sacrifice the interests of the citizens for the sake of benefiting anyone else, whether it be the rulers or the citizens of some other state. For according to the Instrument of Justice View, the proper business of the state is to benefit its members, within the constraints imposed by the natural duty of justice, and these constraints recognize that there are limits on the costs that the citizens of one state must bear to protect the rights of other persons.

Acknowledging that there is a robust natural duty of justice that requires citizens to use their state's resources to help ensure that all have access to a rights-protecting regime is an important theoretical advance in the doctrine of human rights. But from this alone it does not follow that it would be legitimate for the international legal system to *enforce* a duty on the part of states to contribute to the establishment of justice for all persons. For the natural duty of justice might be viewed as an imperfect duty rather than an enforceable one—merely an indeterminate and hence unenforceable duty to do something to help provide just institutions for all persons. Although I can only sketch the argument here, I will conclude by suggesting that a conscientious effort to act on the natural duty of justice will require states to work together to create international legal institutions that will articulate determinate duties and assign them to states in such a way as to distribute fairly the costs of ensuring that all persons have access to rights-protecting institutions. If this were accomplished, the enforcement of duties of humanitarian intervention would be morally justifiable. In effect, the right sort of institutions would perfect the previously imperfect duty.

V. *Special Authorization of Humanitarian Intervention*

The Case for Special Authorization

The prospect of humanitarian military intervention poses, in exceptionally serious form, a basic question that must be confronted once we abandon the Discretionary Association View of the state: how is the commitment to using the state to help fulfill the duty of Natural Justice, where this means helping to

achieve justice for strangers, to be reconciled with the acknowledgment that the state's *primary* obligation is to protect the rights
and further the interests of its own citizens? My suggestion is
that achieving this reconciliation will require institutional innovation. What is needed is some institutional arrangement that
will achieve a proper authorization—compatible with democratic
principles—of humanitarian intervention. Given the gravity of
humanitarian military intervention and the fact that it involves
the expenditure of blood and treasure, not for the good of the
citizens of the state but rather for the sake of strangers, it appears
some extraordinary form of democratic authorization should be
required for undertaking it.

Merely allowing the Executive to make the decision at its own
discretion or authorizing intervention by ordinary legislation
would seem to be inadequate. Such measures would not properly
acknowledge what a serious departure from the presumption that
the state is to act for the good of its own citizens' humanitarian
military intervention is.

Two quite different situations in which the need for institutional innovation might arise ought to be distinguished. In the
first, there is a compelling case for some special kind of authorization because a particular state has an especially poor record
regarding interventions, exhibiting a pattern of errors or abuses
or both. In this situation, the requirement of some extraordinary
form of authorization makes sense as a kind of prophylactic or
self-binding device. The second case is where, even though there
is no particularly dangerous pattern of past mistakes or abuses, it
is recognized that the states generally ought to treat the decision
to engage in humanitarian military intervention as extraordinarily
problematic, given that the primary duty of the state is to further
the basic interests and protect the rights of its own citizens.

With respect to the first situation, it is worth recalling that
both Germany and Japan, in recognition of their past horrifically
destructive decisions regarding the use of military force abroad,
have explicit constitutional measures prohibiting military action

except in cases of national self-defense. So the idea that a particular state's own history might make some form of extraordinary authorization for the use of military force across borders is neither new nor implausible. A state that exhibited a pattern of seriously defective decisions in favor of humanitarian intervention might well require some form of extraordinary authorization.

Consider now the second, general case. The fact that humanitarian military intervention is such a serious and extreme departure from the presumption in favor of a state's partiality toward its own citizens is one reason in favor of extraordinary authorization; but that reason is bolstered by another: even the most democratic states—and those that do the best job of respecting the rights of their own citizens—may be tempted to undertake military interventions in the pursuit of their own interests while rationalizing them in the name of humanitarian goals. Taken together, these two reasons weigh heavily in favor of not regarding the decision to engage in humanitarian military intervention as "government business as usual."

Alternatives for Institutional Innovation

There are at least three distinct institutional arrangements that could express the recognition that humanitarian military interventions are especially problematic for states generally and that as such, the decision to engage in this type of armed conflict requires special institutional arrangements. Each arrangement could be undertaken by a state in recognition that it had an exceptionally poor record on intervention as well. First, a national referendum could be required. A variant of this first proposal would require some measures designed to stimulate genuine public deliberation on the issues prior to the taking of the vote. An additional requirement would be that some court or other relatively impartial body would have to vet a draft of the referendum question to ensure that it is suitably clear and specific. Second, some robustly democratic legislative act could be required in the form of a supermajority in the national legislature in favor of intervention (or that along with concurrence by the Executive). Third, the constitution could include an explicit provision for humanitarian military intervention, with or without some substantive and/or procedural provisions for undertaking it. The constitutional alternative might be preferable for certain states given their histories to a blanket prohibition on any use of military force across borders that is not a clear case of self-defense. However, a constitutional provision allowing humanitarian intervention might be unreasonably subject to abuse and error, in the case of countries that have previously veiled their aggressive wars under the cover of humanitarian intervention, unless it was accompanied by some credible commitment to aptly institutionalizing the decision process for initiating humanitarian intervention. More specifically, the constitutional provision could stipulate that humanitarian military intervention is permissible only if it occurs through participation in a multilateral institution.

My intention in this chapter is not to argue that one of these alternatives is superior to the others, nor to suggest that they are the only possibilities. My goal, instead, is simply to initiate a discussion of institutional alternatives designed to reflect the need to ensure that decisions to engage in humanitarian military intervention are internally legitimate. If humanitarian intervention is in some cases morally required, then a blanket prohibition on it comes at great moral cost. Yet because the humanitarian justification for war has historically been subject to egregious error and abuse, allowing humanitarian intervention carries great moral risk. Neither a blanket prohibition nor a failure to take the risks of allowing humanitarian interventions seems reasonable or responsible. Special institutional authorization of this kind of war seems the best solution: it takes both the need for and the special risks of humanitarian war seriously.

The preceding chapter developed the idea of reciprocal institutional legitimation. This chapter furthers that project by showing how institutionalizing the just war may require not only that states participate in multilateral institutions, but also that they develop new internal institutions. Just as a well-designed multilateral institution can contribute to the legitimacy of states so far as they engage in wars, so the internal legitimacy of participating states can enhance the legitimacy of those multilateral institutions. Other things, being equal, an international regime for regulating humanitarian military intervention whose member states have institutions for ensuring the legitimacy of their own decisions regarding recourse to this type of war are legitimate will itself enjoy greater legitimacy.

CHAPTER 6

Reforming the Law of
Humanitarian Intervention

I. *The Need for Reform*

Taken together, the preceding chapters show that moral improvements in recourse to war behavior will require institutional innovations, both within states and in the development of multilateral institutions. This chapter explores the relationship between the goal of developing multilateral institutions for constraining recourse to war and the commitment to the rule of international law. It offers an answer to a disturbing question: Will some improvements in international law and institutions require violations of existing international law and if so, would such violations be morally permissible?

The Deficiency of Existing Law

The NATO intervention in Kosovo (1999) is only the most recent of a series of illegal interventions for which plausible moral justifications can be given. Others include India's intervention in East Pakistan in response to Pakistan's massive human rights violations there (1971), Vietnam's war against Pol Pot's genocidal regime in Cambodia (1978), and Tanzania's overthrow of Idi Amin's murderous rule in Uganda (1979). Without speculating as to what the dominant motives of the intervenors were, it is accurate to say that in each case military action was aimed at preventing or stopping massive human rights violations—although in each case there may have been other aims as well. All could qualify as instances of humanitarian military intervention according to the definition employed in Chapter Five: the use of military force across state borders by a state (or group of states) aimed at stopping violations of the human rights of individuals other than its own citizens, without the consent of the state within those whose territory force is applied. In all of the instances listed above, the intervention was, according to the preponderance of international legal opinion, a violation of international law. None was a case of self-defense (or the defense of other states) and none enjoyed UN Security Council authorization.

There is, however, an important difference in the case of the NATO intervention. Unlike the previous interventions, the NATO intervention in Kosovo and the ensuing debate over its justifiability have focused attention on the deficiency of existing international law concerning humanitarian intervention. In the aftermath of the Kosovo intervention, there seems to be a widening consensus that there is an unacceptable gap between what international law allows and what morality requires.

This way of characterizing the deficiency, however, is incomplete and even misleading. As Kofi Annan emphasized, the impossibility of gaining Security Council authorization for the intervention indicated a disturbing tension between two core moral values of the international legal system itself: respect for state sovereignty and a commitment to peaceful relations among states, on the one hand; and the protection of basic human rights on the other.[1] The point is not simply that intervention, though illegal, was morally justifiable; in addition, it was consonant with one of the most important values of the UN and of the entire

---

[1] Kofi Annan, "Speech to the General Assembly," SG/SM/7136 GA/9569: Secretary-G, September 20, 1999, 2.

system of international law on its most morally progressive interpretation.[2]

More precisely, the perception is growing that the requirement of Security Council authorization is an obstacle to the protection of basic human rights in internal conflicts. Since the majority of violent conflicts are now within states rather than between them, the time is ripe to consider changing or abandoning a rule of humanitarian intervention that was created for a quite different world. And it is time to confront the question of whether, if change is warranted, it can be achieved solely through legal means.

Three Different Justifications for Illegal Interventions

Many who acknowledge the illegality of the humanitarian interventions listed above nevertheless commend them. Plainly, the strongest justification for intervening despite the illegality of doing so is that intervention was morally permissible—or even morally obligatory. The moral principle to which such justification appeals is among the most fundamental: the need to protect basic human rights.

Often the question of the moral justifiability of illegal humanitarian interventions is framed as a simple choice as to which should take priority: fidelity to law or to basic moral values. Thus NATO leaders and US State Department officials asserted that the situation in Kosovo was a dire moral emergency that justified acting without Security Council authorization. Let us call this the Simple Moral Necessity Justification, according to which basic moral values can trump the obligation to obey the law.

As I have already suggested, there is a second, more subtle moral justification that was suggested from time to time by the

---

[2] The charge that the intervention was illegal is based on the most straightforward interpretations of the UN Charter, Articles 2(4) and 2(7). For a full account of the illegality of the NATO intervention, see J. L. Holzgrefe, "The Humanitarian Intervention Debate," ch. 1, in *Humanitarian Intervention: Ethical, Legal, and Political Dilemmas*, eds. J. L. Holzgrefe and Robert O. Keohane. (Cambridge, UK: Cambridge University Press, 2003), 15–52.

remarks of some public figures during the Kosovo crisis: the intervention was justified (though illegal) because it was necessary if a humanitarian disaster was to be averted *and* was supported by a core moral value of the international legal system itself. What this second justification adds to the first one is the idea that an act can be *lawful*, though illegal.[3] Unlike the Simple Moral Necessity Justification the Lawfulness Justification clearly expresses a commitment to values embodied in the legal system—not just those of morality considered as something external to the law—in this case the protection of international legal human rights.

According to a third line of justification, NATO's illegal humanitarian intervention was undertaken not only to respond to a dire moral emergency and not only to uphold a core value of the international legal system, but also with the aim of contributing to the development of a new, morally progressive rule of international law according to which humanitarian intervention without Security Council authorization is sometimes permissible. Let us call this the Illegal Legal Reform Justification. The idea is that existing international law was violated to initiate a moral improvement in the international legal system. In the case of the Kosovo intervention, the needed reform was to make the international legal system do a better job of serving one of its own core values, the protection of human rights.

The Simple Moral Necessity Justification presents the illegal action as morally necessary, without in any way implying that the international legal system as a whole, or even the particular rule that is violated, is in need of improvement. Employing this first justification for illegal humanitarian intervention is fully consistent with believing that the existing rule requiring Security

[3] This use of the term "lawful" is borrowed from Jane Stromseth: see her "Rethinking Humanitarian Intervention: The Case for Incremental Change," in *Humanitarian Intervention: Ethical, Legal, and Political Dilemmas*, eds. J. L. Holzgrefe and Robert O. Keohane (Cambridge, UK: Cambridge University Press, 2003), 244.

Council authorization is a good rule, even that it is the best rule possible. The Simple Moral Necessity argument in itself is also neutral as to the value of the rule of law. It might consistently be advanced by someone who rejected the entire enterprise of international law.

The Lawfulness and the Illegal Legal Reform Justifications differ in that regard. They both express a commitment to the rule of law. The Lawfulness Justification is based on the assumption that the fact that the values served by the intervention are core values of the legal system matters, normatively speaking, adding weight to the justification of moral necessity. The Illegal Legal Reform Justification validates the illegal intervention as an act directed toward improving the legal system.

There is a difference between the Lawfulness and Illegal Legal Reform Justifications, however: the latter, but not the former, implies that the existing rule requiring Security Council authorization is not optimal, and that a new norm of humanitarian intervention, according to which Security Council authorization is not always needed, is morally preferable. The Lawfulness Justification, in contrast, is compatible with the view that even though it is necessary in exceptional cases to break a particular law in the name of a core value embodied in the system, attempts to change the law would make things even worse.

My focus in this chapter is on the third type of justification, the justification of illegal acts of humanitarian intervention by appeal to the goal of legal reform. However, much of what I say will also be applicable to the Lawfulness Justification. Although I believe that illegal acts directed toward reform may bear a special burden of justification, at least for those who profess to value the rule of law, I will argue that in some cases that burden can be met.

Although the Kosovo intervention stimulated consideration of the need for reform, there has been both a lack of clarity regarding the full range of options for how that reform might come about and an almost total neglect of the question of which paths toward reform are morally preferable. My aim in this chapter is to remedy both these deficiencies. What follows is offered as a contribution to that part of the moral theory of international law that addresses the morality of legal reform, including illegal legal reform.

II. *Why Illegal Action May Be Necessary for International Legal Reform*

The Sources of International Law

The prospect that illegal acts may be necessary in order to achieve significant improvements in the international legal system arises because of the difficulty of achieving reform through purely legal means. The ways in which international law can be made significantly limit the options for achieving meaningful reform through legal means alone.

There are two chief sources of international law: treaty and custom. If the target of moral improvement is the development of a norm prohibiting some form of behavior engaged in by more than a few states or the creation of a new norm that allows behavior that previously would have been a violation of the rights of sovereignty that all states enjoy, reform by treaty may be a very slow process if it occurs at all.

Suppose that the goal of reform is to establish a rule of international law that not only requires states to respect human rights within their own borders and to supply periodic reports on their progress in doing so to some international body (as the major human rights covenants stipulate), but that also obligates, or at least permits, the signatories to intervene to halt massive violations of human rights that occur within other states when less intrusive means have failed. Many states will refuse to sign such a treaty. Others may sign but postpone ratification indefinitely. Some may sign and ratify, but weaken the force of the treaty by stating "reservations" regarding some clauses (thereby exempting themselves from their requirements) or by stating "understandings" that interpret burdensome clauses in ways that make them less inimical to state interests.

As an avenue for moral improvements that are both significant and timely, the process by which international *customary* law is formed is perhaps somewhat more promising, but still very difficult and uncertain. In briefest terms, a new norm of customary law is created as the result of the emergence of a persistent pattern of behavior by states, accompanied by the belief on the part of state actors that the behavior in question is legally required or legally permissible (the *opinio juris* requirement).

There are several aspects of this process that substantially limit the efficacy of the customary route toward system improvement. First, international law allows states to opt out of the new customary norm's scope by consistently dissenting from it. Second, how widespread the new pattern of state behavior must be before a new norm can be said to have "crystallized" is not only disputed but probably not capable of a definitive answer. Third, even if a sufficiently widespread and persisting pattern of behavior is established, the satisfaction of the *opinio juris* requirement may be less clear and more subject to dispute. Pronouncements by state leaders may be ambiguous or mixed, in some cases indicating a recognition that the behavior in question is legally required or permissible, in other cases appearing to deny this.

Given these limitations, the efforts of the state or states that first attempt to initiate the process of customary change are fraught with uncertainty. If the new norm they seek to establish addresses a long-standing and widespread pattern of state behavior, and one in which many states profess to be legally entitled to persist, other states may not follow suit. Or, if other states follow suit, they may do so for strictly pragmatic reasons and may attempt to ensure that a new customary rule does not emerge by officially registering that they do not regard their behavior as legally required (thus thwarting satisfaction of the *opinio juris* condition).

The point is that new customary norms do not emerge from a single action or even from a persistent pattern of action by one state or a group of states. Thus the initial effort to create a new customary norm is a gamble. A new norm is created only when the initial behavior is repeated consistently by a preponderance of states over a considerable period of time and only when there is a shift in the legal consciousness of all or most states as to the juridical status of the behavior. At any point the process can break down. For example, if one powerful states dissents from an emerging norm, other states may decide it is prudent to register dissent as well or to refrain from pronouncements that would otherwise count toward satisfying the *opinio juris* requirement. For all these reasons, significant and timely reform through the creation of new customary norms of international law is difficult and uncertain.

Further, it appears that significant change through the development of new customary law will usually, if not always, require illegality. For example, the first acts designed to help create a new norm that limits sovereignty in the name of protecting human rights or redressing inequities in the distribution of wealth between developed and less developed countries will violate the existing legal rules that define sovereignty. Some would go further, arguing that customary legal change always involves illegality in the early stages of the process. At the very least it appears that significant and expeditious reform through the development of new customary norms without illegality is unlikely.

It has long been recognized that reliance on change through the establishment of new custom is a formidable obstacle to fundamental social change. All of the great proponents of the modern state—the state with legislative sovereignty—from Bodin and Hobbes to Rousseau recognized the severe constraints that adherence to the evolution of customary law imposed on the possibilities for reform. They argued that only the power to issue and enforce rules that can overturn even the most deeply entrenched customary norms in domestic society would suffice; thus their insistence on legislative sovereignty. In the international system, however, there is nothing approaching a universal legislature.[4] To summarize: heavy reliance on customary laws, absence of a sovereign universal legislature, and the obvious limitations of the treaty process together result in a system in which reform without illegality is more difficult than in many domestic systems.[5]

Progress through Illegality: Historical Cases

It can be argued that some of the more fundamental moral improvements in the international legal system have resulted, at least in part, from illegal acts. Consider one of the great landmarks of reform: the outlawing of genocide. To a large extent this was an achievement of the Nuremberg War Crimes Tribunal (though at the time the term "genocide" was not part of the legal lexicon). However, a strong case has been made by a number of respected commentators that the "Victor's Justice" at Nuremberg was illegal under existing international law. In particular, it has been argued that there was no customary norm or treaty prohibiting what the Tribunal called "crimes against humanity" at the time World War II occurred. But quite apart from this, it has been argued that even if (contrary to what some commentators say) aggressive war was already prohibited at the time World War II began, there was no international law authorizing the criminal prosecution of individuals for waging or conspiring to wage aggressive war.

---

[4] The UN Charter can be amended but the prospects for amendment that would result in a rule of humanitarian intervention not requiring Security Council authorization are poor because ratification of an amendment requires a two-thirds majority vote in the Security Council that must include all the permanent members.

[5] The foregoing picture of international law's limited resources for lawful moral reform is, of course, a sketch in broad strokes. There are more subtle modes by which international law can be changed. For example, judicial bodies (such as the International Court of Justice) or quasi-judicial bodies (such as the UN Human Rights Committee) can achieve reforms under the guise of interpreting existing law. However, as a broad generalization it is fair to say that these modes for effecting moral improvements are both limited and slow.

There is no denying that the Nuremberg Tribunal contributed to some of the changes in international law that we regard as epitomes of progress—not just the prohibitions of genocide and aggressive war but also the recognition of the rights of human subjects of medical experimentation.[6] Nevertheless, it can be argued that some of the punishments meted out at Nuremberg were illegal.

One could also make the case that a series of illegal actions over several decades played a significant role in one of the other most admirable improvements in the international legal system: the prohibition of slavery. In the late eighteenth and early nineteenth centuries, Britain used the unrivaled power of its navy to attack the transatlantic slave trade.[7] Britain's overall strategy included legal means, in particular the forging of a series of bilateral treaties; but it also undertook illegal searches and seizures of ships flying under the flags of states that had not entered into these treaties, as well as attempts to get other countries to enforce their own laws against commerce in human beings. It is probable that what success Britain had in persuading other states to cooperate in efforts

---

[6] The Nuremberg Code, which prohibits experimentation on human subjects without consent, was drafted as a direct result of the prosecution of the Nazi doctors for their inhumane experiments on unwilling human subjects. See German Territory under Allied Occupation, 1945–55: US Zone, Control Council Law No. 10, *Trials of War Criminals before the Nuremberg Military Tribunals* (Washington, DC: US Government Printing Office, 1949), II:181–83; William J. Bosch, *Judgment on Nuremberg: American Attitudes toward the Major German War-Crimes Trials* (Chapel Hill: University of North Carolina Press, 1970).

[7] Alfred P. Rubin, *Ethics and Authority in International Law* (Cambridge, UK: Cambridge University Press, 1997), 97–130; Reginald Coupland, *The British Anti-slavery Movement* (Oxford: Oxford University Press, 1993), 151–88. Note that in adducing this example, I am not assuming that the motives of the British government were pure, only that a justification for the forcible disruption of the trans-Atlantic slave trade that could have been given was that these illegal actions would contribute toward a moral improvement in the international legal system. Whether those who instigated the policy of disrupting the transatlantic slave trade were motivated by humanitarian concerns or not is irrelevant.

to destroy the slave trade was due in part to its willingness to use illegal force. The destruction of the slave trade was a milestone in the development of a growing human rights movement that eventually issues in the international legal prohibition of slavery, but which also expanded to include other human rights.

Once the role of such illegal acts is acknowledged, it is unwarranted to assume that continued progress will be achieved with reasonable speed and without illegality. On the contrary, given the system's limited resources for change by legal means—and the fact that it is still a state-dominated system in which many of the most serious defects calling for reform lie in the behavior of states—the question of the morality of illegal legal reform is inescapable. Yet discussions of the morality of illegal humanitarian intervention have generally failed to distinguish between justifications that appeal to the goal of legal reform and those that appeal either only to the necessity of doing what is morally right (the Simple Moral Necessity Justification) or to the idea that what is morally right is also supported by values embodied in the existing legal system (the Lawfulness Justification).

III. *The Main Alternatives for Reforming the Law of Humanitarian Intervention*

New Treaty Law—Within or Outside the UN System?

Attempts to create a new international legal rule allowing humanitarian intervention without Security Council authorization through treaty might take either of two very different forms. The first, which has been suggested by the Independent International Commission on Kosovo, is to work for reform through treaty *within* the UN system. This might be accomplished by a General Assembly Resolution specifying a new rule of intervention combined with amendments to the UN Charter (Articles 2(4) and 2(7)) to make the latter consistent with the former.[8] This

---

[8] Independent International Commission on Kosovo, *Kosovo Report* (Oxford: Oxford University Press, 2000).

route toward reform has two attractions: it would require no illegalities and it would be a broadly democratic or majoritarian
reform, issuing from a broad base of support in the international
community.

For the foreseeable future, however, this strategy is extremely
unlikely to work. Given how jealous states tend to be about
infringements on their sovereignty and given how many states
wish to have a free hand to oppress dissenting groups within
their borders, it is doubtful that the majority of the members
of the UN would vote for such a resolution. Even if the needed
two-thirds majority in the General Assembly were mustered, a
two-thirds majority of the Security Council that includes all the
permanent members is also required for amendment. The same
veto power on the part of the permanent members that results
in a failure to authorize humanitarian interventions would most
probably block such a constitutional change.

If reform through treaty within the UN system is unworkable,
proponents of reform should consider the possibility of a treaty-
based approach that simply bypasses the UN system.[9] The most
likely and morally defensible version of this alternative would be
a coalition of liberal-democratic states, bound together by a treaty
that would specify some well-crafted criteria that must be satisfied for intervention to be permissible in the absence of Security
Council authorization. The constraining criteria would presumably include familiar elements of just war theory, such as proportional force and protection of noncombatants, but might also
make a limited concession toward the UN system by requiring
General Assembly or Security Council resolutions condemning
the human rights violations that provoke the need for intervention. This strategy for reform might be undertaken either as a

---

[9] I am indebted to Jeff Holzgrefe for impressing upon me the importance of
taking this strategy seriously.

result of coming to the conclusion that the UN system is un-workable or in an attempt to spur reform in the UN. In either case, it would involve illegality, since the actions to be undertaken by the liberal-democratic coalition would violate existing UN-based law on humanitarian intervention. The hope would be that what was first an intervention treaty among a small number of states would eventually gain wider participation.

The phrase "UN-based law" is chosen deliberately. Proponents of reform through the creation of a liberal-democratic coalition for humanitarian intervention would stress that the UN is not identical with international law. Rather, it is only one, histori-cally contingent, institutional embodiment of the idea of an in-ternational legal system. International law existed before the UN and may exist after the UN's demise. A probing investigation of the possibilities for reforming international law concerning hu-manitarian intervention should evaluate, not simply grant, the assumption that reform must be achieved within the framework of the UN system. This is especially true given the rather dim prospects for reform through treaty within the UN framework.

One cannot assume without argument that the only alternative for responsible reform efforts is to work within the UN system because only in this way can reform be legitimate. First, the le-gitimacy of the UN system itself is open to dispute, chiefly be-cause it rests on state consent under conditions in which many, perhaps most, states are not sufficiently democratic to be able to claim to represent their citizens. Unless states represent their citizens, it is something of a mystery as to why one should think that state consent in itself (read: the consent of undemocratic state leaders) should carry so much normative weight as to be the sole source of legitimacy, especially in a system that is as de-ficient from the standpoint of substantive justice as the existing international legal system. Second, it should not be assumed that legitimacy is an absolute value. In the case of extremely imperfect legal systems, the need for substantive reform—at least when this involves strengthening protection for basic human rights—could sometimes trump legitimacy. In the next section, I will explore these deeper issues of legitimacy and justice in more detail. Here I only want to indicate that it is a mistake simply to dismiss out of hand the possibility that treaty-based reform might be undertaken in a way that bypasses the UN system.

Reform through the Creation of a New Customary Rule of Humanitarian Intervention

Some who recognize the need to reform the law of humanitarian intervention advocate a gradualist, case-by-case process that will eventually result in a new rule of customary international law that would not require Security Council authorization in all cases. Those who hold this view see the NATO intervention as an important step in the process and also intimate that this adds weight to its justification.

As the NATO intervention illustrates, the reform-through-new-custom approach, like the attempt to create the possibility of intervention without Security Council authorization through treaty that bypasses the UN system, will almost certainly involve illegality. At least the initial state actions that contribute toward the creation of a new customary rule that allows intervention without Security Council authorization will violate Articles 2(4) and 2(7) of the Charter.

In the remainder of this chapter, I will focus mainly on reform through the creation of new custom, for three reasons. First, the NATO intervention in Kosovo did not involve any attempt to create a new treaty-based right of humanitarian intervention. Instead, it is best viewed, if we attempt to understand it as an act directed toward legal reform, as a step in the process of creating a new customary norm. Second, if forced to make a prediction, I would speculate that at present reform through the emergence of new customary law is more likely than reform through treaty outside the UN. For these reasons I will turn shortly to an examination of the morality of efforts at reform through the creation of new customary law concerning humanitarian intervention, focusing on the NATO intervention in Kosovo for concreteness.

It might be argued that there is one final reason to concentrate on reform through the creation of new custom. At least at first blush, it appears that the customary law route to reform enjoys a comparative advantage from the standpoint of legitimacy over the option of creating new treaty law outside the UN system: state action only creates a new rule of customary international law if a preponderance of states come to regard that type of action as legal. In other words, the *opinio juris* requirement does something to ensure that new customary law enjoys the support of states other than those actually engaging in the intervention, and surely this contributes to the legitimacy of an intervention, helping to counterbalance the stigma of illegality. Later I will challenge this assertion, arguing that under current conditions, when so many states are flawed by basic injustices and are so undemocratic that they cannot be viewed as representing their peoples, support by a majority of states does little to assure legitimacy.

IV. *Legal Absolutism: The Blanket Condemnation of Illegal Acts*

Two Objections to Conscientious Law-Breaking

Some prominent legal scholars, including J. S. Watson and Alfred Rubin, roundly condemn illegal acts done in the name of morality, including those done for the sake of morally improving the international legal system.[10] Unfortunately, such critics tend to assume rather than argue convincingly that illegalities in the name of system reform are not morally justified.

It appears that the condemnation of illegal acts of reform stems from two complaints: one is that those who commit them fail to

---

[10] Rubin, *Ethics and Authority*, esp. 70–206; J. S. Watson, "A Realistic Jurisprudence of International Law," in *The Yearbook of World Affairs* (London: London Institute of World Affairs, 1980).

show proper fidelity to law; the other is that they are guilty of moral hubris or moral imperialism, being too willing to impose their own views of what is right on others.[11] It will prove helpful, therefore, to distinguish two distinct questions: (1) What is the moral basis of the commitment to bringing international relations under the rule of law? And (2) Under what conditions, if any, can an agent's judgments about what justice requires count as good reasons for attempting to impose rules on others? In order to answer the first question, we need an account of *fidelity to law* that enables us to determine how a would-be reformer should weight the fact that his proposed action is illegal. In order to answer the second question, we need an account of *moral authority* (or legitimacy) that enables us to determine if the would-be reformer is justified in imposing on others a norm to which they have not consented and which they might reject. My strategy will be to construct and evaluate arguments that can be employed to articulate these two complaints.

The Simple Fidelity to Law Argument

Consider first an argument to show that illegal acts of reform are not justifiable because they betray a failure to show a proper fidelity to the law.

1. One ought to be committed to the rule of law in international relations.
2. If one is committed to the rule of law in international relations, then one cannot consistently perform or advocate (what one recognizes to be) illegal acts as a means of morally improving the system of international law.
3. Therefore, one ought not to perform or advocate illegal acts as a means of morally improving the system of international law.

---

[11] My account of the bases of the complaint of those who condemn illegal acts of reform is somewhat reconstructive.

The first step is to clarify the phrase "the rule of law" in the argument in order to understand just why honoring the commitment to the rule of law is important. There are in fact two quite different ways in which critics of illegal reform may be understanding "the rule of law" in the Fidelity Argument. According to the first, "the rule of law" refers to a normatively rich ideal for systems of rules. According to the second, "the rule of law" means something that may be much less normatively demanding, namely, a system of rules capable of preventing a Hobbesian condition of violent chaos. Let us see how the Fidelity Argument fares under these two interpretations.

Fidelity to the Ideal of the Rule of Law

According to the first interpretation, the rule of law is an ideal composed of several elements: laws are to be general, public, not subject to frequent or arbitrary changes; their requirements must be reasonably clear and such that human beings of normal capacities are able to comply with them; those who adjudicate the law should not be judges in their own cases, like cases should be treaty alike; and so on.[12] These requirements help ensure that a system of law provides a stable framework of expectations, so that individuals can plan their projects with some confidence and coordinate their behavior with that of others. They also help mitigate the risk that the law will serve as a weapon wielded by some against others or an instrument for the furthering of their interests at the expense of the interests of others.

There is another element of the rule of law as a normative ideal, which on some accounts is of special importance: the requirement of equality before the law. The precise import of this requirement is, of course, subject to much dispute, but the core idea is that the law is to be applied and enforced impartially.

---

[12] Lon L. Fuller, *The Morality of Law* (New Haven, CT: Yale University Press, 1964), 33–39.

If we read "the rule of law" in the Fidelity Argument as referring to this normatively demanding ideal, as including the requirement of equality before the law, then the argument is subject to a serious and obvious objection. The difficulty is that the international legal system falls far short of the requirement of equality before the law. The most powerful states (such as China, the United States, and the Russian Federation) not only play an arbitrarily disproportionate role in the processes by which international law is made and applied but also are often able to violate the law with impunity.

According to the first interpretation of the Fidelity Argument, it is our moral allegiance to the rule of law as a normative ideal that is supposed to be inconsistent with advocating or committing what we believe to be illegal acts even if they are directed toward reforming the system. But to the extent that the existing system falls far short of the ideal of the rule of law in one of its most fundamental elements, the requirement of equality before the law, allegiance to the ideal exerts less moral pull toward strict fidelity to the rules of the existing system. Indeed, allegiance to the rule of law as an ideal might be thought to make illegal acts *morally obligatory* in a system that does a very poor job of approximating the requirements of the ideal. More specifically, a sincere commitment to the rule of law might be a powerful reason for committing illegal acts directed toward bringing the system closer to fulfillment of the requirement of equality before the law, if there is no lawful way to achieve this reform.[13]

The point is that one cannot move directly from the commitment to the rule of law as an ideal to strict fidelity to existing law. Whether a commitment to the rule of law as an ideal precludes illegal reform actions will depend in part upon the extent to which the existing system approximates the ideal.

---

[13] The problem of achieving greater equality among states is a complex one. One cannot assume that the best or only way to achieve greater equality is by greater democratic participation in the making and application of international law. One alternative would be a system of constitutional checks on

Notice also that the critics' second complaint has little force against illegal acts of reform directed toward making the system better satisfy the requirements of the ideal of the rule of law, especially that of equality before the law. To say that the core accepted elements of the rule of law are merely the personal moral views of the reformers, and that it would therefore be illegitimate to impose them on others, would be extremely inaccurate. Not only are they widely accepted, but unless they are assumed to be highly desirable it is hard to make sense of the idea of fidelity to the law as a moral ideal. In the next subsection we will see that the question of when an agent is morally justified in imposing moral standards on those who do not accept them—has more bite when the moral principles motivating illegal acts of reform are more controversial.

Substantive Justice

There is another reason why a simple appeal to the ideal of the rule of law cannot show that illegal reform acts are never morally justifiable: the extent to which a system of rules exemplifies substantive principles of justice affects the strength of the pull toward compliance. Approximation of the ideal of the rule of law is a necessary, not a sufficient, condition for our being obligated to comply with legal norms, even if a deep commitment to the ideal of the rule of law is assumed. A system might do a reasonably good job of exemplifying the elements of the rule of law and still be seriously defective from the standpoint of substantive

---

actions of more powerful states. For example, international norms specifying when humanitarian intervention is justified might be crafted to reduce the risk that powerful states would abuse them, in two ways: by requiring very high thresholds of human rights abuses before intervention was permitted, and by requiring international monitoring of the process of intervention to facilitate ex post evaluation of whether the requirement of proportionality was met, etc. I am indebted to T. Alexander Aleinikoff and David Luban for emphasizing this point (personal communication).

principles of justice. For example, the system might be compatible with, or even promote, unjust economic inequalities, depending upon the content of the laws of property and the extent to which the current distribution of wealth is the result of past injustices. Similarly, the elements of the ideal might be satisfied, or at least closely approximated, in a system that failed to meet even the most minimal standards of democratic participation. The elements of the rule of law prevent certain kinds of injustices and help ensure the stability and predictability that rational agents need, but they do not capture the whole of justice. And if justice is to enjoy the kind of moral priority that is widely thought to be essential to the very notion of justice, then one cannot assume that illegal acts directed toward eliminating grave injustice in the system are always ruled out by fidelity to the ideal of the rule of law. Since many, indeed perhaps most, extant theories of justice include more than the requirements of the rule of law, it would be very misleading to assume that any illegal action for the sake of reforming the international legal system by making it more just must be the imposition of the reformer's subjective view of morality or merely personal views.

Nevertheless, a more subtle form of the moral authority issue remains: even if it is true that most or even all understandings of justice take it to include more than an approximation of the ideal of the rule of law, there is much disagreement about what justice requires, and it is appropriate to ask what makes it morally justifiable for an actor to try to impose on others the conception of justice she endorses. I take up the moral authority issue below.

Earlier I suggested that an appropriate conception of the ideal of the rule of law would include the requirement of equality before the law. Some might disagree, limiting the ideal of the rule of law to the other elements listed above. If they are right, then this is further confirmation that the rule of law is not the only value that is relevant to assessing the weight of our commitment to fidelity to law. For if equality before the law is not to be included in the ideal of the rule of law, then there is a strong case for including it among the most basic and least controversial principles of justice, at least for those who value the role that law can play in securing justice. But, if that is so, then whether it is morally permissible to violate a law to improve a legal system must surely depend in part on how unjust the system is.

The Legitimacy of the International Legal System

The international legal system not only tolerates extreme economic inequalities among individuals and among states, it legitimizes and stabilizes them in manifold ways, not the least of which is by supporting state sovereignty over resources.[14] In addition, the international legal system is characterized by extreme political inequality among the primary members of the system (states). As already noted, a handful of powerful states wield a disproportionate influence over the creation, and above all the application and enforcement, of international law. Indeed, it is not wholly implausible to argue that the extreme and morally arbitrary political inequality that characterizes the society of formally equal states robs the system of legitimacy.

To make a convincing case that these defects deprive the international legal systems of legitimacy would require articulating and defending a theory of *system* legitimacy.[15] That task lies far beyond the scope of the present discussion. Yet this much can be said: the more problematic a system's claim to legitimacy, the weaker the moral pull of fidelity to its laws, other things being equal. Neither Watson nor Rubin addresses the issue of

---

[14] Henry Shue, *Basic Rights*, 2nd ed. (Princeton, NJ: Princeton University Press, 1980), 131–52; Thomas Pogge, "An Egalitarian Law of Peoples," *Philosophy & Public Affairs* 23, no. 3 (1994): 195–224.

[15] There are two quite different conceptions of legitimacy that are often confused in the writing of political theorists. The first, weaker, conception is that of being morally justified in attempting to exercise a monopoly on the enforcement (or the making and enforcement) of laws within a jurisdiction. The second, stronger, conception, often called "political authority," includes

whether illegal acts of reform may be justified if they hold a reasonable prospect of significantly improving the legitimacy of a system whose legitimacy is at the very least subject to doubt. Nevertheless, there is a way of understanding their opposition to illegal reform as resting on a conception of system legitimacy that emphasizes adherence to the state consent supernorm, the principle that to be international law, a norm must enjoy the consent of states.

Given the existing international legal system's deficiencies from the standpoint of what is either a cardinal element of the ideal of the rule of law or a basic, widely shared principle of justice, namely, equality before the law, and from the standpoint of a fairly wide range of principles of distributive justice as well, and given that the extreme political inequality among the states poses a serious challenge to the legitimacy of the system, it is implausible to assert that a commitment to the rule of law, as a moral ideal, rules out all illegal action for the sake of reform. The very defects of the system that provide the most obvious targets for reform weaken the moral pull of strict fidelity to its existing law.

So far my analysis shows only that there is no simple inference from allegiance to the ideal of the rule of law to the moral unjustifiability of illegal acts directed to system reform. It does not follow, of course, that everything is morally permissible in a system as defective as the international legal system as long as it is done in the name of reform. An important question remains: Given that a commitment to the ideal of the rule of law does not categorically prohibit illegal acts of reform, under what conditions are which sorts of illegal acts of reform morally justified?

---

the weaker condition but in addition includes a correlative obligation to obey the entity said to be legitimate on the part of those over whom jurisdiction is exercise. I have argued elsewhere that it is the former conception, not the latter, that is relevant to discussions of state legitimacy in the international system. I would also argue that this is true for legitimacy of the system. Allen Buchanan, "Recognitional Legitimacy and the State System," *Philosophy & Public Affairs* 28, no. 1 (1999): 46–78.

As a first approximation of an answer, we can say that, other things being equal, illegal acts are more readily justified if they have a reasonable prospect of contributing toward (a) bringing the system significantly closer to the ideal of the rule of law in its most fundamental elements, (b) rectifying the most serious substantive injustices supported by the system, or (c) ameliorating defects in the system that impugn its legitimacy.

The Rule of Law as Necessary for Avoiding Violent Chaos

Our first interpretation of the "rule of law" in the Fidelity Argument understood that phrase in a normatively demanding way: to be committed to the rule of law is to respect and endeavor to promote systems of rules that satisfy or seriously approximate the various elements of this ideal. We saw that on this interpretation the connection between being committed to the rule of law and refusing to violate existing international law is more tenuous and conditional than the critics of illegal reform assume.

The second interpretation of "the rule of law" as it occurs in the Fidelity Argument owes more to Hobbes than to Fuller. The idea is that even if international law falls far short of exemplifying some of the key elements of the ideal of the rule of law and even if it is seriously deficient from the standpoint of substantive justice and legitimacy, it is all that stands between us and violent chaos.[16] On this interpretation of the Fidelity Argument, we are presented with an austere choice: abstaining from illegal acts of reform or risking a Hobbesian war of each against all in international relations.

This is a false dilemma. As a sweeping generalization, the claim that illegal acts of reform run an unconscionable risk of violent

---

[16] Watson can perhaps be interpreted as endorsing this version of the Fidelity Argument. He strongly emphasizes that international law will only be effective in constraining the behavior of states if it is consensual and rejects illegal acts of reform as being incompatible with the requirement of consent (Watson, "Realistic Jurisprudence," 265, 270, 275). The chief difficulty with this line of argument is that, while it would be extremely implausible to say that there must

anarchy is implausible. It would be more plausible if two assumptions were true: (a) the existence of the international order depends solely upon the efficacy of international law; and (b) international law is a seamless web, so that cutting one fiber (violating one norm) will result in an unraveling of the entire fabric.

The first assumption is dubious. It overestimates the role of law by underestimating the contributions of political and economic relations and the various institutions of transnational civil society to peace and stability in international relations. But even if the first assumption were justified, the second, "seamless web," assumption is farfetched. History refutes it. As we have already noted, there have been illegal acts that were directed toward, and that actually contributed to, significant reforms, yet they did not result in a collapse of the international legal system.

Respect for the State Consent Supernorm

Some critics of illegal reform, including Watson and Rubin, are especially troubled by the willingness of reformers to violate what these critics believe is an essential (constitutional) feature of the existing international legal system: the state consent supernorm, a secondary rule (in Hart's sense of that term) according to which law is to be made and changed only by the consent of states.[17] (As was noted earlier, the requirement of state consent here is understood in a very loose way to be satisfied either by ratification of treaties or through conformity to norms that achieve the status of customary law.) The question, then, is this: Why is the state consent supernorm of such importance that illegal acts of reform that violate it are never morally justified? There appear

---

be perfect compliance with the law for it to be effective, Watson does nothing to indicate either what level of compliance is needed for effectiveness or what counts as effectiveness.

[17] Rubin, *Ethics and Authority*, 190–91, 205, 206; Watson, "Realistic Jurisprudence," 265, 270, 275.

to be three answers worth considering: (1) only if the state consent supernorm is strictly observed will violent chaos be avoided, because only state consent can render international law effective; (2) state consent is the only mechanism for creating effective norms of peaceful relations among states that is capable of conferring legitimacy upon international norms; or (3) the state consent supernorm ought to be strictly adhered to because doing so reduces the risk that stronger states will prey on weaker ones.

Thesis (1)

The general claim that compliance with legal norms can only be achieved if those whose behavior is regulated by the norms consent to them is clearly false. In the case of domestic legal systems, virtually no one would assert that consent to every norm is necessary for effectiveness. So if the importance of consent is to supply a decisive reason against acts of reform that violate the state consent supernorm in international law, it must be because there is something special about the international arena that makes consent necessary if law is to be effective enough to avoid violent chaos.

If the realist theory of international relations were correct, it would provide an answer to the question of what that something special is. According to the realist theory, the structure of international relations precludes moral action except where it happens to be congruent with state interest. The importance of creating norms by state consent, on this view, is that it provides a way for states, understood as purely self-interested actors, to promote their shared long-term interests in peace and stability. Unless realism is correct, it is hard to see why we should assume that consent is necessary for effective law in the international case, while acknowledging, as we must, that it is not necessary for effectiveness in domestic systems.

Realism has been vigorously attacked, most systematically by contributors to the liberal theory of international relations.

Because I believe these attacks are telling, I will not reenact now all too familiar argumentative battles between realists and their critics. Instead, I will focus on the second and third versions of the argument that a proper appreciation of the consensual basis of existing international law precludes justifiable acts of illegal reform.[18]

Thesis (2)

This is the view that what is morally attractive about the existing international legal system is not just that it avoids the Hobbesian abyss, but that it does so by relying upon the only mechanism for creating and changing norms of peaceful interaction that can confer *legitimacy* upon norms, given the character of international relations.[19] (A legitimate norm, here, is understood as one that it is morally justifiable to enforce and whose demands those to whom it is addressed ought to be taken seriously.)

The underlying assumption is that the members of the so-called community of states are moral strangers, that the state system is a mere association of distinct societies that do not share substantive ends of a conception of justice, rather than a genuine community.[20] In the absence of shared substantive ends or a common

---

[18] The literature exposing the deficiencies of the various forms of realism in international relations is voluminous. Of particular value are Charles Beitz, *Political Theory and International Relations* (Princeton, NJ: Princeton University Press, 1979), 3–66; and writings on the liberal theory of international relations by Anne-Marie Slaughter, "International Law in a World of Liberal States," *European Journal of International Law* 6, no. 1 (1995): 503–38; and Andrew Moravcsik, "Taking Preferences Seriously: A Liberal Theory of International Politics," *International Organization* 51, no. 4 (1997): 513–53.

[19] Terry Nardin, *Law, Morality, and the Relations of States* (Princeton, NJ: Princeton University Press, 1983), 5–13; John Rawls, *The Law of Peoples* (Cambridge, MA: Harvard University Press, 1999), 51–120.

[20] Nardin acknowledges that states do share some ends, for example, the flourishing of international trade, but his view seems to be that what is distinctive about international law is that it binds states together in the absence of shared substantive ends.

conception of justice, consent is the only basis of legitimacy for a system of norms. Within domestic societies, there are moral-political cultures that are "thick" enough to fund shared substantive ends or conceptions of justice and hence to provide a basis for legitimacy without consent; but not so in international "society." But if state consent is the only basis for legitimacy in the international system, then illegal acts of reform that violate the state consent supernorm, such as illegal interventions to support democracy or to prevent massive violations of human rights in ethnic conflicts within states, strike at the very foundation of international law and hence are not morally justifiable, at least for those who profess to be committed to reforming that system.[21]

The most obvious defect of this line of argument is that its contrast between international society as a collection of moral strangers and domestic society as an ethical community united by a "thick" culture of common values is overdrawn. Especially in liberal societies, which tolerate and even promote pluralism, whatever it is that legitimates the system of legal rules, it cannot be shared substantive ends or even a shared conception of justice. What Thesis (2) overlooks is that democratic politics in liberal domestic societies includes deliberation—and heated controversy— over which substantive ends to pursue, not simply over which means to use to pursue shared substantive ends.

In particular, liberal domestic societies often contain deep divisions as to conceptions of distributive justice, with some citizens espousing "welfare-state" conceptions and others "minimal state" or libertarian conceptions. Yet such societies somehow manage to avoid violent chaos and also appear to be capable of having legal systems that are legitimate.

An advocate of Thesis (2) might respond relying on Rawls's views in *Political Liberalism* and *The Law of Peoples*, that the members of liberal societies do share what might be called a core

---

[21] Watson, "Realistic Jurisprudence," 268.

conception of justice—the idea that society is a cooperative venture among persons conceived as free and equal—but that there is no globally shared core conception of justice.[22] Hence adherence to the state consent supernorm is necessary in international law, but not in domestic law.

There are three difficulties with this response. First, divisions within liberal domestic societies, especially concerning distributive justice, may be so deep that we must conclude either that (a) there is no shared core conception of justice; or that (b) if there is, it is so vague and elastic that it cannot serve as a foundation for a legitimate system of legal norms. (Even if it is true that welfare-state liberals and libertarians both hold that society is a cooperative endeavor among "free and equal" persons, their respective understandings of freedom and equality diverge sharply.) Second, and more important, even if it is, or once was, true that value pluralism among states is much deeper than within them, there is evidence that this may be changing. As many commentators have stressed, international legal institutions, as well as the forces of economic globalization, have contributed to the development of a transnational civil society in which a culture of human rights is emerging. This culture of human rights is both founded on, and serves to extend, a shared conception of basic human interests and a conception of the minimal institutional arrangements needed to protect them.[23] Moreover, the canonical language of the major human rights documents indicates a tendency toward convergence that may be as good a candidate for a core shared conception of justice as that which Rawls attributes to liberal societies: the idea that human beings have an inherent equality and freedom. So even if it is true that a system of legal norms can be

[22] Rawls, *Law of Peoples*, 51–120; John Rawls, *Political Liberalism* (New York: Columbia University Press, 1993), 89–172.
[23] For a valuable exposition and defense of the idea of a global culture of human rights, see Rhoda E. Howard, *Human Rights and the Search for Community* (Boulder, CO: Westview Press, 1995), 120.

legitimate only if it is supported by a common culture of basic values or a shared core conception of justice, it is not clear that international society is so lacking in moral consensus that state consent must remain an indispensable condition if norms are to be legitimate.

There is a third, much more serious, objection to the proposition that illegal acts of reform that violate the state consent supernorm are morally justifiable because they undermine the only basis for legitimacy in the international legal system: due to the very defects at which illegal acts of reform are directed, the normative force of state consent in the present system is morally questionable at best.

What is called state consent is really the consent of state leaders. But in the many states in which human rights are massively and routinely violated and where democratic institutions are lacking, state leaders cannot reasonably be regarded as agents of their people.[24] Where human rights are massively violated, individuals are prevented or deterred from participating in processes of representation, consultation, and deliberation that are necessary if state leaders are to function as agents of the people capable of exercising authority on their behalf.

But if state leaders are not agents of their people, then it cannot be said that state consent is binding because it expresses the people's will. How, then, can the consent of individuals who cannot reasonably be viewed as agents of the people they claim to represent confer legitimacy? Illegal acts directed toward creating the only conditions under which state consent could confer legitimacy cannot be ruled out as morally unjustifiable on the grounds that they violate the norm of state consent.

This is not to say that the requirement of state consent, under present conditions, is without benefit or that the benefits it brings are irrelevant to the question of whether the system is legitimate.

---

[24] Fernando R. Tesón, *A Philosophy of International Law* (Boulder, CO: Westview Press, 1998), 39–41.

It can be argued, as I have already suggested, that adherence to the state consent supernorm has considerable instrumental value, quite apart from the inability of state consent as such to confer legitimacy on norms. This is the point of the third thesis about the importance of the state consent requirement.

Thesis (3)

This account of why the state consent supernorm is so important as to preclude illegal acts of reform that violate it is much more plausible than the first two. It does not assume that any violation of the norm of state consent poses an unacceptable risk of violent chaos, nor that state consent is supremely valuable because only it can achieve peace through norms that are legitimate. The proponent of Thesis (3) can cheerfully admit that law can be effective without consent and that under existing conditions, state consent is in itself incapable of conferring legitimacy on the norms consented to. Instead, her point is that adherence to the state consent supernorm is so instrumentally valuable for reducing predation by stronger states upon weaker ones that it ought not to be violated even for the sake of system reform. Thesis (3) relies on the empirical prediction that if the international legal system fails to preserve the formal political equality of states by adhering to the state consent supernorm, the material inequalities among states will result in predatory behavior and in violations of individual human rights as well as rights of self-determination that predation inevitably entails.[25]

It is no doubt true that the state consent supernorm provides valuable protection for weaker states. But even if this is so, it does not follow that acts of reform that violate the state consent supernorm are never morally justifiable. Acts of reform that are very likely to make a significant contribution to making the

---

[25] Benedict Kingsbury, "Sovereignty and Inequality," *European Journal of International Law* 9, no. 4 (1998): 599–625.

system more egalitarian—that contribute to increasing the substantive political equality of states, thereby reducing the risk of predation—may be morally justified under certain circumstances, even if they violate the state consent supernorm.

Another way to put this point is to note that the instrumental argument for strict adherence to the state consent supernorm is very much a creature of non-ideal theory. At least from the standpoint of a wide range of theories of distributive justice, the existing global distribution of resources and wealth is seriously unjust. But presumably these injustices play a major role in the inequalities of power among states. If the system became more distributively just, the inequalities of power that create opportunities for predation would diminish, and with them the threat of predation and the instrumental value of the state consent supernorm.

What this means is that there is nothing inconsistent in both appreciating the value of adherence to the state consent supernorm as a way of reducing predation and being willing to violate it in order to bring about systemic changes that will undercut the conditions for predation. The difficulty for the responsible reformer lies in determining when the prospects for actually achieving a significant reform in the direction of greater equality or justice are good enough to warrant undertaking an action that may have the effect of weakening what may be the best bulwark against predation the system presently possesses. While the instrumental (antipredation) argument may be powerful enough to create a strong presumption—for the time being—against violating the state consent supernorm, it is hard to see how it can provide a categorical prohibition on illegal acts of reform.

Furthermore, observing the state consent supernorm is not the only mechanism for reducing the risk of predation. The theory and practice of constitutionalism in domestic legal systems offer a variety of mechanisms for checking abuses of power. For example, a norm requiring that individual states or groups of states may intervene in domestic conflicts to protect human rights only when explicitly authorized to do so by a supermajority vote in the UN General Assembly would provide a valuable constraint on great power abuses.

The results of this section can now be briefly summarized. I have argued that the notion of fidelity to law cannot provide a decisive reason for refraining from committing illegal acts directed toward reforming the international legal system. A sincere commitment to the ideal of the rule of law is not only consistent with illegal acts of reform; it may in some cases make such acts obligatory. Further, it is not plausible to argue that illegal acts of reform always constitute an unacceptable threat to peace and stability. Finally, I have argued that being willing to commit an illegal act of reform need not be inconsistent with a proper appreciation of the need to provide weaker states with protection against predation. I now turn to the other main challenge to illegal international legal reform: the charge that reformers wrongly impose their own personal or subjective views of morality upon others.

V. *Moral Authority*

The Charge of Subjectivism

Opponents of illegal reform, such as Watson and Rubin, heap scathing criticism on those who would impose their own personal or subjective views of morality or justice on others. The suggestion is that those who endorse violations of international law, and especially those who disregard the state consent supernorm, are intolerant ideologues who would deny to others the right to do what they do. It is a mistake, however, to assume, as these critics apparently do, that the only alternatives are arrogant subjectivism or strict adherence to legality.

Internalist Moral Criticism of the System

An agent who seeks to breach international law in order to initiate a process of bringing about a moral improvement in the system need not be appealing to a subjective or merely personal view about morality. Instead, she may be relying upon moral values that are already expressed in the system and, to the extent that the system is consensual, upon principles that are widely shared. In fact, it appears that some who were sympathetic to NATO's intervention in Kosovo, including UN Secretary-General Kofi Annan, believed that this intervention was supported by one of the most morally defensible fundamental principles of the international legal system, the obligation to protect human rights, even though it was inconsistent with another principle of the system, the norm of sovereignty understood as prohibiting intervention in the domestic affairs of the former Yugoslav Republic.[26] To describe those who supported the intervention by appealing to basic human rights principles internal to the system as ideologues relying on a merely personal or subjective moral view is wildly inaccurate.

Two Views of Moral Authority

Since the appearance of Rawls's book *Political Liberalism* there has been a complex and spirited debate about the nature of what I have called moral authority. Two main rival views have emerged. According to the first, which Rawls himself offers, moral authority, understood as the right to impose rules on others, is subject to a requirement of reasonableness. It is morally justifiable to impose on others only those principles that they could reasonably accept from the standpoint of their own comprehensive conceptions of the good or of justice, with the proviso that the latter fall within the range of the reasonable.[27] Rawls has a rather undemanding notion of what counts as a reasonable conception of the good or of justice: so long as the view is logically consistent

---

[26] Kofi Annan, "Speech to the General Assembly," SG/SM/7136 GA/9569: Secretary-G, September 20, 1999, 2.
[27] Rawls, *Political Liberalism*, 136–7.

or coherent and includes the idea that every person's good should count in the design of basic social institutions, it counts as reasonable. As I have argued elsewhere, Rawls's conception of moral authority counts as reasonable grossly inegalitarian societies, including those that include systematic, institutionalized racism or caste systems or systems that discriminate systematically against women.[28]

Grossly and arbitrarily inegalitarian social systems count as reasonable on Rawls's view because the requirement that everyone's good is to count is compatible with the good of some counting very little compared to that of others. To that extent Rawls's conception of reasonableness is at odds with some aspects of existing international human rights law, including the right against discrimination on grounds of gender, religion, or race.

The root idea of the Rawlsian conception of moral authority is respect for persons' reasons in the light of what Rawls calls "the burdens of judgment." To acknowledge the burdens of judgment is to appreciate that, due to a number of factors, reasonable people can disagree on the principles of public order. Like Rubin and Watson, Rawls is concerned about those who assume that their belief that certain moral principles are valid is sufficient to give them the moral authority to impose those principles on others. In that sense, Rawls's reasonableness condition is an attempt to rule out the imposition of purely personal or subjective moral views.

However, Rawls's reasonableness criterion does not rule out imposing moral standards that others do not consent to. What people can reasonably accept, given their moral views, and what they actually do accept or consent to may differ. So, according to the Rawlsian conception of moral authority (or, in his preferred term, legitimacy), acts of reform that violate the state consent

---

[28] Allen Buchanan, "Justice, Legitimacy, and Human Rights," in *The Idea of a Political Liberalism: Essays on Rawls*, eds. Victoria Davion and Clark Wolf (Lanham, MD: Rowman & Littlefield, 2000), 73–89.

supernorm are not necessarily unjustifiable, even if we slide over the problem of inferring the consent of persons from the consent of states.

Rawls's conception of moral authority focuses almost exclusively on one aspect of being reasonable, or of showing respect for the reasons of others: humility in the face of the burdens of judgment. His only acknowledgment that reasons must be of a certain quality to warrant respect and toleration is the very weak requirement of logical consistency or coherence.

A quite different conception of moral authority acknowledges the burdens of judgment and also affirms that part of what it is to respect persons is to respect them as beings who have their own views about what is good and right but places more emphasis on what might be called "epistemic responsibility" as an element of reasonableness.[29] According to this view, respect for persons' reasons does not require that we regard as reasonable any moral view that meets Rawls's rather minimal requirements of logical consistency or coherence and of taking everyone's good into account in some way. In addition, to be reasonable, and hence worthy of toleration, a moral view must be supported by a justification that meets certain minimal standards of rationality.

In other words, to be worthy of respect moral views must be supported by reasoning and reasoning that is of a certain minimal quality that goes beyond logical consistency or coherence. In particular, it must be possible to provide a justification for a moral view that does not rely on grossly false empirical claims about human nature (or about the nature of blacks, or women, or "untouchables") and which does not involve clearly invalid inferences based on grossly faulty standards of evidence. The intuitive appeal of this more demanding conception of what sorts

---

[29] Thomas Christiano, "On Rawls's Argument for Toleration," unpublished paper; Allen Buchanan, *Justice, Legitimacy, and Self-determination: Moral Foundations for International Law* (New York: Oxford University Press, 2007).

of views are entitled to toleration lies in the idea that respect for persons' reasons requires that those reasons meet certain minimal standards of rationality, the underlying idea being that it is respect for persons' reasoning, not their opinions, that matters. Also according to this conception of moral authority, it is a mistake to assume that anyone who tries to reform the international legal system by performing acts that are violations of its existing norms is thereby imposing on others her purely personal or subjective moral views. The charge of subjectivity should be reserved for those views that do not meet the minimal standards of epistemic responsibility. Different versions of this view would propose different ways of fleshing out the idea that epistemic responsibility requires more than mere logical consistency or coherence.

My aim here is not to resolve the debate about what constitutes moral authority (though I have argued elsewhere that the epistemic responsibility view is superior to the Rawlsian view).[30] Instead, I have introduced two rival conceptions of moral authority, in order to show that both create a space between rigid adherence to existing consensual international law and the attempt to impose purely subjective, personal moral beliefs in violation of existing law. So even though it is correct to say that purely subjective or merely personal moral views cannot provide a moral justification for illegal acts of reform, it does not follow that anyone who breaks the law is merely acting on a subjective or personal view.

Watson and Rubin are quite correct to question the moral authority of proponents of illegal reform. Merely believing that one is right is not a sufficient reason for doing much of anything, much less for violating the law or trying to initiate a process that will result in imposing laws on others without their consent. But they are mistaken to assume that those who advocate illegal acts

[30] Buchanan, "Justice, Legitimacy, and Human Rights"; and *Justice, Legitimacy, and Self-Determination.*

of system reform must lack moral authority, and they offer no account of moral authority to show that illegal reformists must, or typically will, lack moral authority.

In addition, as I have already argued, quite apart from whether either the Rawlsian conception of moral authority of the epistemic responsibility conception is correct, those who brand all proponents of illegal reform "subjectivists" entirely overlook the fact that in some cases, perhaps most, the reformer's justification is internalist, appealing to widely shared moral principles already expressed in the system. It does not follow that these internal values of the system are beyond criticism, but they are not purely subjective or merely personal; instead, they are widely held, systematically institutionalized values. In appealing to the internal values of the system in order to justify an illegal act, the reformer is doing precisely what reformers (as opposed to revolutionaries) do: trying to see that the system does a better job of realizing the values it already embodies and is supposed to promote. The proper lesson to draw from Watson and Rubin's worries about moral subjectivism is that the justification of illegal acts of reform must rest upon a conception of moral authority, not that no justification can succeed.

VI. *Reforming International Law Regarding Humanitarian Intervention*

The Need for a Moral Theory of Reform

Assuming that the international law of humanitarian intervention is in need of reform, critical and systematic thinking is needed to determine how reform would best be achieved. Plainly, any proposal for reform should score well on the requirement of feasibility, but that is not sufficient. In addition, proposals for reform must pass the test of moral evaluation. In this section I propose a set of guidelines that those embarking on reform efforts should take into account.

I focus on illegal acts directed toward reform because I believe it is illegal acts that encounter the most resistance and that a special burden of justification must be borne by anyone who proposes to violate existing law in the name of legal reform. In the next subsection, I focus on special guidelines for evaluating the morality of acts directed toward reform through the creation of a new customary law of intervention that applies due to peculiarities of the customary process, in particular the satisfaction of the *opinio juris* requirement.

Guidelines for Determining the Moral Justifiability of Illegal Acts of Reform

The problem of illegal reform is located in the part of non-ideal normative theory of international law that deals with how we are to move toward the institutional arrangements prescribed by ideal theory. We are now in a position to articulate some of the key considerations that such a non-ideal theory would have to include. My aim here is not to offer a developed, comprehensive theory of the morality of transition from non-ideal toward ideal conditions, but only to sketch some of its broader outlines so far as it addresses the problem of illegal acts of reform directed toward the creation of new international law concerning humanitarian intervention. To do this I will articulate and justify a set of guidelines for assessing the morality of proposed illegal acts directed toward the moral improvement of the system of international law.

The guidelines are derived from the preceding analysis of the objections to illegal acts of reform. While none of those objections rules out the moral justifiability of illegal acts of reform, they do supply significant cautionary considerations that a responsible agent would take into account in determining whether to engage in an illegal act aimed at reforming the system. I will then clarify the import of the guidelines and demonstrate their power by applying them to the recent NATO intervention in Kosovo.

An important limitation of the guidelines should be emphasized: they are not designed to provide comprehensive conditions for the justification of humanitarian intervention. Instead, they are to be applied to proposals for illegal interventions directed toward legal reform once the familiar and widely acknowledged conditions for justified intervention are already satisfied. Among the most important of these familiar conditions is the principle of proportionality, which requires that the intervention not produce as much harm (especially to the innocent) as, or more harm than, the harm it seeks to prevent. Much of the criticism of NATO's intervention in Kosovo focuses on the failure to satisfy this requirement.

My concern, however, is with the special justificatory issues raised by the illegality of an act of intervention that is directed toward system reform. To respond to these justificatory issues, I offer the following guidelines.

1. Other things being equal, the closer a system approximates the ideal of the rule of law (the better job it does of satisfying the more important requirements that constitute that ideal), the greater the burden of justification for illegal acts.
2. Other things being equal, the less seriously defective the system is from the standpoint of the most important requirements of substantive justice, the greater the burden of justification for illegal acts.
3. Other things being equal, the more closely the system approximates the conditions for being a legitimate system (i.e., the stronger the justification for attempts to achieve enforcement of the rules of the system), the greater the burden of justification for illegal acts.
4. Other things being equal, an illegal act that violates one of the most fundamental morally defensible principles of the system bears a greater burden of justification.

5. Other things being equal, an illegal act that violates a relatively self-contained body of law within the overall system, and therefore with a lower probability of the violation adversely affecting other parts of the system, the weaker the presumption against violating it.

6. Other things being equal, the greater the improvement, the stronger the case for committing the illegal act that is directed toward bringing it about; and if the state of affairs the illegal act is intended to bring about would not be an improvement in the system, then the act cannot be justified as an act of reform.

7. Other things being equal, illegal acts that are likely to improve significantly the legitimacy of the system are more easily justified.

8. Other things being equal, illegal acts that are likely to improve the most basic dimensions of substantive justice in the system are more easily justified.

9. Other things being equal, illegal acts that are likely to contribute to making the system more consistent with its most morally defensible fundamental principles are more easily justified.

The Rationale for the Guidelines

The basic rationale common to all the guidelines is straightfoward. They provide a way of gauging (a) whether any given illegal act can accurately be described as being directed toward reform of the system and, if so, (b) whether committing it is compatible with a sincere commitment to bringing international relations under the rule of law. The guidelines articulate the considerations that an ideal agent who is committed to pursuing justice through legal institutions, but cognizant of the deficiencies of the existing system, would take into account in determining whether to commit or endorse an illegal act of legal reform. This characterization of such an agent is intended to be abstract, allowing for the fact that different agents may have different views about what justice requires. Thus the guidelines are intended to provide guidance without presupposing a particular theory of justice.

Guideline 1 captures the idea that, for those who are committed to the ideal of the rule of law, the fact that a system closely approximates that ideal provides a presumption in favor of compliance with its rules. Guideline 2 is a reminder that satisfying the formal requirements of the ideal of the rule of law is not sufficient for assessing the moral quality of a legal system and hence for determining the weight of the presumption that we ought to comply with its rules. In addition to satisfying or seriously approximating the ideal of the rule of law, a legal system ought to promote substantive justice. The elements of the rule of law supply important constraints on the sorts of rules that may be employed in pursuit of the goal of substantive justice, but they are not the only factor relevant to assessing the moral quality of the system—how well the system promotes the goal of substantive justice also matters. In the case of the international legal system, it is relatively uncontroversial to say that the most widely accepted human rights norms constitute the core of substantive justice (to call this a subjective or purely personal view would be bizarre). To the extent that the protection of human rights is an internal goal of the international legal system, the appeal for substantive justice is an appropriate consideration in determining whether illegal action is morally justifiable and cannot be dismissed as the imposition of purely personal or subjective moral views.

Guideline 3 rests on the assumption that the conditions that make the system legitimate, including preeminently its capacity to promote substantive justice within the constraints of the ideal of the rule of law, give us moral reasons to support it and that consequently we should be more reluctant, other things being equal, to violate its rules if it scores well on the criterion of legitimacy.

Guideline 4 follows straightforwardly from the fundamental commitment to supporting the international legal system as an important instrument for achieving justice. The reformer, by definition, is someone who is striving to bring about a moral improvement in the system. Accordingly, she must consider not only the improvement that may be gained through an illegal act, but also the need to preserve what is valuable in the system as it is. This same consideration supports guideline 5.

Guideline 6 is commonsensical, stating that the justifiability of the illegal act of legal reform depends upon whether, and if so to what extent, the state of affairs the act is intended to bring about would constitute an improvement in the system. In the case of an illegal act intended to help create a new customary norm, this means that the new norm must actually be an improvement over the status quo.

Guideline 7 acknowledges a fundamental tension in the enterprise of trying to develop a morally defensible system of law: on the one hand, a person who seeks to reform a legal system, qua reformer, values the indispensable contribution that law can make to protecting human rights and serving other worthy moral values; on the other hand, she appreciates that the enterprise of law involves the coercive imposition of rules and that for this to be justified the system must meet certain moral standards. What this means is that the project of trying to develop the legal system to achieve the goal of justice must be accompanied by efforts to ensure that the system has the features needed to make the pursuit of justice through its processes morally justifiable. Thus guideline 7 acknowledges the distinction between justice and legitimacy and emphasizes that anyone who is committed to working within the system to improve it should take the legitimacy of the system itself as an important goal for reform.

Guideline 8, like guideline 3, emerges from my criticism of those opponents of illegal reform who make the mistake of thinking that conformity with the ideal of the rule of law is all we should ask of a legal system. There I argued that whether a legal system achieves, or at least is compatible with, the substantive requirement of justice is relevant to determining the system's moral pull toward compliance. My discussion of alternative views of moral authority showed that, while Watson and Rubin are correct to condemn those who would attempt to impose subjective, that is, purely personal, conceptions of substantive justice on the legal system, illegal reform for the sake of improving the substantive justice of the system is compatible with recognizing a reasonable requirement of moral authority and hence with acting from moral commitments that are not subjective in any damaging sense.

Guideline 8 is also intuitively plausible. A reformer who commits an illegal act that can reasonably be expected to make the system conform better to its own best principles is acting so as to support the system and, to that extent, the presumption against acting illegally that supporters of the system should acknowledge is weakened.

Guideline 9 reflects another desideratum for a system of law. Coherence is important, both from the standpoint of moral justification and because it enhances the ability of individuals to operate effectively under the system's rules by increasing the predictability of the legal consequences of their actions in the absence of fine-grained, expert knowledge of all of the system's complexities. Coherence among the most important elements of the system is of special importance, at least from the standpoint of the system's moral justification.

A word of caution is in order. The guidelines proceed on the assumption that content can be given to the idea of improving the system morally and they employ the notion of justice. However, they are intended neither to provide a comprehensive moral theory nor to supply content for the notion of justice. They are designed to provide guidance for a responsible actor who values the rule of law in international relations and is aware of both the system's need for improvement and the difficulties of achieving expeditious change by strictly legal means. It is inevitable that different agents may reach different conclusions about whether a particular illegal act directed toward system reform is morally justifiable, just as conscientious individuals can disagree as to whether a particular act of civil disobedience in a domestic system is morally justified. In some cases these different conclusions will be the result of different understandings of justice. But without having settled all disputes about what justice is, it is still possible to show that an actor who is sincerely committed to the rule of law in international relations, and who believes the existing system is worthy of efforts to reform it, can consistently perform or advocate illegal acts of reform. And it is possible to develop guidelines for responsible choices regarding illegal acts of reform.

NATO Intervention in Kosovo: A Test Case

The guidelines must be abstract if they are to cover a wide range of possible illegal acts of reform. To appreciate their value and to clarify their meaning, I will apply them to NATO's intervention in Kosovo. I will assume (following what I believe to be the preponderance of informed legal opinion) this was an illegal act. I noted in the first section that three quite different types of justifications could be given for the intervention. My concern in this chapter is with the third type, the Illegal Legal Reform Justification. So the question is: How does this illegal act, justified in this way, fare with regard to the eight guidelines for assessing the moral justifiability of illegal acts of system reform?

It would be difficult to argue that guidelines 1, 2, or 3 weigh conclusively against NATO's intervention in Kosovo. As I have already noted, the existing system of international law departs seriously from the ideal of the rule of law, at least so far as this includes the principle of equality before the law, falls short of satisfying the substantive principles of justice, including those, such as human rights norms, that are internal to the system, and can be challenged on grounds of legitimacy because of the morally arbitrary way in which international law is often selectively applied in the interest of the stronger. The fact that the morally arbitrary permanent member veto has repeatedly thwarted morally plausible humanitarian interventions is also relevant here.

From the standpoint of guideline 4, the intervention in Kosovo initially looks problematic, simply because of the charge that its illegality consisted in the violation of one of the most fundamental principles of the system, the norm of sovereignty articulated in Articles 2(7), 2(4), and Chapter VII of the UN Charter, which forbid armed intervention except in cases of self-defense of Security Council authorization. However, guideline 4 refers to the most morally defensible fundamental norms of the existing legal system. If the new customary norm of intervention that the illegal act is intended to help establish would in fact constitute a major improvement in the system, it would do so by restricting sovereignty, and this implies that the norm of sovereignty in its current form is not fully defensible. In other words, the reformist rationale for acting in violation of the existing norms of sovereignty so as to help establish a new customary norm of intervention is that the existing norm of sovereignty creates a zone of protected behavior for states that is too expansive, at the expense of the protection of human rights. The more dubious the moral defensibility of the principle of the system that the illegal act violates is, the less force guideline 4 has as a barrier to illegal action. In cases where the establishment of a new norm through illegal action would constitute a major improvement because the existing norm that is violated is seriously defective, guideline 4 poses no barrier to illegal action. So whether guideline 4 counts for or against NATO's intervention in Kosovo depends upon whether the change the illegal act is aimed at producing would in fact be a major moral improvement in the system, which is addressed in guidelines 5–8.

The import of guideline 5 for the Kosovo intervention is perhaps less than clear. Nonetheless, even though the UN Charter's prohibition on humanitarian intervention without Security Council authorization is one element of an especially important body of international law, the law of international security, it is not clear that it is very closely connected with many other important areas of international law. In fact, a distinctive feature of international law, as a broad generalization, is that it is highly modularized or, as some would say, fragmented. It is far from being a seamless web, likely to unravel if one thread is severed.

Consider next guideline 6. Recall that the act in question is aimed at the establishment of a new customary norm and that the process by which new customary norms are created is a complex, multistage one in which there are many opportunities for failure. Above all, it is important to remember that whether a new customary norm of intervention will arise will depend not just upon what NATO did in this case but upon whether a stable pattern of similar interventions comes about, upon whether states persistently dissent from the propriety of such interventions, and upon whether those who contribute to establishing a stable pattern of similar interventions do so in a way that satisfies the *opinio juris* requirement. Given these inherent uncertainties of the effort to bring about moral improvement through the creation of a new customary norm, an actor contemplating an illegal act of reform of this sort should be on very firm ground in judging that the new norm would in fact be a major improvement. In the next subsection I will argue that this condition was not met in the case of NATO's intervention in Kosovo.

With respect to guideline 7, it could be argued that since one of the chief justifying functions of the system of international law is now recognized to be the protection of human rights, humanitarian military interventions to protect the most basic human rights actually enhance the legitimacy of the system, even if they are illegal. One reason that guideline 7 is qualified with the phrase "other things being equal," however, is that in evaluating whether a humanitarian intervention was justified—and especially in order to determine whether the special burden of justifying illegal acts was met—one must also consider the violations of human rights caused by the intervention. In the case of the Kosovo intervention, there is considerable controversy as to whether the violence prevented by the intervention clearly outweighed the violence it inflicted—including the killing and wounding of noncombatants.

Guideline 8 is clearly satisfied. The protection of human rights is a fundamental component of substantive justice. It is also, as I have emphasized, a core value of the international legal system.

Consider now guideline 9. It is tempting to assume that, from the standpoint of substantive justice, the Kosovo intervention scores high because the establishment of a norm authorizing intervention into internal conflicts to prevent massive human rights violations would constitute a major improvement in the system. Moreover, the charge of subjectivism (lack of moral authority) rings hollow in this sort of case because, as Kofi Annan suggested, the protection of human rights is a core value that is internal to the system. However, whether or not the NATO intervention can be described as an act of illegal reform that would, if successful, bring about a major improvement in the system depends upon the precise character of the norm that this illegal act is likely to contribute to the establishment of, and upon whether a norm of this character would be likely to be abused. And all of that depends in turn upon *what else is done* by those who undertake an illegal humanitarian military intervention—in particular, whether they take credible steps toward establishing new institutional arrangements that would make a more permissive norm regarding intervention reasonable.

What Sort of New Norm of Intervention?

From the standpoint of its justifiability as an illegal act directed toward improving the system, just how the illegal act is characterized—and just as importantly, how it is perceived— matters greatly. It is not sufficient to characterize the NATO intervention as an act directed toward establishing a new norm of humanitarian intervention in domestic conflicts. Such a characterization misses both what makes the act illegal and what is supposed to make it an act directed toward improving the system by helping to establish a new norm of intervention: the fact that it was undertaken without UN authorization. Those who endorse the act, not simply as a morally justifiable act but as an act of reform calculated to contribute to the creation of a new norm, are committed to the assertion that the requirement of Security Council authorization is a defect in the system. And the fact that the intervention proceeded without Security Council authorization is the chief basis for the widely held view that the intervention was illegal.

For purposes of evaluating the justifiability of the NATO intervention as an illegal act directed toward reforming the system, then, the characterization of the act must at least include the fact that it occurred without Security Council authorization. But something else must be added to the characterization: the fact that the intervention was undertaken by a regional military alliance whose constitutional identity is that of a pact for the defense of its members against aggression. Those who undertook the intervention and their supporters emphasized that it was conducted by NATO, presumably because they thought that this fact made the justification for it stronger than would have been the case had it been undertaken by a mere collection of states.

Note that this appeal to the status of NATO as a regional defensive organization recognized by international law cannot refute the charge of illegality. According to Article 51 of the UN Charter, military action, including action by regional organizations as identified in Article 52, is permissible without Security Council authorization only in cases of the occurrence of armed attacks against a state or a member of such an organization.[31] So the question remains: Would a new customary norm permitting intervention by regional military organizations, or those that qualified as such under Article 52, be a moral improvement in the international legal system?

The answer to this question is almost certainly negative. A military alliance such as NATO is not the sort of entity that would

[31] Barry E. Carter and Phillip R. Trimble, *International Law: Selected Documents* (Boston: Little, Brown, 1995), 14–15.

be a plausible candidate for having a right under international law to intervene without UN authorization. The chief difficulty is that such a norm would be too liable to abuse. To appreciate this fact, suppose that China and Pakistan formed a regional security alliance and then appealed to the new norm of customary law whose creation NATO's intervention was supposed to initiate to justify intervening in Kashmir to stop Hindus from violating Muslims' rights in the part of that region controlled by India.[32]

It is one thing to say that NATO's intervention was morally justified as the only way of preventing massive human rights violations under conditions in which Security Council authorization was not obtainable. It is quite another to claim that the intervention was justified as an act directed toward legal reform. The former justification makes no claims about the desirability of a new rule concerning intervention and is quite consistent with the view that, despite its defects, the rule requiring Security Council authorization is, all things considered, desirable under present conditions. The justification we are concerned with makes a stronger and much more dubious claim, namely, that the current rule requiring Security Council authorization ought to be abandoned and replaced with a new rule empowering regional defense alliances to engage in intervention at their discretion. Perhaps the current rule of intervention ought to be rejected, but it is very implausible to hold that adopting this new rule would be an improvement.

Defenders of the NATO intervention might reply, however, that there is a great difference between the members of NATO, on the one hand; and China and Pakistan, on the other. Unlike China and Pakistan, all members of NATO are liberal-democratic countries, with free presses and political cultures that question government actions. In that respect, NATO is much more accountable and therefore less likely to abuse the right to

---

[32] This example was suggested to me by Hurst Hannum.

intervene than an alliance of repressive, unaccountable states.[33] This reply certainly strengthens NATO's case, but it does not go far enough. The problem is that an action such as the intervention in Kosovo does not wear a unique description on its sleeve. How the action is characterized by the majority of states will make a difference as to what it serves as a precedent for. There is all the difference in the world between regarding NATO's intervention as an intervention by a military alliance and as an intervention by a military alliance of liberal-democratic states, with the accountability that this implies. If NATO's leaders were concerned to take the first step toward a new, more enlightened customary norm of intervention, they should have done more to emphasize their own democratic accountability and thereby reduce the chance that their action would be viewed as a precedent for more dangerous intervention by military alliances whose members were not accountable. In other words, by failing to do all it could have to *specify* the principle it was acting on, NATO ran the risk that its action would come to be viewed as a precedent for a change in customary law that would not in fact be an improvement over the current requirement of Security Council authorization. In the next subsection I argue that there is an interesting relationship between the problem of specification and the satisfaction of the *opinio juris* condition for the emergence of a new customary norm.

Taking the Opinio Juris Condition Seriously

The nine guidelines stated above are quite general. They apply to illegal acts directed toward reforming any legal system, not just international law. But precisely because they are so general, the guidelines fail to make clear something that is crucial for the evaluation of illegal acts directed toward reform through the creation of new customary international law, namely, the fact that

---

[33] This point is due to Robert Keohane.

any such acts must be undertaken in a way that reflects the importance of satisfying the *opinio juris* requirement.[34]

In other words, a conscientious reformer must act in such a way not only so as to help ensure that a morally defensible new pattern of state behavior will emerge regarding humanitarian intervention, but also so as to contribute to a shift in consciousness regarding the legal status of such actions. What sorts of actions might the intervenor undertake that could reasonably be expected to contribute to such a shift?

My suggestion is that, in the case of the NATO intervention, there are at least two dimensions of what I referred to earlier as *lawfulness* that, if taken into account by the intervenors during and after the intervention, could reasonably be expected to contribute toward satisfaction of the *opinio juris* requirement. The first has to do with the nature of the intervening entity. As I noted earlier, NATO does not appear to be the sort of entity that could reasonably be authorized to intervene without UN authorization. The point is not simply that NATO is a self-defense pact and that none of its members was under attack. More important, NATO's charter does not include clear statements committing it to the role of being an impartial protector of universal human rights, dedicated to supporting and, where necessary, supplementing other international legal agencies that have the responsibility for protecting human rights.[35] Had NATO begun an open, publicized process of transforming its juridical character in this way at the time of the intervention and carried through on it in the immediate aftermath, this would have made it much more likely that other states would come to regard humanitarian interventions by entities of *that sort* to be legally permissible, even when they lack Security Council authorization.

---

[34] I am indebted to Jeff Holzgrefe for suggesting this important point.
[35] Omar Dahbour, "Self-Determination and Just War in Kosovo," *Radical Philosophy Review* 2, no. 1 (1999): 14.

Without this public effort to transform its identity, NATO's action is likely to be regarded simply as (at best) a morally excusable violation of international law (as many regarded the interventions in East Pakistan and Uganda), rather than as a prototype for a new, defensible legal norm regarding humanitarian intervention. What sorts of actions come to be regarded as legally required or permitted depends in part upon whether the agents performing them are the sorts of entities that could lawfully do so. NATO lacked the juridical character that could be expected to contribute to satisfaction of the *opinio juris* requirement. And it subsequently did nothing to change this.

Second, if, after the intervention was concluded, NATO had taken a leadership role in orchestrating an inclusive, public deliberation to develop consensus on a better international legal norm and appropriate institutional procedures for humanitarian intervention, this too would have increased the probability of a shift in consciousness regarding the possibility of legal interventions without Security Council authorization. In fact, as I have already noted, the Independent International Commission on Kosovo, not NATO, embarked on this constructive path by suggesting several options for reform that would be an improvement on the current requirement of Security Council authorization.

These options were offered as ways of bringing about the needed reform without illegality. However, the Independent Commission did not go so far as to pronounce that successful reform would occur by strictly legal means. Instead, it suggested that NATO's illegal intervention itself might have played a beneficial role as an insistent "wake-up" call, motivating the international community to explore legal options for legal reform.[36]

My point is that if NATO's goal was not simply to prevent a particular humanitarian disaster but to begin a process of legal reform, then it should have taken steps after the intervention to

[36] See Independent International Commission on Kosovo, *Kosovo Report*; and Michael Perry, personal communication.

increase the probability that a new norm would emerge that states could reasonably regard as a legally binding norm, thus satisfying the *opinio juris* requirement. To accomplish this, NATO should have done at least two things. First, it should have begun the process of transforming itself into an entity of the sort that would be authorized to intervene under a norm of the sort that states would be likely to come to regard as legally binding. Second, it should have facilitated an inclusive, legitimacy-conferring process of international deliberation to devise ways of using or modifying existing international legal procedures and institutions to achieve a responsible specification of the content of the norm, in order to provide appropriate safeguards in the absence of Security Council authorization. A new pattern of state action that is seen to conform to a norm that has been specified by such a lawful process is clearly more likely to come to be regarded as a legal norm.

Some might object that such a process of deliberation about how to codify a new rule of humanitarian intervention is doomed to failure at the present time. However, even if that is so, there may be considerable value in *attempting* to achieve codification. Even if only a limited consensus emerges from such efforts, this may contribute to the eventual emergence of a new customary norm. In other words, it is wrong to assume that the choice is between efforts to codify and the development of new custom.

To engage in a responsible act of illegal legal reform, then, is not simply to perform an action that under some true description of it or another provides the template for a superior norm. It is also necessary to perform the action, to justify it publicly, and to follow through on it in such a way as to facilitate the satisfaction of the *opinio juris* requirement. NATO failed to do this. Whether or not NATO's action was justified simply as a violation of international law for the sake of moral principle, it was not credible as an act directed toward reform of the international law of humanitarian intervention.

VII. *Reform through Treaty That Bypasses the UN*

The preceding analysis shows that the strategy of trying to reform international law regarding humanitarian intervention through the creation of new customary law is a high-risk option, a process that may derail at any number of points or perhaps result in a new norm that is not an improvement over the old one. Given these risks and uncertainties, an agent who attempts to initiate a process of progressive customary change ought to act in such a way as to maximize the changes that the new norm will eventually emerge and that it will be specified in such a way as to constitute an improvement over the status quo. But the process can go awry or not come to fruition, even if the initiator does everything that should be done, because whether a new norm emerges and what its character turns out to be depends upon the responses of the majority of states.

The Moral Limitations of State-Majoritarianism

The majoritarian dimension of the process—the fact that a majority of states must change their behavior and their attitude toward the legality of intervention without Security Council authorization—makes this route to reform vulnerable to the deficiencies of the majority. The same pessimism noted earlier regarding the prospects for reform by treaty within the UN system therefore seems to attach to reform by new custom. In a world in which many states cleave resolutely to their power to abuse their own minorities, achieving reform of the law of humanitarian intervention through the emergence of new custom may be a precarious, or at least a very slow, path toward progress. To overlook this obvious point would be to make the mistake of assuming that the only serious obstacle to reform is the regressive behavior of certain permanent members of the Security Council. The problem goes much deeper.

Reform without Majority Approval

A sober appreciation of the risks and uncertainties of reform through the creation of new custom requires us to consider the option of change through treaty among liberal-democratic states, outside the UN system. The crucial point is that it is a mistake to assume that support by a majority of states, either through treaty or in the process of customary change, is a necessary condition for efforts to achieve reform to be morally justifiable. State-majoritarianism, under current conditions in which many states are not democratic, cannot be viewed as having the same legitimacy-conferring power as the consent of individuals. At most, state-majoritarianism has normative weight as a device for constraining abuses by more powerful states.

However, it is not at all obvious that the only way, or even the best way, to constrain powerful states is by subjecting the process of reforming humanitarian intervention to state-majoritarianism. Instead, the needed constraint might be achieved in a treaty-based coalition among liberal-democratic states by a combination of two factors: first, treaty specification of a fairly demanding set of necessary conditions for intervention; second, the democratic accountability between and within participating liberal-democratic states discussed earlier. And even if it could be shown that state-majoritarianism provides a more effective constraint against great power abuses, reducing the risk of abuse is not an absolute value. Not just the harm, but also the good that a liberal-democratic coalition could do must be considered.

Earlier I suggested that the morality of international legal reform is complicated because, under current conditions, there may be a conflict between the need to achieve gains in substantive justice, namely, better protection of basic human rights, on the one hand; and legitimacy, on the other. I now want to suggest that it is inaccurate to say that pursuing reform through a treaty-based coalition for intervention outside the UN, and hence without the support of a majority of states, offends against the value of legitimacy in the name of substantive justice. State-majoritarianism, as I have just argued, has little to recommend it from the standpoint of legitimacy: the consent of state leaders who do not represent their citizens does not itself confer legitimacy. Instead, under current conditions, state-majoritarianism has normative weight only to the extent that it helps curb greater power abuses in intervention. But I have also argued that attempts to reform the law of humanitarian intervention that require support from the majority of states (whether through constitutional amendment to the UN Charter or through the creation of new custom) do not hold great promise for success. The real issue, then, is whether the commitment to making the system substantively more just is best honored by paths to reform that attempt to check great power abuses through state-majoritarianism or by relying upon devices for constraint that can be built into a liberal-democratic coalition for humanitarian intervention. In the next chapter, the pros and cons of variously structured democratic coalitions for military action across borders are considered, both for the case of humanitarian intervention and for something even more controversial: preventive war. In the eighth and final chapter, a novel alternative to that sort of institutional response is developed: a precommitment regime that would allow democratic governments to authorize in advance other states to intervene to prevent the destruction of democracy or the resumption of large-scale ethno-national violence.

Conclusion

My chief aim in this chapter has been to identify, and to begin the task of developing a solution for, an important but neglected problem in the non-ideal part of the normative theory of international law: the morality of attempts at legal reform. I have focused on illegal acts aimed at developing a new, morally superior norm of humanitarian intervention, for the simple reason that their illegality creates a special burden of justification for the reformer who cares deeply about preventing large-scale basic human rights violations but who is also committed to the rule of international law. However, much of my discussion has implications for broader issues of reform whether it involves illegality or not. As in earlier chapters, I have argued here that moral progress regarding recourse to war will require institutional innovation.

I have also shown the inadequacy of a simple and common response to the problem—the Legal Absolutist charge that such acts are impermissible because they are inconsistent with a sincere commitment to the rule of law or betray a willingness to act without moral authority by imposing purely personal or subjective views of morality on others. By exploring the array of factors that are relevant to determining whether an illegal act of reform is morally justified, I hope to have vindicated the concerns of those such as Watson and Rubin that such illegalities bear a serious burden of justification, while at the same time showing that to reject illegal reform wholesale is to fail to appreciate the complexities of the issues.

My analysis demonstrates that the moral evaluation of an illegal act of humanitarian intervention is more complex than is ordinarily assumed. A responsible agent confronted with the possibility of preventing a humanitarian disaster but aware that doing so is illegal under existing international law will ask not only whether there is a sound moral principle that allows or requires him to violate the law, but also whether he should perform the illegal act in such a way as to try to bring about a beneficial change in the law. If the answer to the latter question is affirmative, then the burdens of responsible agency are extensive for those who would undertake illegal acts for the sake of legal reform. In particular, in the case of attempting reform through the creation of new customary law, acting responsibly requires more than ensuring that the illegal action can, under some favorable description of it or another, provide the template for an improved norm of intervention. In addition, the agent of illegal acts of reform must act in such a way as to promote satisfaction of the *opinio juris* condition. Doing this may require actions that go far beyond the intervention itself, including institutional innovations.

I have also articulated a vexing and momentous issue at the heart of the problem of reform: Is better protection of human rights through a rule-governed practice of intervention best achieved through working within the UN-based system of law, or by creating a treaty-based regime of constrained intervention outside of it?

Facing the problem of justifying illegal legal reform head-on, rather than by pretending that reform efforts are legal by stretching the concept of legality, forces us to probe the morality of attempts to create new customary law, to examine what it is to honor the commitment to the rule of law in an imperfect system, to examine critically the assumption that legitimacy requires endorsement of new norms by the majority of states, and to ponder the nature of the international legal system and the conditions for its legitimacy.

CHAPTER 7

Justifying Preventive War, Institutionally

Original version co-authored with Robert O. Keohane

Since the massive terrorist attacks of September 11, 2001, fears of terrorism and weapons of mass destruction have fueled a vigorous worldwide debate about the preventive use of force. "Preventive use of force" may be defined as the initiation of military action in order to avert harmful actions that are neither presently occurring nor imminent.[1] This chapter first explores the especially problematic nature of preventive war and then proposes a new institutional arrangement that could make preventive war justifiable.

The perspective employed for investigating the permissibility of preventive war is cosmopolitan: a moral standpoint that recognizes the basic human rights of all persons, not just citizens of a particular country or countries. We argue that within an appropriate rule-governed, institutional framework that is designed to help protect vulnerable countries against unjustified

---

[1] The notion of an "imminent attack" is somewhat vague but is usually understood to include not only situations in which missiles or warplanes have been launched but have not yet struck their targets, but also situations in which forces have been mobilized with apparently aggressive intent.

interventions without creating unacceptable risks of the costs of inaction, decisions to employ preventive force can be justified.

In our proposal, states advocating preventive war would have to enter into a contract with a diverse body of states as a condition for authorization of their actions. Both proponents of action and those opposing it would be held accountable, after the fact, for the accuracy of their prior statements and the proportionality of their actions. This institutional arrangement is designed to improve the quality of decisions on the preventive use of force. It does so by insisting that these decisions take place under rules that create incentives for honest revelation of information and responsible conduct, and that they be made by agents that are comparatively morally reliable.

The key to ensuring the fairness of rules governing the preventive use of force is accountability. Our proposed scheme promotes accountability through a combination of ex ante and ex post mechanisms. Prior to taking preventive action, states will be required to enter into a contingent contract that imposes two requirements. First, they must make an evidence-based case for preventive force to the UN Security Council. Second, they must agree in advance to submit themselves to an evaluation by an impartial body after the preventive action occurred.

This body will be charged with determining whether the empirical claims that were employed to justify the preventive action were true. If the ex post evaluation vindicates the recourse to preventive force, then the contract would impose sanctions on those members of the Council who opposed the proposed action. If preventive action were blocked by a majority vote of the Security Council or a veto by one of the permanent members, those seeking to engage in preventive action could then make their case in a different body—a coalition of democratic states— with its own institutionalized mechanisms for accountability. Although our goal is to develop an institutional framework for decisions concerning the preventive use of force, we believe that our general approach can also be used to develop a framework for making decisions concerning humanitarian military inter-vention to stop presently occurring massive violations of basic human rights. We focus more narrowly on preventive force for two reasons: the preventive use of force involves special risks and is thus more difficult to justify; and the Bush administration's re-cent claims that the right of self-defense includes the permission to engage in the preventive use of force have made this an issue of urgent practical importance.

I. *Four Views on the Preventive Use of Force*

Four distinct positions in the current debate on preventive force have emerged: the Just War Blanket Prohibition; the Legal Status Quo; the National Interest; and the Expanded Right of Self-Defense. Clarifying these views and identifying their shortcom-ings helps to illuminate the distinctive features of our proposal.

The Just War Blanket Prohibition

The dominant view in the just war tradition has been that pre-ventive force is strictly forbidden. Force may sometimes be jus-tified in cases in which an attack has not already occurred but is imminent—when, for example, an enemy is mobilizing his forces with clear aggressive intent or when missiles or warplanes have already been launched but not yet struck their targets—but there is generally thought to be a *blanket prohibition* on preventive action.[2]

The Legal Status Quo

States' preventive use of force is generally regarded as prohib-ited in contemporary international law unless they have received

---

[2] Michael Walzer, *Just and Unjust Wars: A Moral Argument with Historical Illustrations* (New York: Basic Books, 1977).

collective authorization by the UN Security Council. Article 2(4) of the UN Charter requires "all states" to refrain "from the threat or use of force against the territorial integrity or political independence of any state," unless authorized by the Security Council (Articles 39, 42, 48) or in self-defense against an armed attack (Article 51). According to the Legal Status Quo view, this highly constrained stance on preventive force ought to be maintained. Preventive force should be used only with Security Council authorization.[3]

The National Interest

Realists hold that states may do whatever their leaders deem necessary to serve the best interests of the state. According to this view, leaders of states may disregard universal moral principles when they conflict with the national interest. More specifically, they may employ force, including preventive force, if they deem it necessary for the pursuit of state interests.[4]

---

[3] In the absence of authoritative judicial determination, international law is subject to a variety of interpretations. Some might hold that under current international law preventive action can be legitimate because the Genocide Convention obligates states/parties to take action to prevent genocide. However, this claim is contestable because, according to Article 103 of the UN Charter, the prohibition against preventive use of force trumps all other treaties, including the Genocide Convention. It might also be held, on the contrary, that preventive force is not permissible under international law even with Security Council authorization, except in order to respond to a "threat to international peace and security." For our purposes, it is not necessary to take a stand on these legal questions. We merely follow most authorities in treating the legal status quo as prohibiting preventive use of force without Security Council authorization, but permitting it if such authorization has been provided.

[4] For the classic statement, see Hans J. Morgenthau, *Politics among Nations: The Struggle for Power and Peace*, 6th ed., revised by Kenneth W. Thompson (New York: Knopf, 1985), 12. Advocates of the National Interest view need not be moral skeptics: instead they may hold that state leaders have one supreme moral obligation—to serve the national interest—and that this obligation overrides all other principles of morality. Those who espouse the National Interest view may disagree among themselves, of course, as to whether a policy of recourse to preventive force, or any particular decision

The Expanded Right of Self-Defense

The George W. Bush administration's "National Security Strategy" articulates a fourth position. It expands the definition of self-defense to include preventive action: "While the United States will constantly strive to enlist the support of the international community, *we will not hesitate to act alone, if necessary, to exercise our right of self-defense by acting preemptively against such terrorists, to prevent them from doing harm against our people and our country*" (emphasis added).[5] The Bush administration's "National Security Strategy" asserts that states possess a right of self-defense that entitles them to take preventive action.

None of these four views provides an adequate basis for governing the preventive use of force. Adherence to the Just War Blanket Prohibition is too risky, given the widespread capacity and occasional willingness of states and non-states actors to deploy weapons of mass destruction covertly and suddenly against civilian populations. In addition, this view requires states to refrain from acting even when they could prevent massive human rights violations at little cost.[6] The National Interest view is also unacceptable. Indeed, it repudiates all progress that has been made in constraining the international use of force. The problem is not simply that the national interest is such a malleable concept that its invocation is likely to provide a rationale for aggression and a recipe for destructive international instability, but also that by reducing the grounds for the preventive use of force to self-defense, this view conceives of the potential aims of preventive action too narrowly. It fails even to consider the possibility that there are circumstances in which the preventive use of force

---

to use preventive force, is in fact likely to serve the national interest or be detrimental to it.

   [5] "National Security Strategy of the United States of America September 2002," 6; available at www.whitehouse.gov/nsc/nss.pdf.

   [6] We explore the flaws of the Just War Blanket Prohibition in more detail below.

would be justified to protect the rights of persons other than one's fellow citizens.

The Expanded Right of Self-Defense view must also be rejected. Allowing states to use force on the basis of their own estimate that they may be attacked in the future, without provision for checks on the reliability and sincerity of that judgment, would make the use of force too subject to abuse and error. Like the National Interest view, it also focuses only on the welfare of those within one's own state, thereby providing no basis for the preventive use of force on behalf of others.

The Legal Status Quo view is quite attractive when compared to the three views described above, since it allows preventive action (with Security Council authorization), including its use to protect persons beyond one's borders, while also providing checks on the judgment of any particular state or group of states seeking to use it. But when compared to a fifth alternative—*the Cosmopolitan Institutional view*—the Legal Status Quo view appears far less compelling. The normative foundation of the Cosmopolitan Institutional view is cosmopolitan in the sense that it takes the human rights of all persons seriously. By basic human rights we mean the most widely acknowledged rights that are already recognized in the major human rights conventions. These include the right to physical security of the person, including the right against torture; and rights against at least the more damaging forms of discrimination on grounds of religion, gender, race, or ethnicity; as well as rights against slavery, servitude or forced labor, and the right to the means of subsistence.[7] A commitment to protecting and preventing massive violations

---

[7] The position we endorse is sometimes called Moderate Cosmopolitanism, which allows one to give a limited priority to the interests of one's own nation and does not require strict impartiality. It is a liberal form of cosmopolitanism, since it emphasizes the basic human rights of all persons. One could imagine other kinds of cosmopolitanism, such as Marxism, that forbid discrimination on grounds of nationality, but do not focus on human rights. For a philosophical justification for the assumption that there are human

of human rights provides a prima facie justification for preventive force as a last resort.

Institutionalizing Cosmopolitan Commitments

These commitments of the cosmopolitan perspective are far from novel. Indeed, they are central to the just war tradition and the current international legal order's allowing human rights to limit state sovereignty. The distinctiveness of the Cosmopolitan Institutional view lies in how it incorporates these normative commitments with an effective *accountability regime* for responsible decision-making concerning the preventive use of force.

A cosmopolitan accountability regime involves both substantive standards and processes. The substantive standards include traditional just war principles, including competent authority, proportionality, noncombatant immunity, realistic likelihood of success, and avoidance of excessive force against enemy combatants. Unfortunately, the chief deficiency of just war theory lies not in its principles but in the failure of the just war theorists to take seriously the need for institutionalizing them in a way that provides incentives for agents to apply them impartially and on the basis of good information. Current international law does institutionalize the important just war principle of competent authority: the requirement that the use of force must be authorized by the Security Council, except in cases of self-defense (when there is no time to consult the Council).[8] And in this sense, the

---

rights, see Allen Buchanan, "Human Rights," in *Justice, Legitimacy, and Self-Determination: Moral Foundations for International Law* (Oxford: Oxford University Press, 2007).

[8] The humanitarian law of war can be seen as an imperfect institutionalization of some of the most important *jus in bello* principles of just war theory. However, given the distinctive risks of the preventive use of force, special institutional arrangements are required for responsible decisions to use force preventively, over and above better compliance with rules of humane warfare that are designed to apply to all uses of force.

Legal Status Quo view can be seen as an important advance from an anarchic situation in which states unilaterally decide whether to use force. But this way of institutionalizing the use of force is seriously inadequate, at least when it comes to the preventive use of force.

II. *The Cosmopolitan Justification for Preventive War*

The Moral Starting Point

We begin with the assumption that it can be morally permissible to use force to stop *presently occurring* massive violations of basic human rights. We then argue from this assumption that there is at least a prima facie case for the moral permissibility of using force to *prevent* massive violations of basic human rights.[9] The core justification for using force to stop rights violations as they are occurring—the need to protect basic human rights—can also justify the use of force to prevent rights violations.[10]

Reflection on two scenarios will help to flesh out the prima facie case for this proposition. In the first case, a group is *already* in the process of releasing a weaponized, extremely virulent, lethal virus into the heart of a major city. Surely, it would be justifiable to intervene forcibly to stop it from releasing more of the deadly concoction. In the second scenario, the intelligence agencies of a state have consistent information from many reliable sources

---

[9] The prima facie argument seems to imply that preventive action to protect basic human rights is not only permissible but also obligatory. However, since we seek to advance a feasible proposal, our discussion of institutional arrangements does not assume such an obligation. The successful implementation of the accountability regime we propose might be an important step toward the more ambitious goal of institutionalizing an obligation to prevent massive violations of basic human rights.

[10] By beginning with the assumption that the use of force is sometimes permissible to stop massive violations of basic human rights already underway, we are of course implicitly rejecting the absolute pacifist view that the use of military force is never justified because it inevitably involves harm to innocent persons. We share this assumption with the four perspectives that we criticize.

that a group that has deliberately killed civilians in the past has in its possession a weaponized, extremely virulent, lethal virus and plans to use it against a civilian population. Suppose further that the current location of the virus is known but the city at which it is targeted is not, and that once the virus leaves its present location it will be very difficult to track. Let us also stipulate that the current location of the virus is in the remote stronghold of the group and that a preventive strike can destroy the virus without killing any persons who do not belong to the group. Under these circumstances, the need to protect basic human rights supports preventive action, regardless of whether the rights endangered are those of our fellow citizens or foreigners. Reflection on such examples supports the conclusion that preventive action can be ethically permissible.

It is crucial to emphasize that this prima facie justification for the preventive use of force does not apply to all cases where harm may be prevented but only to situations in which there is a significant risk of sudden and very serious harms on a massive scale. Such a risk is inherent in weapons of mass destruction but not exclusive to them. Genocides may also erupt suddenly.

In situations characterized by incrementally increasing violence, such as in the former Yugoslavia, however, the case for preventive war is much less compelling. Action to respond to aggression or acts of ethnic violence can feasibly be taken in such contexts with far less uncertainty regarding the need to act after the first human rights violations have already occurred. Thus the force of the prima facie argument is limited and focused. It does not purport to show that force may be used whenever it is likely to stop massive violations of basic human rights.

What the Cosmopolitan Institutional view and the Legal Status Quo view have in common is the assertion that there are some cases in which preventive action ought to be permitted. The prima facie argument for prevention sketched above provides a needed moral foundation for both of these positions.

A Critique of the Just War Blanket Prohibition Argument

Those who endorse the blanket prohibition characteristic of the just war tradition could point out that the prima facie argument ignores a crucial point about preventive force: it is directed toward someone who has not committed a wrong. Thus preventive action violates the rights of its target. Unless this moral objection can be met, both the Cosmopolitan Institutional view and the Legal Status Quo view must be rejected.

This objection is unconvincing, because it rests on a false assumption about the right not to be attacked. There is, trivially, a right not to be attacked *unjustly*. But to assume that this includes the right not to be attacked unless one has already committed, or begun to commit, a wrongful harm is to beg the question at issue—namely, whether preventive force can ever be morally justified.

The Right of Self-Defense

Reflection on the right of self-defense suggests that preventive action need not violate the rights of the target. At common law, an individual may use deadly force in self-defense if a reasonable person in his circumstances would judge that he is in danger of death or serious bodily injury. Of course, other conditions must be fulfilled as well, including the avoidance of excessive force. The point, however, is that there are circumstances in which it is justifiable to use lethal force even if the target against which it is applied has not yet caused harm. If this is the case, then it may also be permissible to use lethal force in cases where a reasonable actor would judge that the behavior of another person or persons pose a serious threat of death or serious bodily harm even if an attack has not yet begun.

In the case of individuals, there is much to be said for restricting the legal right of self-defense so as to require the reasonable belief, by the agent exercising the right of self-defense, that an attack is already under way. This restriction is reasonable in contexts in which there are a well-functioning police force and legal system that serve to reduce the risk that individuals will be attacked by their fellow citizens. In the international arena there is nothing comparable to an effective police force, and the stakes are often much higher, since millions of people may be killed by a sudden deployment of weapons of mass destruction. Under these circumstances, the restrictive interpretation of the right of self-defense seems inadequate. It seems much more plausible to assert that the use of force to prevent great harm can be justified, even if that harm is neither presently occurring nor imminent.

In the second scenario described above, the terrorist group has not yet launched an attack, and the harm it seeks to inflict is not literally imminent. Yet it is incorrect to say that the group has done nothing. It has *wrongfully imposed an especially high risk of serious harm on others*, through its past actions, its current planning to carry out a lethal attack, and its expression of a willingness to kill noncombatants. The group's actions, plans, and avowed intentions have put innocent people at risk for great harms.

As we saw in Chapter One, reflection on the law of conspiracy suggests that using force against someone who has not yet committed a wrongful harm need not violate her rights. The elements of conspiracy include a "specific intention" to do wrongful harm and an "agreed plan of action" to produce the harm.[11] The "specific intention" requirement rules out mere unfocused malevolence as a trigger for criminal liability, while the requirement of an "agreed plan of action" satisfies the condition that a crime must include an act, not merely a guilty mind. There is nothing morally repugnant about the idea of using force against conspirators

[11] See Arnold H. Loewy, "Conspiracy," in *Criminal Law in a Nutshell* (St. Paul, MN: West Group, 2000), 260; and Joshua Dressler, "Inchoate Offenses," in *Cases and Materials on Criminal Law*, 2nd ed. (St. Paul, MN: West Group, 1999), 765.

simply because they have not yet performed the act they have planned. We can dismiss the simplistic allegation that it cannot be right to use force against him because "he hasn't done anything" once we acknowledge that the conspirator has indeed done something by agreeing to a plan to produce wrongful harm.

One plausible explanation of why it can be justifiable to use force against someone who has a "specific intention" and an "agreed plan of action" to do wrongful harm is that she has *wrongfully imposed a risk of serious harm on others*. It is a wrongful imposition of risk if those put at risk have neither voluntarily accepted the risk nor deserve to be subjected to it nor are morally liable to be harmed. The crucial point is that when someone has wrongfully imposed a risk, it can become morally permissible to do things to alleviate the risk that would otherwise be impermissible. This is not to say that one may do whatever is necessary to alleviate the risk. As with the use of force generally, the principles of proportionality, avoidance of excessive force, and demonstration of proper regard for the rights of innocent persons must be observed. Whether the preventive use of force is justified in such cases will depend, as with self-defense against an imminent attack, upon whether it is reasonable to conclude that the target of prevention has wrongfully imposed a dire risk on others.

The analogy with the law of conspiracy and of self-defense takes us only so far, however. It shows only that if similar conditions were satisfied in the case of a state or a terrorist group, it would be justifiable to use force to arrest and punish them. Whether it can be justifiable to use deadly force against them depends on the additional assumption that the wrongful act they plan to commit will be *sudden and will cause massive violations of human rights*. In such cases, the use of military force will often be necessary to alleviate these threats.

One might object that the idea of alleviating an unjustly imposed risk through preventive action justifies inflicting harm only on the one who has imposed the risk, whereas preventive action will inevitably involve a risk of harm to others. As I have already acknowledged, preventive military action (unlike ordinary acts of law enforcement) will almost invariably risk harm to the innocent. This is equally true, however, of intervention to stop a presently occurring genocide and also of the least controversial cases of self-defense against an aggressive attack. Unless one is willing to embrace an absolute pacifist position that rules out the use of military force in self-defense, the fact that a preventive response to the wrongful imposition of dire risk may involve harm to innocent persons does not necessarily render it morally illegitimate.

A High Threshold of Violence

Given that military action typically involves much greater risk of harm to innocent persons than ordinary police action against conspirators, the threshold of expected harm needed to justify preventive military action should be high. From a cosmopolitan perspective, an appropriate threshold is the occurrence of *massive violations of basic human rights*. As noted earlier, by "basic human rights" we mean the most widely acknowledged rights that are already recognized in the major human rights conventions. The requirement of massive violations of *basic* human rights sets a very high threshold for preventive action. As was argued in Chapter One, the best understanding of this requirement is that it is an appropriate heuristic that can serve as a directly action-guiding norm for leaders in their decisions regarding recourse to war. Setting a high threshold makes sense, in other words, given the motivational and epistemic limitations under which war leaders function and the risks of error and abuse that these limitations create.

Advocates of a blanket prohibition on preventive force have one last arrow in their quiver. They can argue that prevention carries special risks that are not present in the case of armed responses to actually occurring attacks. The appeal to hypothetical examples such as that of the sudden release of a deadly virus, it might therefore be argued, glosses over an important distinction between the justification of a particular action and the justification of a rule allowing that type of action. Even if preventive action would be morally justified when certain highly ideal conditions are satisfied, it does not follow that we should replace current restrictions on preventive force with a more permissive rule.

The Uncertainty of Future Harms

The prima facie moral argument for preventive action asserts that preventive action may be undertaken to remove or mitigate a wrongfully imposed dire risk. However, for a dire risk to lead to severe harms, a long causal series of events must typically be completed. Even if the probability of each event in the causal series is high, the probability of the harm will be much lower, since it is the product of all the probabilities of the events in the series. Thus suppose that the causal series anticipated by the potential preventer consists of events A, B, C, and D and that each event has a probability of .8. The anticipated harm (the massive violation of basic human rights) will occur only if the whole series of events occurs; but the probability of this is the product of the probabilities of each of the members of the series: .4096. If the probability of individual events is lower, the joint probability is dramatically reduced. Furthermore, if events are *uncertain*—that is, probabilities are unknown—it is impossible to calculate precise probabilities.

It is not enough to show, the objector would conclude, that there are some circumstances in which preventive action would be morally justified. If these cases are few—and if there is a significant risk that those contemplating preventive action may err in determining whether those circumstances obtain—then perhaps preventive action should be prohibited altogether, as traditional just war theory holds.[12]

---

[12] In one sense, this objection points out the obvious: that trade-offs exist in policy between timely action and certainty about the necessity of action. The

Reducing Uncertainty and Risk through Better Institutions

This argument from the special risks of prevention to a blanket prohibition is fatally incomplete. It overlooks the fact that acceptable risk reduction can be achieved not only by a blanket prohibition but also by a more permissive rule embedded in an appropriate institutional framework. Indeed, a blanket prohibition comes at a high cost, since it rules out action to prevent massive violations of basic human rights even when the costs of prevention are very low and the likelihood of its success is very high. Later, we will argue that this high cost can be avoided, if the right sort of institutional innovation occurs.

A blanket prohibition rule also tends to reduce the effectiveness of coercive diplomacy, which may often be the most promising means of preventing terrible harm as a result of foreseeable future aggression. Coercive diplomacy can be defined as "bargaining accompanied by threats designed to induce fear sufficient to change behavior."[13] It includes deterrence but is more comprehensive, since it also incorporates what Thomas Schelling once called "compellance"—inducing an adversary not merely to refrain from some action but to engage in an action that it would not otherwise undertake.[14] For most states, most of the time illegality is viewed as a cost, if only because of damage to reputation. If preventive force is illegal, states will be less likely to use it and efforts at coercive diplomacy through the threat of preventive force will be less credible.

---

longer one waits, the more information one is likely to gain; but by the same token, one's ability to affect the situation may be reduced. Britain and France had better reason in 1939 than in 1936 to regard Germany as a threat to their security, but the cost of averting the threat was higher in 1939.

[13] Paul Gordon Lauren, "Coercive Diplomacy and Ultimata: Theory and Practice in History," in *The Limits of Coercive Diplomacy*, eds. Alexander L. George and William E. Simons (Boulder, CO: Westview Press, 1994), 23.

[14] Thomas C. Schelling, *Arms and Influence* (New Haven, CT: Yale University Press, 1966), 69–78.

A Critique of the Legal Status Quo View

The Legal Status Quo (Security Council authorization) view and the Cosmopolitan Institutional view both reject the blanket prohibition. Each holds that we can effectively mitigate the special risks of prevention by creating institutional safeguards. Although reliance on Security Council authorization is superior to a blanket prohibition, it is not the best institutional alternative.

The first and most obvious moral flaw of the Legal Status Quo is the moral arbitrariness of the permanent member veto. From a cosmopolitan standpoint, there is no justification for this radically unequal distribution of decision-making authority. The veto seriously impugns the legitimacy of the legal status quo.

Second, the use and anticipated use of the veto can block preventive actions that we have morally compelling reasons to undertake. As the Independent International Commission on Kosovo argued, and as the secretary-general of the UN acknowledged at the time, the case for military action to prevent (further) ethnic cleansing of Albanians in Kosovo was very strong, but no resolution to intervene was proposed in the Security Council because it was known that Russia (and perhaps China as well) would veto it.[15]

Third, the legal status quo lacks provisions for holding the decision-makers who propose preventive force (and those members of the Council who must approve it) accountable for their actions. There is subsequently very little assurance that only morally defensible interventions will be authorized. Without standards for when preventive action is justified and without accountability mechanisms to increase the probability that those standards are met, authorization is likely to be unprincipled rather than guided by a proper concern for human rights.

[15] Independent International Commission on Kosovo, *Kosovo Report: Conflict, International Response, Lessons Learned* (New York: Oxford University Press, 2001).

These flaws constitute a strong prima facie case for rejecting the Legal Status Quo view—but only if a superior alternative is feasible. We have seen that none of the three conventional alternatives—the Just War Blanket Prohibition, National Interest, and Expanded Right of Self-Defense views—is adequate. If the current legal status quo ought to be abandoned, it must be for a new arrangement that provides more, not less, accountability.

A Closer Look at the Risks of Preventive Action

Even though preventive military action is sometimes justified, it creates a number of serious risks, two of which are of special concern with respect to preventive action, even if they are not unique to it. The first is that self-interest masquerading as concern for the common good may lead to decisions that are unjustifiable. The second is that preventive action will undermine existing beneficial institutional norms constraining the use of force. Each of these risks is particularly worrisome, because predictions that violence may occur are generally more subject to error and bias than observations that it is already occurring.

The seriousness of these risks indicates the need for institutional safeguards to make decision-making regarding the preventive use of force more responsible. The more effective these safeguards are, the more the probability of abuse will be reduced, and the more justified it will be to undertake preventive action to cope with massive violations of basic human rights. By reducing the risks of abuse, institutional safeguards can make preventive action more feasible on a greater range of issues, in order to promote basic human rights.

Institutional safeguards therefore take the sting out of the fact that there is no unique, nonarbitrary threshold of probability of harm needed to justify prevention. The risks of unjustified preventive action cannot be reduced to zero, but they can be lowered sufficiently so that preventive action can become a more useful tool of policy. Our institutional analysis in the next section is designed to show that this can be achieved.

III. *Cosmopolitan Institutions for Accountability*

Principles of Institutional Design

We advocate three principles for designing institutions to govern the preventive use of force. The first is *effectiveness*: the institution should effectively promote the responsible use of force to prevent massive violations of basic human rights, regardless of whose rights are threatened. One way to achieve this is to design institutions governing the preventive use of force in which decisions to use force preventively are made by agents who are, comparatively speaking, morally reliable, and who are provided incentives to make these decisions responsibly.

Only those states that have decent records regarding the protection of basic human rights should be allowed to participate in institutional processes for controlling the preventive use of force. Those who have demonstrated respect for human rights over a considerable period of time are generally more reliable decision-makers regarding the use of force for protecting human rights than those who have not. We call this the comparative moral reliability criterion.

Yet even agents that are morally reliable, comparatively speaking, may act unreliably unless they are provided with incentives that induce them to make decisions on the basis of the best available information, and to take actions that are consistent with cosmopolitan principles. In particular, incentives are needed to counter the tendency of those proposing the preventive use of force to overestimate the risk to be averted and the tendency of others to shirk responsibilities to protect basic human rights.

Our second design principle also flows from the core commitment of the cosmopolitan ethical perspective: *mutual respect* for all persons. Being willing to help protect the basic human rights of all persons is one important way in which we show respect. Showing respect also entails being willing to justify one's actions to others. Arrogant dismissal of others' views without providing reasons and evidence is inconsistent with this principle.

Within democratic societies, this principle of mutual respect means that people wielding power and the means of coercion must respond to queries about their use from those who ultimately must authorize these actions—members of the society in question. Those who wield power must also offer justifications of their actions to those who are affected by them, including those who are not members of their societies. In the words of the Declaration of Independence, they must show "a decent respect to the opinions of Mankind."

Our third principle of institutional design, *inclusiveness*, reflects the values of both effectiveness and mutual respect. Effectiveness in world politics depends on the independent actions of many states. Therefore, the principle of effectiveness suggests at least a presumption in favor of maximal inclusiveness, unless countervailing considerations intervene. In addition, the principle of mutual respect implies that institutions should be as inclusive as is feasible, given their goals, since all are entitled to equal regard.

In many cases effectiveness, mutual respect, and inclusiveness will point in the same direction. But it is worth noting that there can be a conflict between promoting effectiveness by selecting agents that possess comparative moral reliability, and inclusiveness. Inclusiveness argues for giving all states access to participation in institutional processes for controlling the preventive use of force, whereas the need to enlist agents who have a sincere commitment to and a sound understanding of human rights favors restricting participation. How the trade-offs between inclusiveness and comparative moral reliability are made is of crucial importance for institutional design, as indicated by our discussion below of possible arrangements for a democratic coalition to supplement the authorization processes of the Security Council.

The Importance of Accountability, Properly Understood

No single state can be counted upon fully to take into proper account the interests of others, particularly when considering the use of military force. Therefore, processes by which states and non-state actors can hold states accountable are essential if the parochial concerns of the most powerful states are not to be allowed to prevail over broader interests and shared values.

Standard definitions of accountability emphasize both information and sanctions. "A is accountable to B when A is obliged to inform B about A's (past or future) actions and decisions, to justify them, and to suffer punishment in the case of eventual misconduct."[16] In our proposal, accountability operates both ex ante and ex post. Those states that propose to use force preventively must, under cosmopolitan principles, consult with other states and make their intentions known to international society more generally before using force. Having used force, they must provide information, answer questions, and subject themselves to sanctions according to rules that have been established in advance.

Inclusion of sanctions (including punishments) is crucial, since there will be little incentive to comply with the requirement to answer questions and provide justifications unless those to whom the action is to be justified can sanction those in power. In addition, accountable institutions require specification of the standards to which agents are to be held accountable, and a willingness on the part of agents to provide information and answer questions about their behavior.

For a cosmopolitan view, the most fundamental standard of accountability is that states must act in ways that are designed to

---

[16] Andreas Schedler, "Conceptualizing Accountability," in *The Self-Restraining State: Power and Accountability in New Democracies*, eds. Andreas Schedler, Larry Diamond, and Mark F. Platner (Boulder, CO: Lynne Rienner, 1999), 17. The word "punishment" could be interpreted in too formal and restrictive a way. We accept this definition only with the proviso that it refers more broadly to a *penalty*.

respect and protect the human rights of all persons. They are only to use force or to authorize its use for the sake of preventing violations of human rights. In addition, justified preventive action must include standards for *how* preventive force is to be applied so that it reflects the cosmopolitan commitment to basic human rights.

Prominent among the substantive standards for determining the way in which preventive action may be conducted will be the traditional *jus in bello* principles—that harm to innocents should be minimized, force must be proportional to the end to be achieved, excessive force is to be avoided, and unnecessary suffering should not be inflicted on enemy combatants. To institutionalize adequately these standards requires mechanisms that help to ensure that they are applied correctly and that there are effective sanctions to increase compliance with them.

To determine whether these standards are met, information is required. Thus the second component of a defensible accountability system is provision for *the sharing of information*. A state proposing to use force must share its information about the risks of large-scale human rights violations that would result from inaction as well as the risks of action, especially regarding harm to innocent persons. The information that it provides must be comprehensive enough for other states to make independent judgments on the costs and benefits of the preventive use of force.

Procedures that ensure information sharing are necessary for providing the appropriate incentives for action. Without such procedures, states could pretend to be using preventive force to protect human rights while in fact acting to preserve their hegemony in a region, to protect weak regimes with which they are allied, or to gain economic advantages. The requirement of information sharing is designed, therefore, not only to correct false beliefs but also to reduce opportunistic use of force. Information sharing is therefore required by the design principle of effectiveness. It is also required by the principle of mutual respect, since mutual respect is evidenced by a willingness to share information with equals rather than to demand deference from those regarded as inferior in the capacity to understand issues and make decisions.

Introducing *sanctions* for the violation of standards is the third element of an accountability system. It is also the most difficult to institutionalize. Different societies hold different values, and states are likely to privilege their own interests, so it is infeasible to rely on voluntary compliance. World politics is often seen as a "self-help" system in which each state is responsible for its own security.[17] Without sanctions, rules for the regulation of the preventive use of force would almost certainly be ineffective. Unless there are sanctions for violations of the requirement to share information, some states will misrepresent the facts, exaggerating the probability of the harm that they propose to prevent. Unless there are sanctions against those who use excessive force, states are likely to discount the harm their forceful actions will inflict on others. Without effective sanctions, the institutions will be ineffective, since in the absence of sanctions, "the strong do what they can and the weak suffer what they must."[18]

Standards, information, and sanctions are all crucial to accountability, but they leave open the question: To whom should agents who are considering wielding military force be held accountable? We have already suggested that a cosmopolitan view entails a presumption in favor of inclusiveness. In addition, the design principle of mutual respect creates a presumption that participation in institutional processes for the use of force to protect the human rights of all should be open to all. This presumption could be rebutted, however, if the effectiveness of the accountability regime requires restricting participation to those agents that are *comparatively* morally reliable.

[17] Kenneth N. Waltz, *Theory of International Politics* (Reading, MA: Addison-Wesley, 1979).

[18] Thucydides, *The Peloponnesian War*, Richard Crawley, trans., bk. V, para. 84 (New York: Modern Library, 1982), 351.

Ex Ante Accountability

With respect to a state's proposal to use preventive force, ex ante accountability requires that all of the issues and options (including nonmilitary options) be discussed, and that states that question the necessity of the intervention have the opportunity to interrogate those who propose it. Consistent with the principle of mutual respect, rational persuasion must be employed. Reliance on principled rational persuasion also means that parties speaking in favor of or against preventive military action must acknowledge that their decisions will have precedential value for future decisions. Both the party contemplating intervention and those who must ratify its decisions must therefore acknowledge at least a prima facie obligation, on future occasions, to follow the principles that they have invoked to defend their actions, regardless of the identities of the intervener and the target of intervention. In this sense, the expectation that current decisions will have precedential value for future decisions serves as a kind of veil of ignorance, making the procedure conducive to fairness and therefore to mutual respect.[19] Even if a very powerful state may not expect to be a target of future preventive action, it may worry that the principles it employs to justify or to oppose preventive action will be used by other powerful states to justify their own preventive uses of force.[20]

Mutual respect also requires that all participants in the process of deciding on the preventive use of force must have equal

---

[19] For a more general argument, see Robert O. Keohane, "Governance in a Partially Globalized World," *American Political Science Review* 95, no. 1 (March 2001): 1–13. See also Geoffrey Brennan and James M. Buchanan, *The Reason of Rules: Constitutional Political Economy* (New York: Cambridge University Press, 1985), 30; and Norman Frohlich and Joe A. Oppenheimer, *Choosing Justice: An Experimental Approach to Ethical Theory* (Berkeley: University of California Press, 1992).

[20] In the World Trade Organization states behave in this way. They are reluctant to put forward legal arguments to defend their own practices that could be used in the future by other states to justify protectionist measures.

standing to pose questions to the potential intervener and offer arguments against intervention. In addition, there is at least a strong presumption against according weighted votes or veto power.

Finally, the process of deliberation ex ante must involve the participation of a group of states with diverse interests. Too much uniformity of interests among the participants would run the risk of bias, perhaps even turning the regime for accountability into a tool for domination. Protection of the human rights of all requires diversity of perspectives.

Ex Post Accountability

It is quite possible that what is discovered after even a successful military attack will not justify the actions that were taken. Ex ante accountability is therefore not sufficient; provisions for ex post accountability are also essential. The attacking states must come back with a full report to the body that authorized their actions. They must also allow an impartial commission appointed by that body to have free and timely access to all places in the country controlled by the attacking states in the course of the preventive action. That is, they must facilitate the generation and publicizing of the best available impartial information about the actual effects of preventive use of military force.

Evaluation of the results of the preventive military action would focus on the consistency of the acting states' behavior with the statements they made in the ex ante accountability process. Two issues are particularly important: (1) Was the information gained ex post about the risk-imposing actions of the target consistent with the statements made by the states proposing action ex ante; and (2) Were the military actions of the attacking states consistent with their assurances ex ante that their actions would be proportional to the objectives being attained? The justification of military action on the basis of risk only justifies action necessary to remove or significantly reduce the risk. It should ultimately be up to the authorizing body, not to the attacking states, to decide how far military action needs to go to attain the agreed objectives.

With respect to the justification of an attack, two contrasting inferences might be drawn from information gathered after the war: one, on the whole, the ex post investigations support the assessments of risk made before the attack; or two, on the whole, the ex post investigations fail to corroborate those assessments. Of course, there would be gradations of judgment between these two poles.

If the situations corresponds more closely to situation one, the attacking states would indeed have performed a public service for the world by eliminating or reducing the threat that weapons of mass destruction would be used or that large-scale violations of basic human rights would be inflicted by some other means. These positive contributions would be counted against their financial obligations. Indeed, it would be presumed that those states that had not shouldered the risk of preventive military action would bear special responsibility for financial support in rebuilding the target country should the preventive use of force have caused extensive damage. Insofar as feasible, they would also bear responsibility for peace enforcement. That is, under these conditions those states that had not supported preventive military action would be sanctioned as "free riders," who were informed about the threat but refused to act in a timely manner. Although the economic obligations of such free riders would be limited by their economic capabilities—poor and weak states would not be unduly burdened in any case—they would, in this situation, be *greater* than those imposed on states with comparable resources that supported the military action.[21]

---

[21] The analogy of conscientious objection may be helpful. Conscientious objectors may avoid military service but are expected to subject themselves to at least equivalent burdens and risks as those who do carry arms, by serving as medics, for example.

However, if the ex post review concludes that the preventive action was unjustified, the attacking states and their supporters would be held accountable. They would have to face sanctions for their actions in much the same way that states participating in the international trade regime are liable for their infringements of its rules. They would be required to compensate those who suffered harm from the preventive action and to provide full financial support for operations that restore the country's infrastructure and enable it to govern itself effectively. Furthermore, the intervening parties would not be allowed to control the political situation in the conquered country, or to determine the allocation of aid or the awarding of contracts to firms offering services for the reconstruction effort. If states know ex ante that these rules are in place, incentives for opportunistic interventions aimed at domination rather than protection of human rights will be diminished.[22]

A crucial component of our proposal is an impartial independent commission, appointed by the authorizing body (such as the Security Council). This commission would have prompt access to the conquered country and would determine the magnitude of reconstruction aid needed. It would also determine the allocation of responsibilities to provide the necessary funds.

One particularly attractive feature of the ex post accountability requirement is that it provides the intervening state with a powerful incentive to comply with the just war principle of using the minimum of force sufficient to achieve the goal of prevention. This requirement places the burden of evidence on the intervening

---

[22] The Fourth Geneva Convention relative to the Protection of Civilian Persons in Time of War of August 12, 1949, and other provisions of international law specify the obligations of occupying powers. These include ensuring respect for basic human rights, including restoration and maintenance of law and order and provision of food and medical care to the population. Under our proposal, these obligations would not be diminished, but occupying powers whose actions had been judged by the ex post review to be unjustified would have their ability to make decisions severely constrained.

state: it must be able to show that its ex ante judgments in support of preventive action were valid, and this requires that evidence to substantiate those judgments be available for all to see ex post. Were the intervener to use excessive force, this could destroy the needed evidence. Ex post accountability thus institutionalizes an important just war principle in such a way as to create incentives for compliance with it.

Similarly, the knowledge that its actions will be subject to an impartial review would give the intervening state an incentive to minimize harm to noncombatants, especially if significant penalties would follow upon a finding that the harm to noncombatants was excessive. These would primarily consist of compensation to those harmed or their families, but might include other sanctions as well.

The key to this mechanism of accountability is a *contingent contract* that applies *both* to states seeking to use force preventively and to states opposing the preventive use of force. States would agree that after the conflict they would abide by the judgments of the authorizing body on the validity of their *ex ante* arguments. They would also agree that, should this judgment go against them and the independent commission determine a level of compensation, they would pay such compensation (subject perhaps to an appeals procedure). It should be emphasized that states opposing preventive action would also be liable to pay compensation if ex post discoveries confirmed the claims made ex ante by the states advocating preventive action and disconfirmed their own ex ante objections. In other words, the contract is double-sided and does not discriminate against potential interveners.[23]

---

[23] Here it might be objected that the strongest states might agree ex ante to pay compensation if an ex post review found their preventive actions to be unjustified, but simply fail to pay up. To avoid this problem, assets could be escrowed ex ante. Such an arrangement was used in the agreements that ended the US-Iran hostage crisis in 1981 and that established the US-Iran Claims Tribunal. See Robert Carswell and Richard Davis, "Crafting the Financial Settlement," in Warren Christopher et al., eds., *American Hostages in Iran: The*

Such a contractual arrangement would decrease the incentives for dishonesty on the part of both proponents and opponents of preventive action in their ex ante presentation of evidence. A major problem facing all but the most powerful states, and all publics, is that they do not have access to privileged intelligence information, particularly with respect to closed societies and dictatorships such as North Korea. They are therefore subject to being deceived about the real state of affairs. And since they are aware that they do not have access to much information, they may become unreasonably skeptical of proposed interventions.[24]

Another advantage of this contractual arrangement is that it would limit abuses of victory in a preventive war. When interventions result in large-scale damage, decisions about how to reconstruct the country, including those relating to its political-economic system and control of its resources, must be made in consultation with the authorizing body. When the states engaged in preventive military action have succeeded in their objective — the elimination of the risks for which they claimed to go to war — they must subject their plans for postwar reconstruction and prevention of recurrence of the risks to the authorizing body.

All states could stand to gain from the implementation of the accountability safeguards that we have described. States not expecting to use preventive military force would gain more reliable information before having to make decisions on its authorization by a collective body such as the United Nations. States expecting to use preventive force could hope to gain credibility for their claims, and therefore be likely to generate broader support, including cost-sharing and the provision of troops, for preventive military actions that are justified. And all could benefit

Conduct of a Crisis (New Haven, CT: Yale University Press, for the Council on Foreign Relations, 1985), 201–34; document in ibid., Appendix D, 405–22.

[24] See George Akerlof, "The Market for Lemons," *Quarterly Journal of Economics* 84, no. 3 (August 1970): 488–500.

from the combination of inducements to avoid dysfunctional deadlock and abuses of authority.

IV. *Alternative Institutional Models for Accountability*

In this section we discuss three alternative arrangements that might reasonably satisfy the requirements of cosmopolitan accountability. We acknowledge that none of these arrangements may be politically feasible at present, even though we have sought to design them in a way that takes a non-ideal world of primarily self-interested states as a given. We hope that people of goodwill and sophistication may be interested in refining and implementing them, or institutions inspired by them. These suggestions therefore fall somewhere between mere idealistic thought experiments and proposals that could be implemented under current conditions.

Institutional Model 1: Accountability without the Veto

The first model relies exclusively on the Security Council but creates mechanisms for ex ante and ex post accountability and removes decisions about preventive force from the scope of the Council's permanent member veto. The veto could still be exercised in other Council deliberations, but it would be abolished in the case of decisions whether to use force preventively.

On this model, the provisions for ex ante accountability described above would structure the Council's deliberations, if time permitted. If nine members of the Council voted in favor, a proposed preventive action would go forward, subject to an impartial ex post review as described. The requirement of a supermajority of nine votes appears reasonable, since it ensures that a diverse group of states would have to agree to the action.

If a state or group of states uses preventive force prior to Council authorization on the grounds that there was no time to seek it, then it would also be subject to an impartial ex post review. Such a review would also determine whether it had been reasonable to go forward without prior approval by the Council. Should the review determine that they were not justified in attacking without prior approval, they would be subject to sanctions at least as severe as those imposed on attackers who received authorization under false pretenses.

There are three major arguments in favor of dropping the veto for these decisions. First, it has no ethical standing, since it is a political artifact of the era in which the United Nations was founded, and offends against the presumption of equality implied by the design principle of mutual respect by giving disproportionate power to some states. Second, removing the veto reduces the inertia in the present system, making it more likely that force could be used preventively when its use would be morally compelling. Third, abolishing the veto would encourage states that resist the use of preventive force to propose constructive alternatives. The lack of a veto would make it necessary for states to persuade others that the preventive use of force is not necessary. In some cases this would require that they present alternatives to its use. At present, those who wield the veto need not persuade, they can simply dictate the outcome.

Despite these attractions, any proposal that includes abolishing the permanent member veto will meet insuperable political resistance to its implementation in the foreseeable future. States that now possess the veto are unlikely to relinquish it, and no one else can make the proposed change. Moreover, it is especially unlikely that they would relinquish the veto over something as important and controversial as the preventive use of force. Even if the permanent members saw some merit in the proposal to relinquish the veto only in decisions concerning preventive use of force, they might fear a slippery slope leading to the loss of the veto in other areas. Finally, there is a danger that removing the veto for states wielding significant force could create military conflict between the United Nations and another great power, which would be a disaster.[25] This alternative for institutional reform, then, is the least feasible of the three alternatives.

Institutional Model 2: Accountability Despite the Veto

A less radical and correspondingly more feasible model would create mechanisms for ex ante and ex post accountability as in model 1 but leave the permanent member veto in place.[26] On this second model, the Security Council would have to approve military action by the procedures currently in the Charter. The Council would appoint an impartial body to determine whether the intervener's ex ante justification for preventive action is confirmed ex post.

Such an arrangement might reduce the likelihood that vetoes would be used, since those states reluctant to endorse preventive action would at least be assured that the results would be impartially reported, with provisions for penalties in the case of malfeasance. In other words, they would not be issuing a "blank check" to those initiating force preventively. To that extent, the second model's provisions for accountability would alleviate the problems that the veto poses. However, it should be emphasized

---

[25] I. L. Claude likens the UN Security Council veto to a "fuse in an electrical circuit," reflecting the wise conviction that "in cases of sharp conflict among the great powers the Council ought, for safety's sake, to be incapacitated." I. L. Claude, *Power and International Relations* (New York: Random House, 1962), 160.

[26] Article 51 of the UN Charter states that Members of the United Nations that respond with force to an armed attack shall "immediately" report their actions to the Security Council. Our institutional model 2 goes significantly beyond Article 51 in three ways: it expands the scope of a reporting requirement beyond the case of self-defense against an actual armed attack to cover preventive force; it specifies that the report must be made by an impartial body and must explicitly address issues of fact and of reasonableness in the justification of the use of force; and it attaches penalties in the case of an unfavorable report. Article 51, in contrast, allows the party using force to report on itself, specifies no criteria of evaluation for the report, and mentions no consequences of an unfavorable report.

that for ex post accountability to work, it would also be necessary for the Council to create suitable penalties to be applied in the case of a negative ex post evaluation.[27] Model 2, like model 1, builds on the existing UN structure, but is more feasible than model 1, since it does not require those with the veto to relinquish it.

Nevertheless, even the measures proposed in model 2 might seem to be too costly for the leader of a coalition for prevention. Why should the coalition leader accept these constraints, if her country is to bear the principal costs of military action? The answer is that only by accepting constraints, ex ante, could the coalition leader make credible the coalition's justification for preventive force and promises regarding its conduct during and after the conflict.[28] And credible promises are essential to induce other members of the Security Council to grant authorization for the use of preventive force. Furthermore, securing a broad coalition ex ante can provide valuable insurance for the interveners, since

[27] This necessity raises the problem of an ex post veto by the intervening state or states of the findings of the impartial commission or penalties implied by those findings. This problem could be solved by adapting a suggestion recently made by Thomas Franck, who points out that Article 27 provides that "decisions of the Security Council on procedural matters shall be made by an affirmative vote of nine members." That is, on procedural matters, the veto is inapplicable. Ex ante the Council could decide that votes on the composition and report of the impartial commission, and on any recommendations for penalties, would be considered procedural. (Professor Franck's proposal concerns specification of what constitutes a "material breach" regarding UN resolutions concerning Iraq. See his "Inspections and Their Enforcement: A Modest Proposal," *American Journal of International Law* 96, no. 4 (October 2002): 899–900.)

[28] When the United States invaded Iraq in 2003 without Security Council authorization, the Bush administration's chief justification for doing so was to destroy weapons of mass destruction, which it said were present in that country. It can be argued that as of nine months after the invasion began, the United States has failed to show either that there were weapons of mass destruction in Iraq at the time of the invasion or that there was good reason to believe that they were present. If this still appears to be the case after all the evidence is in, the problem of achieving credibility for the preventive use of force will be even greater in the future. The case for the ex ante and ex post accountability mechanisms we propose will be all the stronger.

they could otherwise be stuck with bearing the full cost of reconstruction if political conditions in the occupied territories worsen after a successful military operation. States that do not consent to the use of force in the first place are likely to demand a high price for being involved in the post-conflict reconstruction.[29]

Although superior to model 1, model 2 is also unsatisfactory. It avoids the impracticality of model 1, but keeping the permanent member veto comes at a high price, because the veto is both morally arbitrary and facilitates a lack of accountability. The veto gives those who wield it little incentive to persuade others by principled argument or to offer constructive alternatives to the use of force. So long as the decision whether to use preventive force rests exclusively with the Security Council as currently constituted, there will be no recourse against deadlock produced by arbitrary and self-interested use of the veto.

Institutional Model 3: A Role for a Democratic Coalition

The third and most defensible institutional alternative is to implement the Security Council-based accountability mechanisms described in model 2 but supplement them with a supporting role for a coalition of reasonably democratic states. By democratic states we mean those with constitutional, representative governments; competition for elected positions through reasonably fair elections; and entrenched basic civil and political rights. A fairly wide range of political institutions and cultures can meet these minimal requirements. There is no suggestion that democratic states include only US or Western European-style democracies. The point is simply to exclude states that are unambiguous violators of human rights and to include states whose citizens have

---

[29] The United States gained Security Council approval for the first Gulf War in 1991, but not for the invasion of Iraq in 2003. Other countries paid approximately 80 percent of the cost of the former conflict; so far, the United States is paying over 80 percent of the costs of the latter.

significant freedom to exert pressure on their governments to deliberate well and cooperate sincerely in the institutional regulation of preventive force.

Of course there is disagreement as to precisely how these elements of democracy are to be understood. For our purposes, however, there is no need to enter into that debate. Our proposal is to begin with a core group of states whose democratic credentials are uncontroversial, such as the members of the European Union plus states such as Australia, Canada, Chile, Costa Rica, Japan, South Africa, and South Korea. Unlike NATO, the coalition that intervened in Kosovo in 1999, such a coalition would be open to states from all regions of the world. Indeed, we expect that most of its members would not be from Europe or North America. The initial members would be authorized to admit additional countries through a transparent process utilizing publicly stated criteria for membership. Consistent with our overall argument, the democratic coalition would itself need institutionalized procedures for accountability, both with respect to admission to membership and for substantive decisions.

From a principled standpoint, creating a democratic coalition is attractive because it would reinforce the role of states that meet our standard for comparative moral reliability. This is not to say that we believe that democracies always, or even typically, act in ways that are consistent with cosmopolitan morality. Indeed, a key premise of our institutional proposals is that all states often behave in parochial and self-interested ways. We believe, however, that when democracies violate cosmopolitan principles, they are more likely to be criticized by their citizens for doing so, and will be more likely to rectify their behavior in response. They may not be morally reliable agents as measured by some absolute standard, but they are more reliable than autocracies.

The third model is feasible, since formal UN action would not be necessary to implement it. Indeed, if a large and diverse cluster of democracies propose it, no single state could easily block it. The democratic coalition would be based on agreements among its members—not necessarily through a formal treaty. Over time, its practices could become part of customary international law. Furthermore, recent experience with respect to the Anglo-American war against Iraq suggests that democratic countries are capable of making independent judgments about the proposals of a superpower, even when faced with the prospect of bilateral sanctions. Chile and Mexico, for instance, refused to support the resolution authorizing war against Iraq put forward by the United States and United Kingdom in February and March of 2003.

In international law, recognition of new states is awarded by existing states, acting individually or through institutions such as the United Nations. Those entities that are indisputably sovereign states have the authority to determine which other entities will be treated as sovereign. Likewise, the initial core of the democratic coalition would be self-designated states whose credentials as stable democracies are unassailable. They would then develop membership criteria that would determine which other states would be eligible. These criteria would be public, developed and applied through transparent, accountable processes. An additional advantage of a democratic coalition is that accountability is much more institutionalized within democratic societies than in authoritarian ones.

The incentives for joining the democratic coalition would be substantial. Submitting to the coalition's deliberations could enable states proposing the use of military force to gain legitimacy for their actions without Security Council authorization. Furthermore, the accountability arrangements of the coalition would increase the credibility of its arguments, thereby enabling it to gain allies who would share the costs of military action and reconstruction. And other members would receive valuable recognition as democratic states that are regarded as sufficiently trustworthy to participate in important decisions regarding the use of force. More important, they would gain decision-making authority, both with respect to legitimizing the preventive use of force and for determining which other states should be allowed to join. There would also be a powerful incentive to help initiate the coalition or, if others initiated it, to join early, since the original members would have more say in determining the rules under which the coalition would operate.

The principle of mutual respect implies that the rich members of the democratic coalitions would have to offer poorer democracies better treatment than is now the case with respect to both trade and aid. Members of the democratic coalition would extend trade privileges to one another, beyond the requirements of the World Trade Organization, and the richer members would offer particularly generous aid to the poorer ones.[30]

The democratic coalition would not replace the Security Council. Instead, if a state or group of states proposed preventive action to the Council and was unable to gain its authorization, it could then present its case to the democratic coalition. The democratic coalition would have its own ex ante and ex post accountability processes that might differ in detail from those of the Security Council under model 2, but that would likewise be designed to approximate as closely as feasible the design principles for a cosmopolitan accountability regime.

Model 3, then, includes two parts. The first is the existing Security Council arrangement, including the permanent member veto, but importantly modified to include ex ante and ex post accountability mechanisms. The second is a distinct body for decisions concerning the preventive use of force, consisting of a coalition of democratic states, geographically unrestricted in membership, and designed to go into operation only in the event of deadlock in the Security Council.

The most obvious advantage of model 3 is that it provides for the possibility of responsible decisions to use force when the Security Council fails to do so. But another, equally important

---

[30] We are indebted to Michael Doyle for the suggestion that led to this proposal.

advantage is that the possibility that a decision will go to the democratic coalition provides an incentive for the Security Council to act more responsibly. Model 3, then, remedies the chief deficiency of model 2 without requiring the impracticality of abolishing the permanent veto as in model 1. If model 3 were adopted, permanent members of the Council would be more reluctant to veto proposals for preventive action without good reasons and substantial support, if doing so would transfer decision-making authority to an arena in which they did not enjoy veto power—and in which they might perhaps not be represented at all. Model 3 thus illustrates a more general point about institutional innovation: competition from new institutions can stimulate existing ones to improve.

Conversely, the continued operation of the Security Council, with strengthened institutions for accountability of the sort we recommend, could make the idea of a democratic coalition more attractive. It would reduce the likelihood that resort to the democratic coalition would be overused, creating a schism between the democracies and the other members of the UN. In other words, the two institutions could actually enhance each other's legitimacy. This would be an instance of reciprocal legitimation, an idea developed in detail in Chapter Four of this volume.

The third institutional model creates healthy competition with the UN system without bypassing it altogether. More specifically, the democratic coalition provides an incentive for the permanent members to use the veto more responsibly and for all members of the Council to realize that they no longer enjoy an absolute monopoly on the legitimate authorization of preventive use of force.

None of these schemes could function effectively without prior agreement on a threshold criterion for predicted harm to be prevented. We have argued that a starting point for such a threshold is the idea of massive violations of basic human rights. To create a workable criterion would require gaining agreement among the participants in these institutions on a minimal list of basic human rights. The problem of specifying when "massive" violations of basic human rights have occurred would be more difficult. There would, however, be clear cases—for example, where the threatened harm is the detonation of a nuclear bomb in a densely populated area. A solution to this problem would presumably involve a combination of prior agreement on levels of risk sufficient for triggering serious consideration of preventive action and a developing case law that would provide further specificity over time.

The concept of accountability is crucial in thinking about more adequate institutional procedures for decisions concerning the use of force. States advocating preventive war should be subjected both to ex ante and ex post accountability. Ex ante, they must be able to persuade other states of the merits of their case for military action. Ex post, their actions must be subjected to scrutiny and potential sanctions.

Our view might be seen as unduly constraining to states that might otherwise engage in justified preventive intervention. This is indeed a possibility, but it must be emphasized that our argument is *comparative*. Our system for cosmopolitan accountability is less constraining than what we take to be the most plausible of the competing views, the Legal Status Quo view, since our proposal merely envisages a democratic coalition as an *additional* channel for authorization.

Even the most powerful states wish others to view their actions as legitimate. They need allies when undertaking military action and supporters to provide policing assistance, civilian infrastructure, and financial support in the aftermath of war. By meeting the requirements of the cosmopolitan accountability regime, a state proposing preventive military action would gain legitimacy by submitting to the rule of law, and credibility by allaying the suspicions of other states that the justification given for prevention was not sound or that prevention was a pretext for conquest. The cosmopolitan accountability regime should be attractive, then, not only to those wishing to constrain states bent on preventive action but also to those seeking to engage in it. This attraction might be especially strong for a state that has recently engaged in interventions that are widely regarded as illegitimate or ill-conceived.

This is not to say that we regard our proposal as feasible in the short run. There is, as Machiavelli noted, "nothing more difficult to take in hand, more perilous to conduct, or more uncertain in its success, than to take the lead in the introduction of a new order of things."[31] Considerable discussion and refinement would be necessary for our accountability regime to be accepted by states. Countries in the Global South will have to be reassured that the rich countries are really following cosmopolitan principles of mutual respect. Potential interveners will have to come to recognize that the advantages of accountability outweigh constraints on their freedom of action.

Even the process of discussing accountability in this way would be an advance, by focusing attention on the problem of eliciting accurate information in situations of potential military conflict.[32] Such discussions could themselves enhance the reputational and credibility costs of ex ante dissimulation. Over time, we hope that our proposal could provide an intellectual resource for reformers seeking to promote effective multilateral action, with safeguards against its abuse. Establishing an institutionalized system of accountability for preventive war would constitute a progressive step in international governance.

[31] Niccolo Machiavelli, *The Prince* (1532), chap. VI.
[32] We are indebted to Jeremy Waldron for this point.

CHAPTER 8

Precommitment Regimes for Intervention

Original version co-authored with
Robert O. Keohane

I. *Expanding the List of Institutional Options*

The world currently lacks reliable multilateral arrangements both to prevent humanitarian disasters and to protect fragile democratic governments against coups and other violent attempts to overthrow them. The need to provide better protection of fragile democracies is especially important. It is a valid question whether democratic publics should rely on the Security Council, with its particular composition and permanent member veto, to serve as their principal external guarantor. We argue that the Security Council is a legitimate institution for making these decisions, but that it does not possess unconditional *exclusive* legitimacy. That is, under some conditions, multilateral coercive intervention to resolve a humanitarian crisis or to counter the use of violence against democratic governance could be legitimately authorized through other means. Nevertheless, the dangers of unilateral intervention, or intervention by a relatively small set of powerful states, are sufficiently great that these other options should be quite carefully restricted. In the final section of this chapter we evaluate proposals for institutions other than the Security Council to authorize the multilateral use of force.

We are skeptical about the authorization of force by a democratic coalition unless it meets the standards of inclusiveness and accountability proposed in Chapter Seven. Since those standards may not be met in the foreseeable future, it is important to consider alternative institutional arrangements. In the present chapter, we consider one promising alternative: "precommitment regimes." Such regimes would enable states to preselect groups of other states to intervene legally, without Security Council authorization, in cases of well-defined contingencies involving threats to struggling democracies or major violations of human rights. This chapter, therefore, should provide an attractive alternative for those who either think that an inclusive democratic coalition is not currently feasible or that it would be dominated by a few powerful countries or by the United States.

To begin, we set out a conceptual framework for assessing the legitimacy of the Security Council. We distinguish between normative and sociological legitimacy and between justice and legitimacy, and we explain the distinctive practical function and value of legitimacy assessments. We then proceed to discuss the legitimacy of Security Council action, concluding that, despite some serious flaws, the Security Council is arguably a legitimate institution for making decisions regarding the use of force across borders.

Next we focus on the problem of Security Council *inaction*. This problem became salient in the 1990s in the context of such humanitarian emergencies as those in Somalia, Bosnia, and Rwanda. These concerns led to a now famous report, *The Responsibility to Protect*,[1] and to almost a decade of discussions in the United Nations about the principle of the responsibility

---

[1] International Commission on Intervention and State Sovereignty (hereafter ICISS), *The Responsibility to Protect* (Ottawa, Canada: International Development Research Centre, 2001).

to protect and how it should be implemented. These discussions culminated in a three-day debate in the UN General Assembly in July 2009, which has provided a clear indication of the support of most UN members for the principle of RtoP (Responsibility to Protect) as interpreted by Secretary-General Ban Ki-moon, as well as the range of concerns and objections to its institutionalization. RtoP may ultimately lead to broader international agreement on the conditions under which humanitarian intervention is justified, but it does not resolve a crucial issue: If the Security Council refuses to act due to the exercise of a Great Power veto, may other means legitimately be used to authorize the use of armed force?

As mentioned above, in the final section we consider possible reforms that would help to make RtoP more meaningful, including reforms circumventing a Security Council veto. In our view, desirable reforms must meet three criteria: (1) they must facilitate prompt action that promises to be effective and not to worsen the situation; (2) they must not undermine the near consensus formed, in the discussion of RtoP, on the principle that under some conditions coercive multilateral intervention is justifiable; and (3) they must not overlook the crucial significance of building state capacity to prevent avoidable humanitarian crises.

II. *A Conceptual Framework*

Normative and Sociological Senses of "Legitimacy"

It is important at the outset to recall the distinction introduced in Chapter Three between the normative and sociological senses of "legitimacy." An institution is legitimate in the normative sense if and only if it has *the right to rule*, broadly described. A legitimate institution is justified in issuing rules and seeking to gain compliance with them by attaching costs and benefits, and if those to whom it directs its rules have content-independent reasons to comply. In other words, the fact that the institution issues the rules itself counts as a reason for compliance, irrespective of the substance of the rule.[2] In addition, legitimate institutions are presumptively entitled to noninterference with their proper activities.[3] Generally speaking, the proper response to the defects of a legitimate institution is to try to reform it, rather than to overthrow it.

Legitimacy in the normative sense is not to be confused with legality. Agreement that the Security Council has exclusive legal authority under international law does not settle whether it has exclusive legitimacy; indeed, having legal authority may even be compatible with its lacking legitimacy tout court. Similarly, whether the NATO intervention in Kosovo was illegal is one question, and whether it was legitimate is another, as the Goldstone report noted.[4]

In contrast to the normative conception, to say that an institution is legitimate in the sociological sense is merely to say that it is generally *believed* to have the right to rule. An institution

[2] This claim that legitimate institutions are generally authoritative—that is, that those to whom they direct their rules have content-independent reasons to comply with *all* of their rules or policies—requires qualification. For it can be argued that if an institution issued a policy that directly and unambiguously was at odds with the very functions that are used to justify its existence or that clearly violated the most basic human rights, then there would not even be a prima facie duty to comply. In other words, in such extreme cases the content of a policy could undercut authoritativeness. For example, if we suppose that the European Court of Human Rights satisfies all reasonable criteria for being a legitimate institution, and if we further suppose that it has issued a ruling declaring that EU states may deprive their Roma citizens of all civil and political rights, there would be no content-independent reason for anyone to comply with this ruling. It would be a mistake to say that in this case there was a content-independent reason to comply but that it was *outweighed* by considerations of content. Instead, the content of the policy is so unacceptable that it *negates* any content-independent reasons for complying. We rely here in part on an unpublished paper by Bas van der Vossen on legitimacy.

[3] This analysis of normative legitimacy as the right to rule is elaborated and defended in Buchanan and Keohane, "Legitimacy."

[4] Independent International Commission on Kosovo, *The Kosovo Report* (New York: Oxford University Press, 2000).

might be legitimate in the normative sense even if it was not legitimate in the sociological sense—if, for example, there was a widespread erroneous adverse belief about how it came to be or how it was currently operating. Conversely, an institution might be widely believed to be legitimate but lack legitimacy in the normative sense, if, for example, it succeeded in hiding certain damaging information about itself. Whether an institution is legitimate in the sociological sense can be determined by surveys of opinion and observation of the behavior of agents subject to its authority. Whether it is legitimate in the normative sense is a moral question that can only be answered on the basis of a defensible account of what characteristics an institution must have in order to have the right to rule.

There is an important connection between the two senses of legitimacy. To function effectively, an international institution usually needs to be widely regarded as legitimate. This is particularly true of international institutions that are not simple bargains for mutual advantage and where free riding cannot be avoided by tit-for-tat strategies. An institution that is not regarded as legitimate is more likely, other things being equal, to provoke a backlash that may have serious consequences. So designers of institutions should not simply aim for ideally best arrangements, but must consider tradeoffs between moral desiderata and sociological legitimacy. In the remainder of this chapter we will first focus on normative legitimacy, but then go on to consider its relationship to sociological legitimacy in our assessment of proposals for alternatives to the Security Council.

A Standard of Legitimacy for Global Governance Institutions

As Chapter One also emphasized, legitimacy is not the same as justice. An institution can fall short of being fully just and yet be legitimate (although it is true that severe injustices can rob it of legitimacy). When there is pervasive disagreement and uncertainty about what justice requires, the concept of legitimacy can play a uniquely valuable role by making possible support for the institution that is based on moral reasons, not merely on self-interest or the fear of coercion. People who disagree about what justice requires may be able to agree in their judgments of legitimacy. If there is considerable agreement on a standard of legitimacy, or at least on some basic necessary conditions for legitimacy, then legitimacy judgments can identify an effective normative coordination point in the absence of agreement on justice.

There are two weighty reasons not to insist that global governance institutions must be just if they are to be recognized as having the right to rule. First, there is sufficient disagreement and uncertainty about what global justice requires that demanding such a high and ambiguous standard for legitimacy would frustrate the reasonable goal of securing coordinated support for valuable institutions on the basis of moral reasons. Second, even if there were much less disagreement and uncertainty, withholding support from a valuable institution because it fails to meet standards of justice would undermine progress toward justice, which requires effective institutions. The concept of legitimacy, then, can be seen as an expression of a realistic normative stance: it reflects both an awareness that some institutions, though morally flawed, are so beneficial that we need them despite their imperfections; and a commitment to holding institutions to a higher standard than their mere benefit relative to the non-institutional status quo.

In our view, the legitimacy of global governance institutions, including the Security Council, should be assessed according to what we call the Complex Standard. We advance the Complex Standard as a proposal for criteria that individuals and groups can use to determine whether particular global governance institutions ought to be regarded as authoritative in their domains of operation. That is, should those to whom they address their rules and policies work on the presumption that they should be obeyed, or at most reformed, and that they should not be interfered with or overthrown? The Complex Standard is not offered as a discovery of the necessary and sufficient conditions for the legitimacy of global governance institutions, but rather as a reasonable basis for a valuable practice. It has three substantive criteria and three epistemic criteria.[5]

The first substantive criterion is *minimal moral acceptability*. Global governance institutions, like other institutions, must not persist in perpetrating serious injustices that involve violations of basic human rights. This requirement seems especially appropriate for the Security Council, since in recent times it has increasingly portrayed the protection of basic human rights as one of its major tasks.

The second substantive criterion is *institutional integrity*. If there is a gross disparity between an institution's performance and its self-proclaimed goals or procedures, its legitimacy is seriously called into question. Similarly, it undermines an institution's legitimacy if its constitution predictably thwarts the pursuit of the very goals on which it bases its claims of authority.

The third substantive criterion, *comparative benefit*, is more complex, but intuitive nonetheless. Because the chief justification for having global governance institutions is that they supply important goods that cannot be achieved without them, failure to supply these benefits calls the legitimacy of these institutions into question. Unless they do a reasonably good job of supplying the benefits invoked to justify their creation, the constraints on sovereignty they impose and the removal of decision-making to bodies remote from democratic citizens would be unacceptable. Achieving the comparative benefit criterion requires providing net benefits exceeding those that would be possible without the institution in question. However, if an institution provides only marginally better benefits than would be available in its absence, and if there is good reason to believe that it should be able to

[5] For a more complete list of substantive criteria, see Chapter Two of this volume.

provide much more substantial benefits but persists in failing to do so, its legitimacy will be questionable.

This is *not* to say that an institution loses legitimacy whenever there is a feasible alternative that could be marginally more efficient at delivering the benefits in question. Such a criterion for legitimacy would be too demanding and would foster excessive instability, defeating the practice's goal of achieving moral reason-based coordinated support for valuable institutions. Yet if an institution persists in seriously suboptimal performance, with little prospect for improvement, *and* there is a morally acceptable alternative institution that would do a significantly better job of securing the benefits in question and that could be created without excessive transition costs, the institution's legitimacy would be called into question.

Fourth, legitimate institutions are fair or at least are not characterized by deep and pervasive unfairness in their substance and procedures. If there are serious problems of unfairness, institutional legitimacy may still be maintained, provided that there are credible public commitments on the part of the institution to remedying these deficiencies.

The four substantive criteria are best conceived as what John Rawls calls counting principles: the more of them an institution satisfies and the higher the degree to which it satisfies them, the stronger its claim to legitimacy. In addition to the four substantive criteria, there are three epistemic virtues that are critical for the legitimacy of global governance institutions.

First, because their chief function is to achieve coordinated action among states and other actors, institutions ought to generate reliable information about coordination points and make it available to relevant actors; otherwise they will not satisfy the criterion of comparative benefit. Second, a degree of transparency concerning the institution's operations is necessary in order to achieve satisfactory terms of accountability. By "terms of accountability" we mean the specification of who the accountability holders are and of the standards to which they are to hold the institution's operations. For the terms of accountability to be met, the operations of the institution must be reasonably transparent to the accountability holders and other relevant stakeholders. Third, institutions must have the capacity to revise their goals and processes over time as circumstances dictate, and this in turn requires the capacity to revise the terms of accountability through a process of principled deliberation.

Because there is considerable disagreement and uncertainty as to what global justice requires and about the proper division of labor between international and national institutions for achieving it, there is continuing controversy about the appropriate terms of accountability for global governance institutions. Epistemic virtues are therefore of crucial importance. Institutions should facilitate principled, factually informed deliberations about these matters and should help ensure that they utilize input from all who properly have a stake in the outcomes.

III. *Assessing the Legitimacy of Security Council Action*

In evaluating the performance of the Security Council, we begin with our three epistemic criteria. On the criterion of transparency, the Security Council gets low marks. Its most important negotiations take place in secret.[6] Despite talk of transparency, the effectiveness of the Council, as essentially a Great Power club, actually depends on its *lack* of transparency. It can therefore be argued that to achieve the objectives of international peace and security, the Security Council must be non-transparent: that is, a transparent Security Council would fail on the criterion of comparative benefit since it would simply become a forum for

---

[6] For a recent comprehensive review of Security Council action on issues of war and peace, see Vaughan Lowe et al., *The United Nations Security Council and War: The Evolution of Thought and Practice Since 1945* (Oxford: Oxford University Press, 2008). In almost all important situations, the most critical negotiations took place privately rather than publicly.

appealing to outside audiences rather than reaching Great Power agreement to take effective action. We do not dispute this argument, but note that non-transparency can affect the sociological legitimacy of the Security Council with states other than Great Powers, and with the publics of democratic Great Powers.

From the standpoint of accountability, the Security Council also falls short, in two respects. First, the UN Charter provides no checks on the Security Council: there are no constitutional constraints on what it can do. Indeed, when the Security Council acts, with the approval of all Great Powers and sufficient other support, its legal powers are essentially unlimited, and there is no provision for judicial review of its decisions by the International Court of Justice or any other judicial body.[7] Second, there is little in the way of incentives for responsible use of the veto by the five permanent members. The permanent members most likely to use the veto against humanitarian intervention are extremely powerful and not likely to suffer severe political or economic consequences for using it to thwart such interventions.

The Security Council scores better on our third epistemic criterion—the capacity of an institution to revise its goals in light of experience and changing values. The institutional goals of the Security Council have changed somewhat over time, with the protection of basic human rights coming to occupy a larger place in the institution's mission. On the other hand, the permanent member veto seems firmly entrenched, despite the lack of a compelling moral justification for it.

We now turn to our four substantive criteria. When taking measures under its own control, the Security Council has generally met the minimal moral acceptability requirement. And

[7] We are not suggesting that such a provision would be a good idea, since the International Court of Justice (ICJ) is too weakly institutionalized to take on such a burden; if it had this authority, it would surely become even more politicized than it is, and there is little reason to believe that the ICJ would dare to overrule a united Security Council or that such an adverse ICJ decision would be heeded by the Great Powers.

although there have been occasional reports of rape and killing by UN forces, forces under UN command do not seem to exhibit a systematic pattern of serious human rights violations. They have not, however, always been effective. For example, as an international commission reported, "poorly armed and ill-disciplined UN troops were an inadequate response in the face of atrocities in Sierra Leone."[8] There have recently been much more serious problems with operations carried out by forces nominally under state control, working in cooperation with UN peacekeeping forces. A recent report by Human Rights Watch has documented mass rapes and murders by Congolese forces supported logistically by the United Nations Peacekeeping Department.[9]

The Council's record is mixed and ambiguous on the second criterion, institutional integrity. Integrity requires a lack of "egregious disparity" between the goals of an institution and its actual practices.[10] Every complex organization engages in some form of "organized hypocrisy," and the UN is no exception.[11] The "Oil-for-Food" program, which was marred by corruption, is a case in point. So weaknesses can be identified on this standard. But unlike many national-level and local institutions in a variety of countries, the Security Council does not seem to be consistently corrupt. On the other hand, the failure to take serious steps toward stopping the massive killing and other human rights abuses in Bosnia, Rwanda, Darfur, and Congo, and perhaps somewhat more controversially in Kosovo, reveals a marked discrepancy

[8] ICISS, *The Responsibility to Protect*, 109.

[9] See Human Rights Watch, "Eastern DR Congo: Surge in Army Atrocities," November 2, 2009; available at www.hrw.org/en/news/2009/11/02/eastern-dr-congo-surge-army-atrocities. See also Jeffrey Gettleman, "U.N. Told Not to Join Congo Army in Operation," *New York Times*, December 10, 2009. The moral status of Security Council *in*action is more questionable, as we will see, than that of Security Council action.

[10] Buchanan and Keohane, "Legitimacy," 422.

[11] Stephen D. Krasner, *Sovereignty: Organized Hypocrisy* (Princeton, NJ: Princeton University Press, 1999).

between the professed goals and the behavior of the Security Council.

On the criterion of fairness, the Security Council is also deficient. Disproportionate and arbitrary power is wielded by the permanent members, due to their possession of the right to veto any proposed action or authorization. And there is no sign that this unfairness is likely to be remedied, because each permanent member has the right to veto any proposal to eliminate the permanent member veto.

Finally, assessing how well the Security Council fares according to the criterion of comparative benefit is probably most difficult because it requires the assessment of a counterfactual—that is, what would have been the case in the absence of the Security Council. It should not be taken for granted, as if it were self-evident, that the use of force across borders would be more common and more often wrongful if the Council did not exist. Few informed observers would give the Council major credit for the reduction in the scale and destructiveness of warfare in the second, as compared to the first, half of the twentieth century, since factors other than the existence of the Security Council (such as the possession by states of nuclear weapons and changing views of the acceptability of war as a means of national policy) could account for the improvement. By all accounts, UN peacekeeping operations and Security Council–authorized interventions have had much more modest effects. Nevertheless, the most systematic recent studies of peacekeeping conclude, after careful analysis that takes account of these inferential difficulties, that the net effects are positive: "peacekeeping works."[12]

---

[12] Virginia Page Fortna, *Does Peacekeeping Work? Shaping Belligerents' Choices after Civil War* (Princeton, NJ: Princeton University Press, 2008); and Michael W. Doyle and Nicholas Sambanis, *Making War and Building Peace* (Princeton, NJ: Princeton University Press, 2006). Both of these studies are impressive pieces of scholarship. It is important to note, however, that efficacy at peacekeeping does not imply overall effectiveness, particularly if an institution often fails to act when human rights are at stake.

Based on these empirical findings, we believe that the Security Council provides significant benefits from the standpoint of international security and the protection against human rights abuses relative to the status quo ante, the condition in which there was no supranational institution capable of exercising significant constraint on the use of force. We conclude, perhaps somewhat charitably, that the Security Council sufficiently realizes the substantive criteria of the Complex Standard to be considered legitimate (in the normative sense), although its performance is in many respects highly flawed. So far, we have attempted an overall assessment of the Security Council, an evaluation of its legitimacy taken as an institutional whole. It is also appropriate to attempt more fine-grained, specific legitimacy assessments, judgments focused on some particular aspect of the institution's performance—in this case, its inaction in the face of massive violent human rights violations.

The Security Council's Inaction and the Responsibility to Protect

During the 1990s the Security Council's failure to act effectively, for years in the former Yugoslavia, and with devastating consequences in Rwanda, drew much more criticism than its authorization of peacekeeping actions in troubled societies ranging from Angola and Mozambique to Guatemala. Responding to this concern, in 2001 the International Commission on Intervention and State Sovereignty (ICISS), initiated by the government of Canada, issued a report, *The Responsibility to Protect*, which has resonated in the United Nations system ever since.[13] As co-chair of the commission, Gareth Evans—the former foreign minister of Australia—has played an active role in explaining and promoting the concept of the "responsibility to protect," and the

---

[13] ICISS, *The Responsibility to Protect*, n. 1, *supra*.

World Summit of 2005 endorsed the report's recommendation in the following terms:

> The international community, through the United Nations, also has the responsibility to use appropriate diplomatic, humanitarian, and other peaceful means, in accordance with Chapters VI and VIII of the Charter, to help to protect populations from genocide, war crimes, ethnic cleansing and crimes against humanity. In this context, we are prepared to take collective action, in a timely and decisive manner, through the Security Council, in accordance with the Charter, including Chapter VII, on a case-by-case basis and in cooperation with relevant regional organizations as appropriate, should peaceful means be inadequate and national authorities are manifestly failing to protect their populations from genocide, war crimes, ethnic cleansing and crimes against humanity.[14]

Building on this resolution, in January 2009 Secretary-General Ban Ki-moon articulated three "pillars" of the responsibility to protect: (1) state responsibility; (2) international assistance and capacity building; and (3) timely and decisive response "when a State is manifestly failing to provide such protection."[15] The secretary-general emphasized that all three pillars had to be strong. A subsequent General Assembly debate in July revealed some dissent to the principle, but also an increasing convergence of views among many countries. There was support for the secretary-general's view that RtoP was not open for renegotiation, but needed to be implemented; for his articulation of the three pillars strategy; and for his view that the scope of RtoP should be narrowly confined to four crimes: genocide, war crimes, ethnic cleansing, and crimes against humanity. Notably,

---

[14] UN General Assembly, Sixtieth Session, "2005 World Summit Outcome," A/RES/60/1, October 24, 2005, para. 139.
[15] UN General Assembly, Sixty-third Session, "Implementing the Responsibility to Protect: Report of the Secretary-General," A/63/677, January 12, 2009, 9.

it should not extend to inadequate responses to natural disasters or civil war. The Nicaraguan president of the General Assembly, joined by Cuba, Venezuela, Sudan, and on some issues other delegations, tried to cast doubt on the legitimacy of RtoP by linking it to unilateral intervention, but without much success. In contrast, India, Indonesia, Japan, Brazil, and South Africa came to its defense.

The secretary-general's report, and the subsequent debate, did reveal some ambivalence about the role of the Security Council in implementing the RtoP agenda. The secretary-general urged the five permanent members "to refrain from employing or threatening to employ the veto in situations of manifest failure to meet obligations relating to the responsibility to protect."[16] To our mind, this statement can be interpreted as an attempt to cast doubt on the legitimacy of such a veto. In the General Assembly the caution about RtoP expressed by many developing countries suggested that there would be little support in that body for more expansive authorization for humanitarian intervention. As noted above, a radical minority saw RtoP as a license for unilateral intervention, but there was more general caution about intervention without the consent of the state involved, expressed by China, Pakistan, and Sri Lanka. On the other hand, thirty-five states supported the secretary-general's recommendation that the five permanent members refrain from employing the veto in situations covered by RtoP. And, not surprisingly, a number of delegations expressed (in varying degrees) skepticism about the Security Council's ability to discharge its responsibilities and declared the need for General Assembly oversight.[17]

[16] Ibid., para. 61.

[17] We rely here on two valuable reports on the General Assembly debate: Global Centre for the Responsibility to Protect, "Implementing the Responsibility to Protect—The 2009 General Assembly Debate: An Assessment" (August 2009); and International Coalition for the Responsibility to Protect, "Report on the General Assembly Plenary Debate on the Responsibility to Protect" (September 15, 2009).

Exclusive versus Non-exclusive Legitimacy

We have argued that the Security Council is a legitimate institution taken as a whole and that this implies a presumption that its activities are legitimate. Nevertheless, as noted, in recent years the Council has been criticized more severely for *inaction* than for action. Although no interventions by the Security Council have led to large-scale human rights abuses, its inaction in Rwanda in 1994 contributed to a death toll estimated at between 500,000 and 800,000.[18] The central problem with the Security Council is, therefore, not what it does, but what it fails to do. So the most serious questions about Security Council legitimacy are not those of non-exclusive but of exclusive legitimacy.

An institution has exclusive (normative) legitimacy with regard to a domain of action if and only if it is legitimate with regard to that domain *and it is impermissible for any other agent to attempt to act in that domain* (without its authorization). Thus, if the Security Council had exclusive legitimacy with regard to intervention decisions, every other agent would be under a moral obligation not to make such decisions. Our contention is that the Security Council does not have exclusive legitimacy. It would be permissible, we argue—and in fact would be highly desirable—to develop a superior (on the basis of the Complex Standard) institution for the making of intervention decisions when the Security Council fails to make them.

The core of our argument that the Security Council does not possess exclusive legitimacy can be outlined as follows, in the form of four premises and a conclusion.

Premise One: The Security Council has sometimes failed to authorize justified humanitarian interventions against genocide, war crimes, crimes against humanity, and ethnic cleansing; and

---

[18] For a gripping account by an academic who was at the United Nations during these crucial times, see Michael Barnett, *Eyewitness to a Genocide: The United Nations and Rwanda* (Ithaca, NY: Cornell University Press, 2002).

there is no evidence that this disposition toward unacceptable inaction has been rectified. By claiming exclusive authority, the Security Council not only fails to discharge its avowed function of protecting basic human rights but also poses a serious obstacle to states fulfilling the responsibility to protect. Furthermore, there is no prospect of the Security Council reliably protecting weak democratic governments from violent overthrow.

Premise Two: Because it lacks systematic procedures for accountability and is recalcitrant to reform by way of eliminating the permanent member veto, the Security Council has little prospect for substantial improvement. If the permanent members were to accept the secretary-general's advice not to use the veto in situations covered by RtoP—and were somehow to institutionalize this promise—this premise could be rendered invalid; but such self-abnegation is highly unlikely.

Premise Three: If an institution repeatedly fails to discharge one of its primary justifying functions (in this case, the protection of basic human rights), acts as an obstacle to other parties fulfilling that function, and has little prospect for substantial improvement in these regards, then it is permissible to try to develop a superior alternative, if there is a reasonable probability that the alternative can be successfully created and sustained and the risk that the attempt to create the alternative will have negative unintended consequences is acceptably low.

Premise Four: There is a reasonable probability that at least one alternative institution for making humanitarian intervention decisions and decisions concerning the restoration of legitimate government that would be superior to the Security Council could be created and sustained, and the risk that the attempt will have bad unintended consequences is acceptably low.

Conclusion: Therefore, the Security Council does not possess exclusive legitimacy with regard to humanitarian intervention decisions, and it is permissible to try to develop a superior institutional alternative.

The first three of these premises enjoy considerable intuitive plausibility, given our analysis of legitimacy and our account of the distinctive function and practical value of legitimacy assessments. Premise Four, however, requires more support, since we have not discussed alternative institutions. Therefore, we will next explore two candidates for alternative institutions that could prove superior, on the basis of the Complex Standard of legitimacy, to the status quo: a democratic coalition and a precommitment regime.

IV. *Alternatives to the Security Council*

A Democratic Coalition

The first alternative that we consider is a coalition of democratic states. "Democratic" here means liberal constitutional democracies: states with constitutions that embed majoritarian voting processes in a system of party competition and entrenched civil and political rights and that have an independent judiciary. In addition, such states have strong civil societies, with a variety of organizations, institutions, and practices that provide sources of information that are relatively independent of the state, which help create a political culture that is willing to question the state's policies, and that exert significant influence on state action. One prominent example of the idea of a democratic coalition is the proposal for a "concert of democracies" advanced by John Ikenberry and others.[19]

The key idea of this proposal is that democratic states are *relatively reliable decision-makers* when it comes to decisions concerning humanitarian intervention. Their relative reliability has

[19] G. John Ikenberry and Anne-Marie Slaughter, "Forging a World of Liberty Under Law: US National Security in the 21st Century," Final Report of the Princeton Project on National Security (Princeton, NJ: Woodrow Wilson School of Public and International Affairs, Princeton University, September 27, 2006).

two main sources. First, if the coalition's membership is restricted to well-established liberal constitutional democracies, the shared commitment to human rights and to democratic government will be relatively strong—entrenched in political cultures and empowered by constitutional orders. Second, liberal democracies are epistemically superior in ways that are relevant to making good decisions. They feature free media, traditions of organized political activism, access to accurate information, and powerful channels of accountability that constrain state action.

Drawing on the discussion in Chapter Seven, we can say that the most plausible proposals for a democratic coalition to authorize intervention share three features.[20] First, the coalition could begin its formal deliberations only after a failure by the Security Council to authorize an intervention and could act only after advising the Security Council that it is about to do so, in order to give that body a chance to reconsider its own inaction. Second, the coalition's deliberations would be guided by a relatively uncontroversial set of substantive criteria for intervention that set a high threshold for what counts as a socially created humanitarian emergency—namely, massive violation of the most basic human rights, genocide being the clearest example. Third, the democratic coalition would include provisions for *ex ante* and *ex post* accountability. Ex ante accountability requires that all of the issues and options (including nonmilitary options) be discussed, and that states that question the necessity of the intervention have the opportunity to interrogate those who support it. Provisions for ex post accountability are also necessary. The interveners must publicly commit in advance to allowing an independent body to have free access to the state into which

[20] In our view the proposal for a concert of democracies by Ikenberry et al. does not include sufficient provisions for accountability. The provisions outlined here are drawn from Allen Buchanan and Robert O. Keohane, "The Preventive Use of Force: A Cosmopolitan Institutional Proposal," *Ethics & International Affairs* 18, no. 1 (2004): 1–22.

the intervention is to occur and to facilitate the generation and publicizing of the best available information about (1) the actual effects of the intervention and (2) whether the pre-intervention assessment of the humanitarian emergency on the basis of which the case for intervention was credible. The independent body's ex post evaluation of the intervention would focus on whether the behavior of intervening states was consistent with the statements they made in the ex ante accountability process.

There are two quite different types of objections to the democratic coalition proposal. The first is that its combination of membership criteria and substantive criteria is not adequate to ensure responsible decisions. Although it is true that well-established democratic states have a stronger commitment to human rights and democracy than other states, this commitment is not a guarantee against flawed decision-making in the case of humanitarian interventions. For example, the democratic states willing to participate in an intervention coalition may use such an opportunity to pursue their own geopolitical interests under the guise of humanitarian concern, either in a calculated fashion or through self-deceiving rationalizations. Also, the channels of accountability provided by democratic political processes are designed to make leaders accountable to their own fellow citizens, not to foreigners. This implies a risk that when democratic states deliberate about intervention, they may seriously underestimate or unduly discount the costs of an intervention to the intended beneficiaries or other "outsiders." Taken together, these objections imply that a democratic coalition may lack adequate provisions for responsible decision-making: the combination of membership criteria and substantive criteria is insufficient, so additional provisions for accountability are needed. The inclusion of ex ante and ex post accountability provisions to simple democratic coalition proposals is designed to address this first type of objection.

The second type of objection is from the standpoint of sociological legitimacy, and it remains even if ex ante and ex post accountability provisions are included. Unless the criteria for membership are so undemanding as to undercut the claim that democracies are relatively reliable decision-makers, many states, including some powerful ones, such as China and Russia, will be excluded from participating. Non-democratic states tend to be especially adamant about the inviolability of sovereignty, and may regard a democratic coalition as a military alliance against them. Specifically, Russia and China are likely to find the idea of such a coalition especially repugnant, because it repudiates the exclusive legitimacy of the Security Council, in which they both hold veto power. Indeed, the Chinese reaction to the idea of a democratic intervention coalition has been extremely negative.[21] A new institution for intervention that is greeted with hostility by two or more major powers as well as by a number of less powerful non-democratic states would be lacking in sociological legitimacy. The proposal for a "concert of democracies" by Ikenberry and others is perhaps especially unlikely to enjoy broad sociological legitimacy because of a provision of its draft enabling treaty, whereby members of the coalition are obligated not to use force against each other. Thus, the proposal for democracies to use force against states controlled by non-democratic governments at the same time exempts the interveners from possible intervention.[22]

The lack of sociological legitimacy is a serious matter for three reasons. First, it may hamper the effectiveness of the coalition. States that regard the coalition as illegitimate will not cooperate (by not granting rights to traverse airspace, and so forth), and may exert pressure on their allies and clients to

[21] One of the authors was present in Shanghai and Beijing in January 2007, when the Princeton Project report was discussed in meetings involving American and Chinese participants. The Chinese participants were vociferous and sustained in their criticisms of the idea of a democratic coalition that could authorize intervention. It was clear that they viewed this proposal as entirely unacceptable.

[22] Ikenberry and Slaughter, "Forging a World of Liberty Under Law," App. A, n. 7.

refrain from cooperating as well. Second, there is the risk of an adverse defensive reaction: the perceived threat of a democratic coalition could strengthen militant nationalism in powerful non-democratic countries, and might even lead to the forging of new alliances among them. Third, the institutionalization of a democratic coalition could inhibit cooperation between democratic and autocratic states on important issues other than humanitarian intervention—such as global economic stability, orderly international trade, and effective actions to limit climate change. The protection of human rights through intervention is an important objective for policy, but does not necessarily trump effective cooperation on other issues that affect billions of people and, indeed, prospects for a healthy atmosphere for human life. In brief, where sociological legitimacy is lacking, institutionalizing a democratic coalition could have bad consequences. It could be argued that on balance, the expected gain in the quality of decisions relative to the Security Council does not seem great enough to justify the risk that the lack of sociological legitimacy will undercut the effectiveness of the coalition, provoke an unacceptable backlash, and disrupt cooperation on other important issues. That conclusion seems all the more forceful if effective implementation of the very stringent measures for ex ante and ex post accountability detailed in Chapter Seven in the proposal for the institutional regulation of preventive war decisions should turn out not to be feasible. Hence it is worth considering an alternative institutional arrangement that could avoid these drawbacks.

IV. *A Precommitment Regime for Democracy-Protecting Intervention*

The Idea of a Precommitment Contract for Intervention

The precommitment regime we shall outline is designed to achieve greater sociological legitimacy than the democratic coalition proposal by explicitly respecting state sovereignty while facilitating intervention when necessary to protect democracy against violent overthrow. This institutional arrangement could also enhance the probability of timely intervention to stop the resumption of ethno-national violence that some countries have suffered. It is not designed in the least to expand democracy to societies that have not experienced it—certainly not by force—but only to help maintain democracy where the people of a country have already managed to institute it themselves. It is our hope that this respect for democratic sovereignty would enable such a regime to go beyond the present RtoP mandate to respond to sustained and widespread violence against civilians, as in cases of genocide or ethnic cleansing, to achieve a further desirable objective: helping to protect nascent democracies against violent overthrow.

Under a precommitment regime for democracy protection, a set of democratic states could enter into a contract by which a democratic government would authorize intervention in its own territory in response to violence that the government was unable to control, either due to incapacity or to having been dislodged from power by force. Conceptually, we think of this contract as between the guarantor states, on the one hand; and the people, or *demos*, of the vulnerable state, on the other. The existing democratic government would be regarded as the agent of the demos.[23] Some would argue that in existing international law states cannot consent to the use of armed force against themselves; but the fact that this contract is with the demos gets around that objection: armed force would not be used against the demos but only against a regime that had violated democratic processes and disempowered the public.

If the Security Council failed to authorize an intervention in response to a grave humanitarian crisis involving massive violations of human rights, as a result of a loss of effective control by the elected government, its partners in the precommitment regime

---

[23] We thank an anonymous referee for raising the question of with whom the contract should be made.

could intervene. If the contract so provided, a precommitment regime could also be designed for less extreme situations: for example, when the elected government is violently overthrown in a military coup, or when a violent revolution (with the violence not forced on the revolutionaries by state repression) takes place, with or without aid from abroad. But precommitment regimes could not be activated in the absence of violent actions or tangible and substantial threats. Claims of "creeping authoritarianism" on the part of an elected government could not trigger intervention, since in such circumstances the criteria for judgment on whether such actions should be regarded as antidemocratic or as an implementation of democracy are too unclear.

It is important to emphasize that pre-authorization for intervention would be available only to democratically elected governments that at the time of the precommitment contract held power through means consistent with democratic legality. Authorization for intervention would not be extended to situations in which a popular movement had arisen to contest state power. The reason for these conditions is to ensure that a precommitment regime did not become a means for autocratic regimes to maintain themselves in power in spite of popular opposition. We are not proposing a return to Count Metternich's Concert of Europe.

Furthermore, precommitment contracts would have to include provisions to strengthen the capacity of those democratic states that are to be protected to maintain order within their territories. Such provisions would be in the interest of the potential interveners by reducing the likelihood that they would have to act, as well as in the interests of the governments arranging to be protected. These provisions would also be sovereignty-reinforcing, and therefore consistent with the emphasis that we observed in the RtoP debates on maintaining state sovereignty and building state capacity.

Because we are not international legal specialists, we can only sketch the legal arrangements we envisage, hoping that if international lawyers find these ideas worthwhile, they could devise appropriate modalities. As we envision them, precommitment contracts would be reported to the Security Council under Article 51 of the UN Charter and registered with the Secretariat of the United Nations under Article 102. Each precommitment regime would have a provision for designating which of its guarantor members would undertake the intervention, should the triggering conditions be fulfilled. And any valid precommitment contract would have to incorporate ex ante and ex post accountability mechanisms, as sketched above. Such precommitment regimes could be justified as easily as defensive alliances, such as NATO. Article 51 of the Charter says that "nothing in the present Charter shall impair the inherent right of individual or collective self-defense if an armed attack occurs against a Member of the United Nations, until the Security Council has taken measures necessary to maintain international peace and security."

Any precommitment contract would also have to include provisions for revoking the authorization. Precommitment contracts should be revocable at will by legitimate governments, since any other provision would be likely to be seen by most states as inconsistent with an appropriate understanding of sovereignty. However, if a precommitment regime specified as a triggering condition the violent overthrow of the democratically elected government, then clearly an attempt to revoke the authorization for intervention by those who had unlawfully seized control could not be regarded as legitimate.

The Security Council could invalidate the precommitment agreement through a procedural vote, requiring nine of the fifteen Council members, with the veto not applying (Article 27(2)). This provision is designed to ensure that precommitment agreements regarded by a majority of the Security Council as inconsistent with international peace and security would not be valid. An agreement could be invalidated if in the judgment of the Security Council the incumbent government did not permit fair contestation for public office through free and fair elections, or if it systematically repressed the ability of those outside the government to speak, write, and organize politically. The Security Council could, in making these judgments, rely on impartial measures of democracy, such as those used by scholars.[24] The Security Council could take such action at any time, taking into account the possibility that signatory governments, even if democratic when the original contract was concluded, could become non-democratic over time.

There are at least four situations in which a state might find a precommitment regime an attractive option: (1) a new democracy that had not gained control of its own military could select a precommitment regime as a way of deterring a military coup and, if unsuccessful at deterrence, responding to it; (2) a state that had just made the transition from authoritarian rule to democracy could opt for the precommitment contract as an insurance policy against authoritarian counterrevolutionaries forcing it back into its previous condition;[25] (3) a state that has either recently emerged from a period of violent ethnic conflict or has good reason to believe that it is likely to suffer this great harm could engage in measures designed to prevent it by signing the precommitment contract; (4) any state whose leaders thought that it was likely to be a target of uninvited intervention in the future could, by signing the precommitment contract, at least control who the interveners would be. This latter measure might be critical in a situation in which there was reason to fear that a neighboring state might be poised to invade one's country (to secure resources or annex part of its territory, perhaps) under the pretext

[24] The most common such measure is the Polity IV measure. See "Polity IV Project: Political Regime Characteristics and Transitions, 1800–2009," available at www.systemicpeace.org/polity/polity4.htm.
[25] Andrew Moravcsik has made a similar argument about human rights regimes: that "governments delegate self-interestedly to combat future threats to domestic democratic governance." See Andrew Moravcsik, "The Origins of Human Rights Regimes: Democratic Delegation in Postwar Europe," *International Organization* 54, no. 2 (Spring 2000): 217–53. The quote is from the abstract, which appears in the unpaginated front material of the journal.

of a humanitarian intervention or an intervention to restore democracy. In the 1990s, for example, interventions in West Africa by the Economic Community of West African States (ECOWAS) in Sierra Leone and Liberia were both ineffective in dealing with resource-fueled civil wars, and provided the opportunity for pillage by some ECOWAS units.[26] The civil war in Rwanda spilled over into the Congo in 1994, and by 1998 several African countries had intervened, resulting in massive human rights abuses.[27]

In certain situations, the incentives for opting for precommitment could be increased by the actions of other states. For example, in cases of new states emerging through secession from or dissolution of existing states, where the risk of humanitarian crises or authoritarian takeovers was high, other states could make the signing of a precommitment contract a condition of recognition of the new state or of its membership in valuable trade regimes or military alliances.

A precommitment regime would not require prior authorization of the Security Council and would therefore sidestep the veto. But by providing that the Council could invalidate agreements, this institutional innovation—unlike a democratic coalition—would not directly challenge the authority of the Council. Furthermore, it would be consistent with a strong interpretation of the notion of sovereignty, because it would not authorize intervention without prior state consent. To put the same point differently, whereas the democratic coalition is in direct competition with the Security Council in cases in which the Council fails to authorize an intervention, the precommitment regime would operate in a complementary way, without repudiating the Security Council's decisions. Note that the Security

---

[26] See Adekeye Adebajo, *Building Peace in West Africa: Liberia, Sierra Leone, and Guinea-Bissau* (Boulder, CO: Lynne Rienner, 2002).

[27] Joe Bavier, "Congo War-Driven Crisis Kills 45,000 a Month: Study," *Reuters*, January 22, 2008; available at www.reuters.com/article/idUSL2280201220080122 (accessed July 7, 2010).

Council could always preempt action by the precommitment regime if it decided to take action itself.

Such a precommitment regime does carry the potential danger that it would become an oppressive alliance, enabling a protected state more readily to repress domestic opposition or to threaten its neighbors. Domestic repression would contradict the democracy-enhancing purpose of a precommitment regime, and threats to neighbors could generate protective reactions leading to a spiral of conflict. Precommitment contracts would therefore remain valid only as long as their beneficiaries continued to adhere to democratic standards, including an absence of systematic bias against any internal ethnic group; and as long as they maintained nonaggressive and non-expansionary foreign policies, firmly eschewing alliances that could be threatening to their neighbors. Great care would have to be taken that pre-authorization arrangements, within the spheres of military capacity of major states, were clearly not threatening to those states, since such measures would be a recipe for multilateral warfare rather than peacekeeping or peacemaking. The provision that the Security Council could void a dangerous contract is designed to mitigate the risk that states protected by precommitment contracts could become internally repressive or externally aggressive.[28]

We do not propose a precommitment regime as a panacea, since the creation of this institutional option would not necessarily significantly change state behavior. Established democracies with the capacity to intervene on behalf of threatened democracies are not always inclined to do so. Indeed, there could be a problem of time inconsistency: even states that had taken on the role of guarantor under a precommitment arrangement might renege when the time came to fulfill their commitments. Shifts in international alignments or domestic opinion could undermine even genuine

[28] See Inis L. Claude, *Power and International Relations* (New York: Random House, 1962), esp. chap. 5, "A Critique of Collective Security."

intentions to become engaged.[29] In response to these worries, we do not contend that legal obligation automatically transfers into political action. But a precommitment regime would remove one constraint, by providing a clearly institutionalized path for pro-democratic intervention without formal action by the Security Council—and one that does not violate sovereignty.

In addition, having joined a precommitment regime as a guarantor, a state would have some reputational stake in fulfilling its commitment. This consideration would not necessarily be decisive, but it would generate an additional reason to act. In view of the time inconsistency problem, however, it would be important for the criteria for intervention to be very clear, so that reputational costs of reneging would be high and so that democratic leaders in vulnerable states would not place confidence in arrangements that turned out to be ephemeral. Indeed, one of the advantages of a precommitment regime would be to enhance clarity about whether, and under what conditions, democratic regimes could expect external protection against threats of force against them.

On the side of vulnerable countries, there could also be reservations: governments could be reluctant to signal weakness, or to seem to reduce their own sovereignty, by entering into precommitment contracts. Yet if faced with real dangers from potential coups, they would have the incentive to seek some guarantees of protection. Reluctance on the part of vulnerable countries (as well as other countries) could be reduced, furthermore, by placing part of a package of capacity-building measures under the responsibility to protect.[30] The package as a whole would provide opportunities for states to fulfill their responsibility to protect

[29] We are grateful to three anonymous referees for emphasizing this point in their comments on a draft of this paper.

[30] We are indebted to Laurence Helfer of Duke Law School for this suggestion.

in a rule-governed, responsible manner, taking sovereign consent very seriously, without being hamstrung by the veto.

At present, precommitment regimes are likely to be most valuable in Africa, a region far from the borders of any permanent member of the Security Council, and in which democracy is fragile. Between 1960 and 2005, there were sixty-seven *constitutional* changes of leadership in Africa, of which 21–31 percent were followed within four years by attempted military coups. Moreover, the proportion of constitutional changes of leadership that are followed by military coups seems to be fairly steady over time.[31] These facts suggest that there is a major problem to which an international solution could be appropriate. To some extent, coups have been inhibited by continuing ties with the prior colonial powers; but a precommitment regime would regularize and institutionalize such inhibitions, increasing accountability for such protective actions through publicity and through the operation of the Security Council.

In general, the incrementalist option of precommitment regimes is likely to enjoy more sociological legitimacy than the status quo because it makes it possible to fulfill better the responsibility to protect. It is more a supplement than an alternative to existing arrangements for joint military action. In addition, the precommitment proposal should be less threatening to non-democratic states, such as Russia and China, because, unlike the democratic coalition proposal, it does not provide a special exemption for democratic states to act contrary to existing UN Charter–based international law. The execution of precommitment contracts, as we have argued, is permissible under existing law.

---

[31] Kristen A. Harkness, "Dangers to Democratization: Military Responses to Constitutional Changes of Leadership in Africa" (paper presented at the Midwest Political Science Association conference, Chicago, April 2010), esp. Table 2, p. 12.

The Risk of Unintended Consequences

Those who assume that the Security Council is not only legitimate but also has exclusive legitimacy regarding humanitarian intervention typically claim that any attempt to create an alternative institution for these decisions would be too risky. Three different risks need to be distinguished: (1) the risk that the new institution would make bad decisions concerning intervention; (2) the risk that the existence of the new institution would erode the sociological legitimacy of the Security Council; and (3) the risk of other unintended consequences, such as undermining efforts to institutionalize the UN's Responsibility to Protect doctrine. Although one can never provide guarantees against human error and self-interest, the specifications that beneficiary governments must be democratic, the absolute right of a legitimate government to revoke its precommitment authorization, and the fact that the Security Council can void such agreements, are designed to reduce the first sort of risk. Compared to a veto-ridden Security Council, unjustifiable *inaction* would be less likely.

With respect to the second issue, we have already noted that because of provisions for Security Council preemption, arrangements for precommitment regimes would not be likely to erode the Council's perceived legitimacy. Indeed, they might reduce justifiable criticism of the Council that results from its frequent inaction in the face of humanitarian crises and the internal use of force.

The third risk—that a precommitment regime would generate other bad consequences—is potentially the most serious; and in comparing the proposal for a democratic coalition with that of a precommitment regime, we have tried to take this into account by specifying limiting conditions—in particular, that the regime being protected must be democratic to prevent the bad consequence of keeping authoritarian regimes in power, and that the Security Council can void precommitment regimes by a procedural majority of nine states. By contrast, the much more open-ended proposal for a democratic coalition could provoke a serious backlash from a coalition of post-imperialist countries and authoritarian regimes that would wave the "anti-imperialist" banner to defeat its efforts. Nonetheless, we acknowledge that our preferred alternative might have deleterious consequences that we have not anticipated. We hope, by offering this proposal, to elicit criticisms and suggestions to improve the formulation presented here.

Notes

We are grateful for comments on earlier versions of this paper by Charles Beitz, Curtis Bradley, Michael Doyle, Laurence Helfer, Andrew Hurrell, Richard Steinberg, and Laura Valentini, and to three anonymous referees. Edward Luck was especially helpful at an early stage in the development of our ideas.

INDEX